The SOCIALIST IDEAL in the LABOUR PARTY

The SOCIALIST IDEAL in the LABOUR PARTY
from Attlee to Corbyn

MARTIN R. BEVERIDGE

MERLIN PRESS

First published in the UK in 2022 by
The Merlin Press
Central Book Building
50 Freshwater Road
Dagenham
RM8 1RX

www.merlinpress.co.uk

ISBN 978-085036-776-8

© Martin R. Beveridge, 2022

Martin R. Beveridge asserts the moral right to be identified as the author of this work in accordance with the Copyright, Designs and Patents Act 1988

A catalogue record for this book is available from the British Library

Printed in the UK by Imprint Digital, Exeter

Dedication

For Leo Panitch
1945-2020

Contents

Acknowledgements	vi
Abbreviations	vii
Introduction	1
Chapter One: Orthodox Socialism	9
Chapter Two: The Changing Political Status of Organised Labour	32
Chapter Three: Labour in Power	53
Chapter Four: Bevan and the Crisis of Orthodox Socialism	75
Chapter Five: Harold Wilson in Office and the Rise of a Labour New Left	98
Chapter Six: New Labour's 'Modernisation' Project	124
Chapter Seven: Jeremy Corbyn and the Resurgence of the Socialist Ideal	150
Appendix: Labour Members and Supporters Speak	178
Further reading	184
Notes	187
Index of names	207

Acknowledgements

A book is always the result of a collective dialogue, and this one builds on the experiences and reflections of many left campaigners and thinkers. Apart from those whom I have cited in the references, there are many more who influenced me than I can hope to recount.

I am immensely grateful to the Labour Party members and supporters who shared their thoughts about socialism with me in 2016, as well as my brother Ian for our conversations and his feedback on the manuscript. The librarians at the British Library and the Du Bois library at UMass Amherst were, as always, extremely helpful. Simon Pirani and Terry Brotherstone generously took the time to give me critical comments on early drafts of the manuscript. I would also like to thank Hilary Wainwright for her encouragement of the project, and my editor at Merlin Press, Tony Zurbrugg. Above all, I thank *mi compañera* Joselyn M. Almeida for her support and developmental editing at every stage of writing.

Sections of chapter five were originally published online as a tribute to Tony Benn in *Jacobin* magazine.

Abbreviations

AES: Alternative Economic Strategy
AEU: Amalgamated Engineering Union
ASLEF: Associated Society of Locomotive Engineers and Firemen
BMA: British Medical Association
CLP: Constituency Labour Party
CLPD: Campaign for Labour Party Democracy
CND: Campaign for Nuclear Disarmament
CP: Communist Party
ERM: Exchange Rate Mechanism
GEC: General Electric Company
GMB: General, Municipal, Boilermakers and Allied Trade Union
GMWU: General and Municipal Workers Union
ILP: Independent Labour Party
IMF: International Monetary Fund
IWC: Institute for Workers Control
JPC: Joint Production Committee
NASD: National Association of Stevedores and Dockers
NATO: North Atlantic Treaty Organisation
NCB: National Coal Board
NEB: National Enterprise Board
NEC: National Executive Committee
NUM: National Union of Mineworkers
NUR: National Union of Railwaymen
OFSTED: Office for Standards in Education, Children's Services and Skills
OPEC: Organisation of Petroleum Exporting Countries
PFI: Private Finance Initiative
PLP: Parliamentary Labour Party
SAP: Social Democratic Party of Sweden
SDP: Social Democratic Party (UK)
SLL: Socialist Labour League
SPD: Social Democratic Party of Germany
T&GWU: Transport and General Workers Union

TSSA: Transport Salaried Staffs' Association
TUC: Trades Union Congress
UCS: Upper Clyde Shipbuilders
UKIP: United Kingdom Independence Party
UNISON: Public sector workers' union formed by the amalgamation of local government and health service unions.
UNITE: Union formed by the merger of the T&GWU with Amicus, the amalgamated electricians' and engineers' union.

Introduction

As of this writing, the lives of millions of people across the globe have been disrupted by the twin crises of climate breakdown and the Covid-19 pandemic. In Britain, they have cast a vivid spotlight on the indifference of the government, the inadequacy of the social safety net, the defunding and privatisation of the National Health Service, and the relative importance of essential workers who are low-paid and undervalued. While Covid-19 did not create new social and economic problems, it compounded those that already existed. What is new about these crises is that the solutions to these problems are literally matters of life and death. They demonstrate the urgency of fundamental structural change.

The Labour Party under Jeremy Corbyn campaigned in 2017 and 2019 on ambitious policies that addressed the very problems the pandemic highlighted: it advocated increased state spending to counter the financialisation of social care and health care and to reduce unemployment through a Green New Deal intended to create one million new jobs. Through fairer taxation it planned to fund upgrades to schools, hospitals, care homes and council houses. The shortages of doctors and nurses would be alleviated by expanding training places and restoring bursaries. In addition, the party committed to bringing utilities, water, the railways, and Royal Mail back into public ownership, and to democratising the economy through alternative models of ownership. However, Labour's 2019 election defeat left the party searching for direction, despite surveys of voters and opinion polls that show its manifesto policies remain popular and relevant.[1]

The strategies embodied in these manifestos only became party policy because a stunning upsurge of Labour supporters from both inside and outside the party propelled Corbyn into the leadership in 2015. The following year, I travelled to the UK from my home in Amherst, Massachusetts, to discover why there was such a strong response to his politics, since he did not seem to be advocating anything startlingly new. In interviews with Labour members and supporters, I discovered that, irrespective of their opinion of Corbyn as party leader, most shared his ethical socialist values of collective solidarity, respect and equality. For example, Geraldine, a retired teacher in Liverpool, maintained that whatever their situation, 'people should be treated with the same respect, the same dignity'.² Although not often stated overtly, these values form an underlying unity among party members without any need for further political discussion. They show how a socialist ideal has persisted despite the defeats and setbacks the labour movement has suffered over recent years.

It is the persistence of this ideal that has held the Labour Party together despite factional struggles and leadership changes. But the beliefs about socialism I encountered among Labour supporters – such as the right to a more equal distribution of opportunities and wealth, a decent standard of living for all, special provision for families and social care for the sick and elderly – did not fall from the skies. They were established through the historical struggles and experiences of the labour movement and reflect a resistance to the domination of extreme individualist values in the contemporary world. However, they also contain a fundamental ambiguity, in that the demand for a fairer economy does not specify a necessary change in social relations. There is a continuum of ideas about socialism in Britain, from advocating a limited redistribution of wealth that leaves the social order intact, to envisaging a serious attempt to change the structure of exploitation and class power that underlies inequality. The two poles of this continuum form an opposition that is at the root of the tensions between the left in the constituencies and the right-leaning parliamentary party. The paradox is that, throughout Labour's history, the very ambiguity of socialist beliefs has enabled opposed political tendencies to coexist uneasily within the party, while apparently speaking the same language.

My focus in this book is primarily on the way socialist ideas have been articulated in the Labour Party, although there have been other popular approaches to socialism. For example, the revolutionary syndicalist movement in the years before the First World War envisaged a society built on the basis of democratic workshop organisation. However, its notion of the anatomy of a future socialist society – the common ownership and control of land and industry – was imagined in a way essentially similar to that of the early Labour Party. Clement Attlee's 1922 election address expressed the same idea: 'Instead of the exploitation of the mass of the people in the interests of a small rich class,' he said, 'I demand the organisation of the country in the interests of all as a co-operative commonwealth in which land and capital will be owned by the nation and used for the benefit of the community.'³ I am using the term 'socialist ideal', then, to refer to the conception of how society could be structured under socialism, rather than to whether it should be achieved gradually or through revolution, and the term 'social democracy' to the coalition of interests whose aim is to move society in a socialist direction through parliamentary means. As a case in point, the social democracy of the 1945 Labour Party was held together by a common socialist ideal, although leaders and members differed substantively over how far and how fast the government should go to bring it into being.

The reforms of the post-war Labour government were undoubtedly a milestone in the development of the socialist ideal, but to grasp the extent of that government's influence on the consciousness of the labour movement, it is first necessary to recover the idea of socialism prevalent in the grassroots prior to the party's accession to power. An important guide to the thinking of labour activists before 1945 was the popularity of Robert Tressell's famous novel, *The Ragged Trousered Philanthropists,* which was a virtual handbook for socialists in the years between the First and Second World Wars. It expounded a description of socialism based on the writings of the early socialists Robert Blatchford and Edward Bellamy. As industries became increasingly concentrated in monopolies at the turn of the century, these writers contended that industrial concentration formed the basic requirements of a socialist state, a theory that was highly influential among labour activists from the 1900s into the 1940s. Socialism, they thought, consisted of the state taking over all forms of production and distribution, a conception I will describe as 'orthodox socialism'.

This early version of the socialist ideal went through two important transformations: the first was brought about by the initial successes of the 1945 Labour government in bringing to an end the years of mass unemployment and absolute poverty, leading to the conviction that the government's programme of nationalisations was a 'first step' to socialism. As a result, the institution of state-centric nationalisation, social welfare, and full employment became identified with the idea of socialism. The Attlee government's legacy of welfare laws and institutions created an expectation of state responsibility for individual well-being as of right, as the property of any British citizen, which dominated social thinking in the form of a moral imperative until the end of the 1970s.

The second transformation came after the attempts by the Wilson governments of 1964-1970 to impose incomes control disillusioned many of Labour's members, including cabinet minister Tony Benn. Basing himself on the militancy of the organised working class in conflict with the anti-union legislation of the Heath and Wilson governments, together with the ongoing fight for democracy within the Labour Party, Benn began to advocate for radical democracy in the form of cooperatives and workers' control, as an answer to the immediate problems of industrial rationalisation and factory closures. However, the defeat of the Bennite left in the 1980s paved the way for the rise of New Labour.

The suppression of socialist discourse by New Labour accommodated the financialisation of the economy and concentration of wealth and power in London and the southeast. However, after the crash of 2008, the leadership of Blair and Brown lost authority, and the labour movement's tradition of ethical socialism revived with Jeremy Corbyn's candidacy for party leader. Corbyn's emphasis on the importance of extra-parliamentary protests merged with the social movements campaigning against austerity that brought with them ideas of horizontal and participative democracy, reacting to the precarity of life in neoliberal society. These ideas combined to bond Corbyn with Labour's radical rank and file, creating the political space for a further transformation of the conception of socialism.

Prioritising the bottom-up empowerment of communities, the new iteration of the socialist ideal envisages the central state transformed into an agency that creates an overarching framework for participatory democracy. Its aim of fundamental structural change to the functioning of the economic system, by decentralising economic power in order to rebuild and stabilise regions and localities, devolving Treasury powers to local councils, and using the power of the state to support community organising, is extremely relevant to the problem of how society can be reconstructed in the aftermath of the pandemic. It challenges activists to participate in social movements within the communities of which they are a part.

The structure of the book is chronological: The first chapter analyses the most influential novel of the interwar years, *The Ragged Trousered Philanthropists*, which fused a compelling depiction of working-class life with an exposition of socialist ideology. Its ideas formed an important subtext to the consolidation of Labour's electoral agenda during the 1930s. Socialism was understood to be an ultimate goal that coexisted with both the labour movement's day-to-day struggles over wages and conditions, and Labour's moderate policies for the amelioration of unemployment and grinding poverty.

The second chapter shows how organised labour's essential role in war production in the Second World War changed class power relations. The incorporation of the Labour leaders into the coalition government allowed them to insist on trade union recognition in the factories; for them, state direction of industry appeared to coincide with the economic ideas of orthodox socialism. The public responded enthusiastically to the egalitarian aspects of the Beveridge Report, which were adopted wholesale by the party and the Labour left as the foundation for welfare reform. Labour's adoption of the report was a major factor in the party's election victory at the end of the war.

The 1945 Labour government, with its contradictory policies of social reform and the simultaneous restoration of the capitalist basis of the economy, is the focus of chapter three. The government consolidated the collectivist gains made during the war to create a new social consensus based on bureaucratically managed nationalised industries, Keynesian approaches to economic planning, and welfare provision on the basis of economic expansion. Although confined to obsolete and failing industries, nationalisation appeared to be a 'first step' in the direction of a socialist society. The perceived change in the role of the state transformed the party's idea of socialism from the vision of a fully socialised economy into the acceptance of a mixed economy with full employment and social welfare.

The fourth chapter reviews the ideological conflicts that developed in the Labour party after 1948 as the government retreated from its nationalisation programme, creating the Bevanite movement that became a pole of attraction for the left in the 1950s. The Bevanites were caught between the orthodox ideal of a socialist planned economy and the Attlee government's creation of a mixed economy, resolved on the rhetorical plane with the demand for control of its 'commanding heights'. The political stalemate between the dominant right wing and the Bevanite left contributed to the development of a New Left outside the party that began a re-evaluation of the bureaucratic form of nationalisation implemented after 1945.

The disillusion of Labour supporters with the Wilson governments' policy of wage restraint between 1964-70 resulted in the emergence of a Labour new left within the party, as chapter five explains. Led by Tony Benn, this new left forged a relationship with the industrial militancy and factory occupations of the 1970s, out of which came the development of an industrial strategy that stressed industrial democracy and social control of the economy. With the encouragement of Benn, Lucas Aerospace shop stewards pioneered a concrete experiment in bottom-up planning based on extensive shop-floor involvement, pointing to a solution to the defence of jobs against industrial rationalisation.

Chapter six discusses how the neoliberal political paradigm established by successive Thatcherite governments shaped the rise of New Labour. A precondition for the centralisation of the party leadership under Kinnock was the defeat of the left in the party, paving the way for the rise of Tony Blair and Gordon Brown and the acceptance of a globalised market economy.

New Labour increased spending on public services but imposed on them the principle of market competition, and it encouraged a financial bubble that crashed in 2008, destroying the basis of Blair's 'Third Way' politics.

In the final chapter I trace how the party membership rejected the Blairite leadership and joined with anti-austerity protest movements that turned to Labour politics after Jeremy Corbyn was nominated in the 2015 leadership election. His tenure as leader saw the overturning of the Tory government's majority in 2017, aided by a highly popular manifesto that put forward common-sense alternatives to neoliberalism, but subsequently was subverted by the politics of Brexit. I analyse the 'new politics' that emerged as socialist theorists worked out concrete policies aimed at facilitating a participatory democratic relation between the state and community-based social movements. A re-thinking of the Labour left's strategy following the 2019 election defeat of the party and its subsequent rightward turn requires an appreciation of these policies' transformative potential.

The history of the socialist ideal shows that it has not developed out of its own internal logic, but has been reshaped through social struggles and historical events that have been absorbed into political culture. There is a plurality of intersecting histories that are equally crucial for the fulfilment of the ideal in its totality: for example, the campaigns for women's equality or for racial justice, which cannot simply be reduced to fundamental class antagonisms. A full account of them is beyond the purview of this book, but wherever possible I have incorporated them into the narrative.

Orthodox socialism had assumed that the establishment of a socialist society would automatically end all forms of social oppression. This belief coexisted with the hostility of the trade union movement to women in the workplace during the interwar years, and its resistance to family allowances before 1942. However, the provisions of the welfare state that particularly benefited working-class women were enacted because of the way public pressure for change during wartime was assimilated by Labour, despite its trade union affiliation. Traditional gender relations were later undermined by the impact of post-war affluence on family life, as women began to enter the economy in greater numbers. Labour was slow to adapt to these changes: the male-dominated party's obliviousness to gender issues continued despite the apparently progressive legislation of the Wilson governments. It was not until the 1980s that the rise of the women's movement initiated a rethinking of the political position of women within the party.[4] New Labour's Equality Act outlawed discrimination on the basis of gender or sexual orientation, but likewise followed changed social attitudes after the fact, and did little to encourage women's independent agency. The great merit of Corbyn's leadership was its ability to engage with social movements of class, gender and racial emancipation in real time and motivate socialist theorists to explore ways of extending solidarity and participatory democracy, so as to lay the foundations for building social relations of equality and mutual respect.

The endeavour to resolve Labour's ambiguity over policy and practice has translated historically into a succession of ideological conflicts that cumulatively have redefined the idea of socialism. These conflicts are chronicled in the following chapters, which also trace the interaction of the political and social events that formed the context of the disputes. Activists will recognise many parallels between the struggles within the Labour Party today and past tensions between the grassroots and the actions of the trade union and party bureaucracies. They will also discover the nearly-forgotten ruthlessness of the Labour right wing in suppressing the oppositional Bevanite movement in the 1950s. Moreover, the originality of the 'new politics' devised by socialist thinkers supporting the Corbyn left is thrown into sharper relief by a history of the beliefs that motivated earlier generations to fight for a more equal society and a better world.

I have based the book's narrative on an original reading of major political texts and on recent scholarship on Labour Party history. My work has benefited from the feedback of fellow activists and scholars in the US and Britain who demonstrate the ideal's continued vitality during the most challenging epoch in recent world history.

Chapter One

Orthodox Socialism

'Instead of the exploitation of the mass of the people in the interests of a small rich class, I demand the organisation of the country in the interests of all as a co-operative commonwealth in which land and capital will be owned by the nation and used for the benefit of the community.'[5] Clement Attlee, general election address 1922.

The Cooperative Commonwealth

In 1945 a war-weary British public elected a Labour government with an overwhelming parliamentary majority. A watershed in British political history, it established a social consensus lasting over thirty years, setting the parameters of a tripartite compromise between unions, employers and government that served as the foundation of the welfare state. Post-war governments of all complexions have grappled in one way or another with the Attlee government's institutional legacy.

Its manifesto called for nationalisation of major industries and the establishment of welfare institutions like the health service and state pensions, and the government's achievement of these aims had a marked impact on the way the idea of socialism was understood. As John Saville, an important theoretician of the New Left, commented: 'This identification of social welfare legislation and full employment with the road to a socialist state has become embedded within the understanding of the labour movement in Britain; and no period of its history was more powerful in its influence than the years of the Attlee administration.'[6] Not only does the welfare state remain a fundamental element in British national identity, its interpretation also underlies today's political schisms. For New Labour, as much as the Conservative New Right, the Attlee government's legislation created public debt and welfare dependency. For the left, Clement Attlee was thought to have mobilised the public behind a clear policy of reform – and over seventy years later Labour's policy to counter austerity-driven government aimed to restore these reforms.

Attlee's speech about national insurance in 1946, when he was prime minister, has a contemporary resonance. In reply to the hypothetical question of whether or not the country could afford it, he told parliament that he could not accept that 'the sum total of the goods produced and the services rendered by the people of this country' would not be sufficient to provide for 'the very modest standard of life' represented by the legislation. 'I cannot believe that our national productivity is so slow, that our willingness to work is so feeble or that we can submit to the world that the masses of our people must be condemned to penury.'[7] The significance of Attlee's statement lies in the ethical, not economic, nature of his justification for social security's expense: we cannot tell the world that the masses must be condemned to penury because of our unwillingness to work. It forms a link between the Labour government's legislation and prewar socialist rhetoric.

Political scientist Samuel Beer discerns a unified doctrine or 'orthodoxy' within the party's speeches and literature which 'persists without fundamental change through the interwar period and into the years after 1945.'[8] The orthodox doctrine expressed a moral critique of a dehumanising society dominated by class exploitation, and opposed to it an ethical ideal symbolised by the notion of a 'New Jerusalem,' one that was voiced by Labour politicians throughout the first half of the twentieth century. It embodied a vision that 'an unselfish and caring community would one day replace an indifferent and cruel social order,' a vision encapsulated in the idea of a Cooperative Commonwealth.[9] This concept was essentially utopian, since it did not address the realities of the class domination of the British state, but by separating the practical and the imaginary it enabled the everyday activities of trade unionism to coexist with the ultimate goal of eliminating private ownership of industry. This goal remained a core aspiration of the party's rank and file, even though a short experience of government in the 1920s took the Labour Party leaders towards a more pragmatic appreciation of what could be achieved under the existing state structure. The inherent dualism of the tradition accommodated the discrepancy between the socialist ideal of completely replacing private property with public administration and the practical steps the leadership introduced into the party's policies to deal with mass unemployment.

The leadership's ameliorative plans were fairly close to the rank and file's hard-headed appraisal of practical possibilities, however. Sociologist G.H. Armbruster, who surveyed a Welsh mining town in 1939, concluded that, aside from the moral ideal of 'brotherhood,' its residents' idea of practical socialism 'is really more akin to the programme of the Liberal Party than that of a clear-cut socialism as we understand it; the security of their jobs, adequate wages, the improvement of housing conditions, increased pensions, social insurances etc. are the tangible contents of these aspirations. The question of common ownership of production is even looked upon with a healthy scepticism.'[10] The miners' scepticism is doubtless related to the unsuccessful fight of their union throughout the interwar years for nationalisation of the industry. But their ideal of 'brotherhood,' which Armbruster notes as an aside, was central to the movement's socialist tradition.

Labour's understanding of society in the interwar period located the source of all social ills in the capitalist economic system. Socialism therefore required a fundamental reconstruction of the system, not a patchwork of reforms, and the moral basis of the new society was to be 'fellowship' – the 'brotherhood' of the Welsh miners. The party's ethical vision underlay its view of how the economy should operate: cooperation would replace competition and the public service motive the place of the profit motive, while wealth would be equally distributed and labour shared fairly among all. The vocabulary of 'planning,' adopted by the Labour leadership from the early 1930s, implied that a public administration under democratic control could manage the economy in place of the market. This concept imbued nationalisation with its socialist character, and the two were closely connected in Labour thinking; Attlee was later to say: 'Fundamental nationalisation had to go ahead [in 1945] because it fell in with the planning, the essential planning of the country.'[11]

Working-class aspirations for job security, higher wages, better housing and social insurance were incorporated into a new social agenda that culminated in a popular radicalism that swept Labour into power in 1945. Labour's success channeled hopes of a more egalitarian society after years of mass misery and political exclusion; as historian David Howell points out, the election saw 'the triumph of a radicalism that went far beyond the [Labour] party ... The dualism that characterised the party also characterised a large section of the electorate – "bread and butter plus a dream." That was the secret of 1945.'[12]

The dream, or the ideal of a better and more humane world, was sustained by the resistance of much of the population to the coercive power of wage-labour, and inspired the labour movement's day-to-day struggles over wages and conditions. To the extent that a novel can embody the ideas of society in a particular historical period, Robert Tressell's *The Ragged Trousered Philanthropists* expresses vividly the notion of a Cooperative Commonwealth that was widespread in the labour movement before Labour's victory in 1945. In the following sections, I explain how the loyalty of the rank and file to this notion formed an important subtext to the consolidation of Labour's political agenda during the turbulent politics of the 1930s. After the severe electoral setback of 1931, the moderates in the Labour leadership had to defend their commitment to 'practical socialism,' or amelioration of workers' conditions within the structure of the existing state, while continuing to pay lip-service to the grassroots' ideal of 'full socialism.'

The Ragged Trousered Philanthropists

Although Tressell claimed to have written only a 'readable story full of human interest,' with the subject of socialism treated incidentally, his work is infused with the categories of orthodox socialism, containing a passionate denunciation of the poverty, exploitation, and dehumanisation caused by the capitalist system. The immediate popularity of his novel demonstrated the power of the utopian idea of an egalitarian community, and many workers found in it compelling arguments for 'socialism as we understand it.' Its evocation of Edwardian wage-discipline and the catastrophic effects of unemployment rang a chord from its publication in 1914 through the 1940s and still resonates in these days of zero-hours contracts.[13]

'Robert Tressell' was the pen name of sign-writer and painter Robert Noonan, whose daughter Kathleen gave his hand-written manuscript to children's author Jessie Pope after his death in 1911. She recommended it to her publisher, Grant Richards, and at his behest abridged the 250,000-word manuscript considerably before its first publication in 1914; she further shortened it to 90,000 words for a reissued edition in 1918. Despite her bowdlerisation of its socialist message, the novel became and remained extremely popular; it is even held that it contributed substantially to Labour's landslide victory in 1945.[14]

Tressell begins his novel by describing 'The Cave,' a large and dilapidated old house that is to be renovated and remodeled. This delimits the space for the collective labour of about twenty-five men, who fill the air with 'the sounds of hammering and sawing, the ringing of trowels, the rattle of pails, the splashing of water brushes, and the scraping of the stripping knives used by those who were removing the old wallpaper.'[15] At the end of the working day, each worker leaves this collective space and returns to the private space of the family (sometimes via the public house). Tressell's depiction of these private spaces casts more light on the character of each individual, whom he makes representative of workers at different ages and stages of life.

The workers are introduced to the reader through a break-time discussion of the causes of poverty, which demarcates the socialist Frank Owen from the other men, who repeat arguments they have picked up from newspapers that blame immigrants, overpopulation, and machinery. Their banter and backchat is rendered in a way that illuminates the relations between them, Crass the site foreman, and the general foreman, Hunter, nicknamed 'Old Misery,' who wields the power of fear over the men since he can sack them at a moment's notice and return them to unemployment. An older worker, Jack Linden, is fired in order to make way for a younger man to work at a cheaper rate, even though because of his age Linden is unlikely to find other work and eventually dies in a workhouse. Class relations are depicted in the collective space through the petty tyranny of Rushton and Sweater, the owner of the decorating firm and the house respectively.

The concreteness of Tressell's descriptions of the work process makes unmistakable the employer's drive to get work done as cheaply and shoddily as possible, a theme that runs throughout the book and which is further emphasised by the Dickensian names he gives to the bosses. A contrast to this scenario is Frank Owen's delight in being given a task that involves some creative artistry. He gets a great deal of pleasure from the planning and execution of this decorative work, while Rushton's only thought is how much profit could be made from it.[16] This evokes William Morris's ideal of 'joyful labour' as an expression of the creative impulse, rather than the degradation of work in the pursuit of profit.

Time is measured by the whistle for break times, the succession of working days, the seasons (in winter the reduced hours of daylight limit the number of working hours and wages are diminished), and by the unfolding of the debates between Owen and the men on the causes of poverty. As the work on the house nears completion, the men become fearful of a great purge or 'slaughter,' and in the event fifteen of them are laid off. During the winter months, hours are irregular and few, until in spring and summer work recommences with a quantity of smaller jobs and 'the crowd of ragged-trousered philanthropists continued to toil and sweat at their noble and unselfish task of making money for Mr. Rushton.'[17] Even after one of them is killed in an accident with a ladder, Hunter and Crass scheme to exploit his funeral arrangements.

The dramas that unfold in the private spaces of the family, the struggle to survive with low wages, rented rooms, and the constant fear of unemployment, encompass the daily exertions of the women in the novel to find enough resources to feed their families and ward off sickness. Tressell frames these dramas with the relations established in the collective space of work. For example, after Linden is sacked, Owen arranges help for his children; a co-worker, Easton, takes to joining his workmates in the pub after work and neglecting his wife, Ruth, who finds it impossible to make ends meet. She is seduced and raped by another co-worker, their lodger Slyme. After she gives birth she attempts suicide, but is able to turn to Owen's family for support and is eventually reconciled with her husband.

Tressell permeates his account with a moral condemnation of a system that prevents the unemployed from creating the necessities of life because of their separation from the privately-owned means of production. What is of significance is the weight Tressell gives to ideology – especially the influence of newspapers – in persuading workers to support Liberal or Tory politicians against their own class interests; he is critical of them for not seeing how they are being duped, while explaining this from the constant propaganda that teaches them they are not fully human beings with the same rights as their betters. The workers are 'philanthropists' because they justify the very system that is the cause of their poverty.

Its combination of a genuine working-class perspective with arguments for socialism aided its political impact, acknowledged by readers who later became prominent in the labour movement. Jack Jones, later general secretary of the T&GWU, was given a copy by an old-time socialist, Bill Bewley, in the 1930s. 'I couldn't life [sic] my eyes from its pages. It was so real in its exposure of much of the life around me and which I was beginning to experience in my first job after leaving school. But the great significance of the book for me was the simple, clear explanation of socialism.' The book 'was passed from hand to hand' and it 'had a profound effect on me as it did on tens of thousands of working people in my time'; but it was 'the criticism of our class that affected me most.'[18]

Left MP Eric Heffer was lent it when a young apprentice carpenter. '[The character] "Misery" the foreman was very real. Good workers were often sacked because "they were not fast enough". ... Tressell's book had an enormous influence on me. It helped me to understand that Tories and Liberals were really different sides of the same capitalist coin. It explained simply but intelligently how capitalism worked, and why it was essential to get rid of it.' John Sommerfield was an RAF fitter who took it with him to Burma. Recounting the experience of many in the armed forces during the Second World War, he recalls that it 'was only a Penguin edition and, unfortunately, didn't last long, being handed around and read and re-read until it literally fell to pieces.'[19]

The book was a best-seller in 1918; during the 1926 General Strike it was reprinted eight times, culminating in a special TUC edition in 1927. The novel continued to sell in huge numbers during the Depression, and in 1934 sold 200 copies on one Putney building site after a strike.[20] In April 1940, during the Second World War, Penguin republished the 1918 edition as a sixpenny paperback in what was probably a standard edition of 50,000 copies. It sold out in one month and was reprinted in May – feeding into 'the market formed by the [Left Book Club] whose July 1940 offering, *Guilty Men*, by Michael Foot and others, lambasted the prewar National Government and went on to sell 220,000 copies.' Penguin reprinted again in 1941 and 1944, while the Richards Press reissued the 1914 edition in August 1943 and reprinted it in April, July and December 1944.[21]

In his introduction to the restored complete edition, Peter Miles writes: 'Bearing in mind what Jessie Pope cut ... the fact that for the first half of its life *The Ragged Trousered Philanthropists* exercised its spell over readers on the basis of a mere shadow of its full form and political trajectory remains one of the more remarkable aspects of its remarkable history.' Pope cut out large sections of the manuscript, toned down many of Owen's criticisms of capitalist society, and rearranged its chapters to make it resemble a more conventional account of working-class immiseration; she made the book's conclusion a moment when Owen contemplated suicide, rather than Tressell's optimistic vision of a future Cooperative Commonwealth.[22]

Despite this editing, the novel retained its popular appeal, partly because of Tressell's depiction of workers as human and their oppression inhuman, but also because of its accurate portrayal of how the threat of unemployment meant the prospect of devastating poverty for entire families. This resonated both with struggles against the hardship of unemployment in the 1930s and concerns about a return to prewar unemployment in the 1940s. Miles comments that Tressell 'condenses the threats [of being laid off] into the tragi-comic play between them and the foreman Hunter ... There is much to savour in the depiction of the worker-foreman relationship (which many will recognise).' The fact that this social relation remains so recognisable is another reason for the book's continuing success. Roland Sheppard got a copy in Christmas 1968, and found himself 'surprised at how the actual working conditions for painters has not changed. I had higher wages and a shorter work day/week, but painters were, and are still, harassed by the boss and his agents in the same manner as in England in the early 1900s.'[23]

The novel is rooted in a popular socialist tradition; there are many references to the arguments and ideas of the early socialist Robert Blatchford in Tressell's work, which he incorporates into many of the scenes and dialogue of the book. Blatchford's *Clarion* newspaper and other publications, such as his book *Merrie England*, were extremely well-received in the late nineteenth and early twentieth century; historian Noel Thompson comments that the circulation figures of the *Clarion* and the million copies of *Merrie England* that were sold 'suggest that his socialism

... was also representative of the aspirations and thoughts of many within the Labour Movement.'[24] It was also the nexus of an alternative socialist culture of outdoor communal activities, like the Clarion choirs, bicycling and rambling clubs, and the Clarion propaganda vans which traveled across the country spreading the message of socialism, which feature in a chapter of *The Ragged Trousered Philanthropists*.

Even though Tressell wrote the novel in an era of burgeoning trade union militancy, he refers only obliquely to the organisation of workers at the point of production. Instead, he criticises workers' attachment to the ideology of the ruling class, from the point of view of an isolated socialist in the workforce. Indeed, it could be said that it was written as a manual for socialist propagandists, from one of whom Tressell probably borrowed the 'Great Money Trick' that Owen uses to demonstrate the way capitalists extract profit from workers by virtue of their ownership of the means of production.[25] His exposition gives a good indication of how Marxist ideas were understood and how they circulated within the working class.

The intellectual case for socialism is presented in a 'great oration' in the latter part of the book, substantially based on ideas from Blatchford and Edward Bellamy's 1888 novel *Looking Backward*, expounding the solution to poverty and unemployment as the 'Public Ownership of the Machinery, and the National Organisation of Industry for the production and distribution of the necessaries of life, not for the profit of a few, but for the benefit of all!'[26] In the oration, Tressell argues that just as the community has organised an army and navy to protect itself from external danger, it can also organise to protect itself against the domestic danger of mental and physical degeneration from the lack of proper food and clothing. 'Socialists say that the community should undertake and organise the business of producing and distributing all these things; that the State should be the only employer of labour and should own all the factories, mills, mines, farms, railways, and fishing fleets. ... Socialists say that the community should undertake the business of providing proper dwellings for all its members, that the State should be the only landlord, and that all the land and all the houses should belong to the whole people.'[27]

Tressell deals with the problem of the transition to socialism by asserting that the rational organisation of production by the community will ensure the triumph of state manufacturing through its greater efficiency: 'As for the factories, shops, and other means of production and distribution, the State must adopt the same methods of doing business as the present owners. I mean that even as the big Trusts and companies are crushing – by competition – the individual workers and small traders, so the State should crush the trusts by competition. It is surely justifiable for the State to do for the benefit of the whole people that which the capitalists are already doing for the profit of a few shareholders.'[28]

A state-run 'National Service Store' would employ all those who are unemployed and would provide 'an abundance of everything' to only those who work for the state. Unemployment would be done away with because 'the nation will be the sole employer of labour ... every mentally and physically capable person in the community will be helping in the great work of production and distribution. ... there will be no unemployed and no overlapping of labour, which will be organised and concentrated for the accomplishment of the only rational object – the creation of the things we require...'[29]

These are the organisational principles of the 'Co-operative Commonwealth' of the future, says Tressell. A socialist society, in other words, would retain the contemporary industrial structure but with the capitalist class replaced by the state as the unified representative of 'the whole people,' 'the community,' which would carry out the organising of production and distribution of goods and the employment of labour. Society would be levelled by removing the economic function of businessmen and the unnecessary labour of clerical and retail workers; facing the more efficient competition of state industries, capitalists would soon go out of business.[30]

Rather than collective struggle or revolution, Tressell followed Blatchford in envisaging the passage to socialism as one of patient persuasion. In *Britain for the British*, Blatchford writes: 'Let us once get the people, or a big majority of the people, to understand Socialism, to believe in Socialism, and to work for Socialism, and the real revolution is accomplished ... the first thing to be done is to educate them ... our method is persuasion.' His publications, like Tressell's, provided a moral and economic critique of capitalist society together with a depiction of a utopian alternative as a persuasive argument to convert the reader to socialism.[31]

Tressell's argument that the state can simply take the place of the capitalist class in a socialist society reproduces Blatchford's definition of 'practical socialism' as 'a kind of national scheme of cooperation, managed by the State.'[32] While pointing out the class domination of the ownership of land and industry, Tressell's exposition of a moral economy, where production is carried out on the basis of need rather than profit, embodies an assumption that the state can act as a neutral instrument to express the popular will of a frictionless society, once public ownership of the means of production has been achieved.

This abstract conception of the state did not support any specific programme for how a future cooperative commonwealth was to be achieved, and so complemented both the propaganda of socialist activists and the parliamentary aspirations of the early Labour Party. Winifred Blatchford wrote in *The Clarion* a month after the book's publication: 'All the chapters on economics and politics are high above the rest of the book in power and in craftsmanship. All these chapters are indeed of great ability and skilfully written and present the case clearly and strongly. These chapters taken from the rest would give us a book invaluable for propaganda work.'[33] The Labour MP for Stepney, Clement Attlee, confessed to prefer literary rather than Fabian accounts of poverty that relied heavily on statistics, and, according to his biographer, one of his favourites was *The Ragged Trousered Philanthropists*.[34]

Attlee's first parliamentary speech in 1922 echoed Tressell's sources. Attacking the waste of human life due to unemployment in his constituency, he asked: 'Why was it that in war we were able to find employment for everyone? It was simply that the Government controlled the purchasing power of the nation.... That is what we are demanding shall be done in time of peace. As the nation was organised for war and death, so it can be organised for peace and life if we have the will for it.'[35]

His speech clearly paraphrases the American socialist Edward Bellamy's *Looking Backward*. The nation in Bellamy's conception, or in his words 'the universal partnership of the people,' was identified with an industrially organised society and retained the hierarchies that were necessitated by industrial production, with an emphasis on the contemporary vogue for 'scientific management' in pursuit of efficiency, excluding non-producers like landowners and bankers. Attlee had read *Looking Backward* before the First World War and been greatly influenced by its vision of a centralised state 'organising industry upon the mutual obligation of citizen to nation, and nation to citizen, [where] duty has wholly taken the place of contract, as the basis of industry and the cement of society.' Attlee took from Bellamy the perspective of making the state a positive agent for improving social conditions, through government control of the economy, and it was Attlee's own sense of public duty that had led him to work among the working class of London's East End.[36]

Aligning himself with Bellamy's statist conception of socialism, Attlee rejected the ideas of Ruskin and Morris who saw the answer to workers' alienation as changing the nature of work itself, with the conditions of craft production as a model of how the worker could feel pride in his work. 'Most of the work that has to be done today is on the whole dull,' thought Attlee: improvements in basic working conditions, like wages and working hours, should be the first priority of the labour movement, rather than imposing on it a middle-class view of how people should live.[37] Attlee's indifference to workplace alienation was reflective of the belief of the labour leadership that workers' ongoing struggle in the factories for control over the work-process was separate from the campaign for parliamentary legislation that would ameliorate basic working conditions.

The challenge of syndicalism

The labour leaders' statism was challenged in the years before the First World War by the syndicalist movement. Syndicalists typically ruled out any involvement with the capitalist state through the political process, instead advocating social representation through workers' organisation in the large industrial plants that had emerged at the end of the nineteenth century. Like Tressell, they subscribed to the idea of public ownership of the means of production and distribution, but rejected a state structure for directing it. The Irish revolutionary James Connolly, who when in the US had collaborated with Daniel De Leon in founding the Industrial Workers of the World (IWW), argued that a future socialist commonwealth should be democratically organised from the bottom up through assemblies of workplace delegates, which would elect a national body. The working class organised on the lines of large-scale industry would become the 'real holding and administrative force of the world' if it was part of an industrial union that would function as 'an industrial republic inside the shell of the political state' that would then crack open this shell and replace it.

Connolly wrote that 'under a social democratic form of society the administration of affairs will be in the hands of representatives of the various industries of the nation; that the workers in the shops and factories will organise themselves into unions, each union comprising all the workers at a given industry; that said union will democratically control the workshop life of its own industry, electing all foremen, etc. ... that representatives elected from these various departments of industry will meet and form the industrial administration or national government of the country. ... In other words, social democracy must proceed from the bottom upward, whereas capitalist political society is organized from above downward.'[38]

The notion of bottom-up workers' control became widespread from 1912-22, and through the expansion of syndicalist influence came to pose 'a serious alternative to nationalisation as the main conception of socialisation.' Workshop committees had displaced the official structure of union authority by 1911-12, linked to a powerful shop stewards' movement in the engineering industry, and syndicalists had made deep inroads into every major union by 1914. Guild Socialists like G.D.H Cole, who were influential in the early Labour Party, also propagated the ideas of workshop control in place of parliamentarism. They joined in opposing 'the state collectivism and social welfarism that dominated progressive thought before 1914.'[39]

The greatest success of the syndicalist movement in Britain was the work of activists in the South Wales Miners' Federation who were linked to Tom Mann's Industrial Syndicalist Education League. In 1910 they led 30,000 miners on strike over conditions and wage cuts; although they were defeated, they summarised the lessons of the strike in a famous pamphlet, *The Miners' Next Step*. It was published in 1912 to coincide with the start of the national miners' strike over the minimum wage. The document aimed for the 'elimination of the employer', but also suggested various tactics short of an all-out strike to make the mines unprofitable. In this way, the miners could take over the industry and institute direct workers' control. The pamphlet imagined a central production board that would ascertain social needs and formulate requirements for the different departments of industry, 'leaving to the men themselves to determine under what conditions and how the work should be done. This would mean real democracy in real life.'[40]

The onset of the First World War raised acutely the class character of the national state. Social democratic parties throughout Europe that were committed to reforming capitalism through the existing state structure reneged on their professed internationalism and ended up capitulating to jingoistic war hysteria. In Britain, both Labour Party and union leaders actively encouraged the suspension of strikes in an 'industrial truce', despite the passionate anti-war campaigning of revolutionary syndicalists like Tom Mann, John Maclean, and J.T. Murphy. But while opposing the war and leading unofficial and illegal strikes that threatened to disrupt the production of munitions, shop stewards' leaders abstained from agitating politically against the war because they believed it would undermine workers' unity on industrial issues. By contrast, James Connolly continued the political struggle to free the Irish nation from British colonial rule and led the tragically defeated 1916 insurrection in Dublin. As Murphy was later to acknowledge, relying exclusively on the industrial struggle in Britain 'had the effect of handing the political initiative to the "patriotic" reformist labour leadership' and isolating the workshop movement in the engineering industry.[41]

As the munitions industry was run down at the end of the war, rising unemployment led initially to widespread industrial militancy, but undermined the shop stewards' movement and the workshop movement which were both defeated by the early 1920s. The subsequent decline of militancy facilitated the hegemony of the more bureaucratic leaders in the labour movement, who had embraced a philosophy that the industrial strength and political representation of the working class should be kept separate, later to be characterised as 'Labourism.'[42]

Historian Richard Price comments that after 1919 'the political credibility of Labourism was increasingly enhanced as the plausibility of alternative tendencies like direct action declined. ... the failure to achieve nationalisation of the railways or mines, the disastrous episode of Black Friday, and the subsequent defeats of the miners' strike in 1921 and of the engineers in 1922 were matched by the growing success of the Labour Party in national politics. Thus, the ultimate triumph of political Labourism depended as much upon the economic defeat of Labour as it did upon the internal manoeuvrings of the political leaderships.'[43]

The defeat of the general strike marginalised industrial and political militancy and established the domination of Labourism in the interwar years. Ideas of using industrial strength for political ends were taken off the agenda. Aneurin Bevan, who had been a follower of *The Miners' Next Step*, considered that the unions had been decisively defeated before 1926. He relates that when the leaders of the miners, railwaymen and transport workers, the so-called 'Triple Alliance', met with Lloyd George in 1919, the prime minister asked them if they were ready to accept the consequences of a victorious strike and take on the authority of the state. The miners' union leader, Robert Smillie, told Bevan he knew at that point they were beaten, and the alliance fell apart on 'Black Friday' in 1921 when the transport workers and railwaymen failed to strike in support of the miners. 'After this, the General Strike of 1926 was really an anticlimax,' Bevan remarked; his subsequent career as well as that of Tom Mann epitomised activists' turn away from revolutionary syndicalism to Labourist or Leninist politics respectively.[44]

The changing political alignments of the 1930s

In the 1920s Labour leaders were able to combine impassioned expositions of orthodox socialism in their speeches with capitalist economic policies in practice, until in 1931 the minority Labour government under Ramsay MacDonald capitulated to the Treasury's and international bankers' demands for cuts in unemployment benefit. The Labour ministers' vague belief that the state could somehow be redirected to facilitate a gradual evolution from advanced capitalism to a socialist society left them helpless in the face of the economic crisis and accompanying capitalist onslaught, and MacDonald's decision to join the Tories in a National government left the party in political confusion. In the summary judgment of Henry Pelling, 'On 25th August 1931 the TUC and the extra-parliamentary party took control of the parliamentary party and disavowed the leadership of MacDonald.'[45]

The electoral carnage in October that year severely weakened the parliamentary party and diminished its influence relative to the party's National Executive Committee, now dominated by the TUC. It was a traumatic experience that was formative in the outlook of party leaders until at least the 1970s. In its literature of the time, Labour revived the rhetoric of socialism and economic planning, emphasising a swift transference of power to the state; its 1931 manifesto proclaimed 'The decay of capitalist civilisation brooks no delay.' Socialist reconstruction, meaning nationalisation of major industries and banks, was now 'imperative': state planning became the way to achieve mastery over the capitalist economy.[46]

Left and right wings of the party fought over competing narratives of the government's collapse. The left concluded that capitalism was in its terminal crisis and socialism was potentially at hand, while the right considered that capitalism would continue for some time to come and what was more urgent were practical measures to alleviate unemployment. Commenting on his own political evolution, Attlee later wrote: 'The revulsion from MacDonaldism caused the Party to lean rather too far towards a catastrophic view of progress ... and to underestimate the recuperative powers of the capitalist system.'[47]

In 1932 the ILP broke away from the Labour Party with the intention of presenting an undiluted socialist message to the masses – but its membership thereafter disastrously declined. A large section of the ILP decided not to alienate themselves from the broader labour movement, and instead joined with left intellectuals such as Harold Laski and Stafford Cripps to form the Socialist League within the Labour Party. The League called for an immediate transition to the complete socialisation of industry and the banking system under a Soviet-style five-year plan. The power of the capitalist class had to be quickly neutralised through emergency powers taken on the first day of office of a Labour government; coercion was thus to be implemented constitutionally.[48]

The trade unions, led by Bevin and Citrine, had no enthusiasm for centrally planned jobs and wage rates and considered Cripps' plan to seize emergency powers liable to lose the party votes. An advocate of 'practical socialism,' Bevin was also influential in encouraging Labour's slow absorption of Keynesian economics. He had worked closely with Keynes in the MacDonald government and learnt that his ideas proved the burden of the crisis need not fall exclusively on the working class, even within the existing capitalist system.[49] Bevin and the NEC were concerned to steer the party in a direction that would make it more electable and undo Tory prime minister Stanley Baldwin's efforts to shut Labour out from power. Under Bevin's counsel, the new policy committee set up by the NEC attracted a number of liberal intellectuals concerned with the technical and legislative details of economic planning, investment and capital reconstruction. The two leading members of the committee were Herbert Morrison and Hugh Dalton. Dalton had gathered around him a circle of professional economists, including Hugh Gaitskell, Evan Durbin and Douglas Jay, who were to elaborate the objectives and machinery of socialist planning. They maintained that the market should continue to play a key role, even in a socialist system. 'Fervently anti-Marxist in domestic politics, the Dalton kindergarten was none the less profoundly influenced by the example of Soviet planning ... they were not Keynesians, but apostles of strong legal and physical controls over the economy.'[50]

The committee began to reconcile the socialist ideal of complete state control of the economy with the experience of the actual state Labour had encountered in its short experience of government, countering the left's priority of socialist reconstruction by changing the emphasis of policy to that of practical social provision of the necessities of life for working class families. Public ownership was retained in the party's platform, but it was reformulated: the idea of a state monopoly of employment, industry, and housing as the socialist answer to unemployment was re-mapped onto a programme of nationalisation of basic industries accompanied by centralised planning, a concept ambiguous enough to encompass both government participation in the economy and the ideals of the party membership.

Women did not receive equivalent voting rights to men until 1928, but forged a presence for themselves in Labour grassroots politics, aided by the growth of local constituency parties in the early 1930s. Up until that time women's roles within the party had followed the conventional gender division in the household, but while women's individual membership increased after 1931, support for the party's women's sections and the Women's Cooperative Guild went into relative decline.[51] Women were turning to broader class issues such as housing and unemployment and the threat of fascism and war, 'relinquishing those campaigns that sought to advance women's status within the party, or that focused on specifically gendered issues.' At the same time, Labour councils became closely associated with public ownership of amenities, housing, and municipal employment. As women were elected onto local councils, so their scope for political participation grew – reforms such as health clinics, maternity centres, washhouses, parks and playgrounds extended Labour's appeal and provided women 'with a distinctive place within Labour and municipal politics.'[52] A regional network of constituency parties developed around their role in local government, which encouraged the constituencies to become more assertive, and to protest their lack of representation on the NEC and their disquiet over the unions' block vote.

To Herbert Morrison, at the time leader of the London County Council, nationalisation meant a more rational form of capitalist industry, to be run by a commercially-minded board of governors appointed by a minister, in the form of a public corporation. He opposed workforce representation on the board since he considered workers did not have the necessary managerial expertise. However, he advocated this within the rhetorical framework of orthodox socialism, writing in 1933 that future Labour governments should socialise 'industry after industry under a management which can be broadly relied upon to go on with its work.' Attlee also believed that publicly-owned industries should be removed from direct political control, and advocated instead that the government should exercise its overall influence through planning, which was the 'essential new constructive idea which Socialism has to offer.'[53]

The stress in the party's literature during the 1930s changed from the importance of planning for the interests of 'the people' or 'community' to the interests of 'the nation.' Dalton formulated a policy that allowed for competition in a mixed economy, directed by the state, a plan that was a major break from the ideal of a cooperative commonwealth. Influenced by Keynes, the right-leaning intellectuals had changed calls for state ownership of the economy to a policy for financial planning of a mixed economy in which the public sector was to be predominant. Members of Dalton's circle 'combined a distaste for what they regarded as the self-indulgent expressivism of the Labour left with an intellectual scorn for demands for wholesale nationalisation and workers' control which seemed to them naïve and irrelevant to the main job of abolishing poverty.'[54]

In the years 1935 to 1937, the leadership reinforced its control of the party with the aid of the block union vote. As Addison puts it, 'the Bevinite school of thought ... put the Left in quarantine.' What exercised the left was the danger of fascism, which they perceived as an existential threat to be combatted by mobilising workers for direct action against Oswald Mosley in Britain and in support of the Republicans in Spain. Ernest Bevin, on the other hand, made the defence of the national state his priority and steered the party in the direction of supporting the government's steps to rearmament, despite the scepticism of the membership.[55]

After the Soviet Union began supplying weapons to the Republicans in Spain, many on the Labour left became convinced that an alliance with the Communist Party (CP) would strengthen the movement against fascism. However, a wave of unofficial strikes resulting from rising prices and increased mechanisation were blamed by union leaders on communist militants. The CP was denounced for 'leaving the trade unions to deal with the difficult situation created by their pernicious intervention in union affairs.'[56] At a national level, the hunger marches organised by the Unemployed Workers' Movement in 1934 and 1936 were shunned, despite pressures from Cripps and MPs like Aneurin Bevan. Moreover, 'while many Labour and trade union members joined with communists, Jews and non-party workers to do battle with the blackshirts – in Cable Street, Bermondsey and elsewhere – the official Labour line was to demand government action to prevent fascist parades and incitement to violence.' The Labour Party's MPs did not support the republican cause in Spain, lining up behind the National government policy of non-intervention – despite many local branches becoming active on the issue.[57] The Labour executive began to take disciplinary measures against those who supported demands for a United Front with the CP. However, it dared not act against Cripps. 'His standing in large sections of the Party was too high. The constituency parties loved him.'[58]

While the disputes over the United Front and rearmament continued to occupy the party's leading bodies, there was a revolt among the rank and file over internal governance. Grassroots activists began a campaign to get representation for local constituency parties on the NEC, pushing back against the trade union block vote that dominated conference decisions. Against the active opposition of the party leadership, it sought to create regional federations and organise constituency opinion. A consequence of the increase of the party's individual membership from 215,000 in 1928 to 431,000 in 1936, despite the debacle of 1931, was that 'the individual membership had become a powerful collectivity in its own right, able to insist on direct representation to the NEC. What is significant is that the Constituency Parties Movement ... succeeded in its demands because of its view of the role of the rank and file: not as the educators of the masses nor as the vanguard of the proletariat, but as people who selected candidates, raised money for elections, knocked on doors, licked envelopes, and got voters to the polls.'[59]

Unlike the Socialist League, the Constituency Parties Movement was able to gain support from the vast majority of constituencies, and at the 1936 annual conference in Edinburgh won the changes it sought in the party constitution. It succeeded by mobilising 'the great army of fundamentally loyal constituency activists in a *united* campaign against the discipline imposed by the general staff at Transport House. ... It was Transport House, not the constituency parties' association, which was shown to be out of touch with rank and file feeling.'[60]

Attlee's ideological intervention

The political authority of the Labour leadership at this time, then, was by no means assured. The constituencies were still strongly supportive of Cripps, although because of the trade union block vote this was not reflected in conference decisions. Orthodox socialist philosophy had advocated persuasion through propaganda of the mass of workers; workers' ideas and votes were the key to achieving a just society, not the direction of an enlightened elite. This tradition remained strong among the party membership, and was at the root of a potential conflict between the rank and file and the Fabian assumptions of Bevin, Morrison and Dalton. Attlee, although no theoretician, played a key role in marshalling the membership behind party policy. He had the advantage of an intimate understanding of Labour's institutions and membership gained by working his way up from the party's base.

Attlee's biographer states that Attlee sought to 'gain control' of the party through his 1937 book, *The Labour Party in Perspective*, which 'rejected the ideas of united fronts or popular fronts (hence Cripps and *Tribune*); it sold over 50,000 copies and set the tone for the Bournemouth party conference.'[61] What is interesting about the book is the structure of Attlee's political arguments, which reveals his sense of the attitudes of the party membership. He was able to accommodate a justification of the leadership's policies within the vision of orthodox socialism, by continuing to stress nationalisation as the foundation of a rational economy, and Bellamy's vision of individual 'duties to the community' as an alternative to state coercion.

Attlee constructs a narrative of the 1931 collapse that blames MacDonald for losing touch with the party rank and file because of his personal 'vanity' – not his policies – thus distancing the party leadership from responsibility, framing the episode as an individual act of disloyalty to the movement. An anti-fascist Popular Front coalition with non-socialist parties could not work, Attlee says, because of the fundamental disagreements between socialists and Liberals over nationalisation and the control of trade and industry. A United Front with the CP was equally impossible because of the principle 'that the socialist movement must be democratic, and that the will of the majority must prevail.' Making clearer the intended audience for his arguments, he goes on to say that a rapid growth of individual membership will increase the party's influence, and 'those who enter its ranks will accept the conditions and discipline of democracy.'[62]

Attlee is invoking here the principle of enforcing majority decisions on party members, what Eric Shaw calls 'social-democratic centralism,' based on workers' experience of trade union collective action in which the values of solidarity, unity and loyalty are paramount, and personal opinions are of necessity subordinated to the joint effort.[63] Attlee used this argument to criticise the ILP for refusing to follow majority decisions of the party conference, and the CP which, he said, would institute rule by an intellectual elite. He was then able to denigrate Cripps and the Socialist League for continuing to campaign for a United Front, against the party's majority decision; he himself would 'fall into line' behind a majority, he said, because he had 'great faith in the wisdom of the rank and file.'

He had more difficulty in reconciling the leadership's backing for rearmament in Britain with the party's history of support for international disarmament. He achieved this by reference to the disagreements over the imposition of sanctions and potential use of force after Italy invaded Abyssinia in 1935, that had forced Labour's former leader, the convinced pacifist George Lansbury, to resign. Attlee compared the use of force to uphold the rule of international law to a police action rather than military war. In building up defensive capability in Britain, Labour would be 'providing the forces necessary for the preservation of peace through the League of Nations.' His objections to the National government's programme were over its unsound foreign policy of alliances and the balance of power, not the principle of rearmament itself.[64]

The divisions over rearmament must be seen in light of the left's belief that the Tory-dominated National government 'would use force not to uphold the collective security of the League of Nations, but to defend and pursue its own national and imperialist interests.' TUC leaders Bevin and Citrine sympathised with Labour distrust of the National government, but for them the threat of fascism was of more pressing concern. The TUC general council recommended that Labour support the government's arms programme in 1935 after Hitler had reintroduced conscription and announced his intention to disregard the Versailles agreement over rearmament in Germany. The left of the party continued to argue against support for the government plan: Aneurin Bevan famously told the party conference in 1937, 'We are not going to put a sword in the hands of our enemies that may be used to cut off our own heads.'[65]

The ethical socialist notions of justice, equality and social improvement are prominent in Attlee's vision of the transformation of society, which he combined with a re-centering of the definition of socialism on improving the living standards of working class families. However, he reiterated the contemporary gender preconceptions of women as primarily housewives, mothers and consumers: the party aimed to represent the 'women in the home' who would be provided with the latest electrical appliances, rather than advocate for men to share the housekeeping: 'The aim of socialism will be to see that every family in the country has a house with electric light and power for cooking, central heating, refrigerator and plenty of floor space, one in fact that is well-furnished with everything that a modern housewife needs.'[66]

Attlee repeated the idea of state ownership of industries in a mixed economy as a substitute for the socialist notion of complete public ownership and control of industry, arguing that socialist planning 'will envisage a steady progress towards greater equalisation of wealth,' which is what distinguishes it from capitalist proposals for planning. He again stresses the role of the party membership in this transition. 'The existence in this country of thousands of men and women who give freely of their time and labour for the cause in which they believe is the thing which has enabled the workers, despite all the advantages of money, education, economic power, and social privilege which belong to their opponents, to create a political party able to contend for power. It is this army of active Socialists which will in due time achieve power and create the Britain which they desire.'[67]

Attlee and the Labour leaders believed as sincerely as the party rank and file in the ideal of the Cooperative Commonwealth. But in his argument for socialism, Attlee drew on the trade union movement's practice of separating 'immediate' from 'ultimate' aims: a Labour government 'has its general objective—the establishment of the Socialist Commonwealth,' he wrote. 'It must take the first steps for its realisation, but at the same time it has to deal with immediate and pressing evils which call for remedy.'[68] Attlee reiterated this idea at the 1937 party conference: Labour's programme was a 'table of priorities' to take Britain part of the way towards a socialist commonwealth.[69] Here is the first appearance of the argument that would be heard after 1945 that the government was taking the 'first steps' to socialism.

The Bournemouth conference rejected decisively any kind of joint action with the Communist Party against fascism. At the same time, it passed a resolution demanding a major programme of rearmament, calling for a government 'strongly equipped to defend this country to play its full part in collective security, and to resist any intimidation by the Fascist Powers designed to frustrate the fulfilment of our obligations.'[70] Even after 1939, when Labour support for a war against fascism found favour amongst the majority of its members and supporters, this was only reluctantly accepted. The Colne Valley Labour Party resolved: "The war we have dreaded for months back has come to pass and we are again at war. Our young men are being trained in the use of weapons of destruction with which to maim and kill their fellow workers in other lands. Apparently, no useful lesson was learnt by our rulers from the last war.'[71]

Although Bevin and Dalton are credited with the policy successes of the 1937 conference, Attlee was closely involved in the drafting of the party's election platform, and even wrote his own version. He insisted it was a practical programme which 'necessarily combines both ameliorative measures and fundamental changes,' and told the conference 'there is no new decision on Policy. It is made up from the decisions you have already taken.'[72] *Labour's Immediate Programme* gave more details of planning through the nationalisation of the Bank of England, coal, power and transport. A 40-hour week and paid holidays would be introduced. Prosperity depended on production conforming to 'a national plan under the guidance of the State;' state control of food prices, improved wages, statutory holidays, and 'vigorous measures' to increase employment were promised, but the programme was vague on the details of improved pensions and health services. While radical in promising public ownership and a more equal society, it contained a series of pragmatic measures to ameliorate unemployment and poverty, emphasising industrial policy over social welfare. 'As *Labour's Immediate Programme* made clear, the reconstruction of finance, land, transport and power would *lead* to benefits in food, wages, leisure and security.'[73]

While Labour's 1937 platform could be understood as advocating the gradual improvement of society rather than its overturn, it also promised a future of common ownership and a more equitable society in line with the party's constitutional commitment 'to secure for the workers by hand or by brain the full fruits of their industry ... upon the basis of common ownership of the means of production, distribution, and exchange.'[74] It provided the basis of the 1945 government's orientation, assuming a plan defined at the centre and implemented through Westminster and Whitehall with local governments taking a subsidiary role.

After continuing to campaign on a Popular Front platform, Cripps was expelled by the NEC in 1938 (as well as – briefly – Bevan), leading to what Dalton called 'a fight to the finish.' Cripps had little support from trade unionists, who placed a premium on loyalty and discipline. In the constituencies, however, Cripps had built up a large number of admirers. Richard Crossman was one; he wrote: 'We know that we are not living in a world which is evolving towards Socialism, and in which there is time to wait. ... [Cripps] knows the urgency of the situation and realises that Labour cannot jog along in the old traditional way.' But he got no support from those with a union background, to whom 'Cripps' flagrant defiance of Party decisions seemed disloyal, insolent and egotistical – symptomatic of a middle and upper class individualism which was really a kind of snobbery.' Middle-class intellectuals 'did not accept easily the dictates of long established leaders whom they regarded as their intellectual inferiors.'[75]

The political differences between left and right were not as great as the party's internal conflict made them appear. Influenced by a positive appreciation of bureaucratic planning in the Soviet Union, both sides accepted the idea of planning by a small body of experts, and of bringing unions into the process of government – but not of workers' control. The vocal opposition of the Socialist League to Dalton, Bevin and Morrison 'disguised an underlying agreement with the Labour right about the nature of planning which was [later] to serve as a basis for an agreement among all sections of the party on the fundamentals of a socialist state.'[76] Both sides agreed that reform should be carried out by the central state, overcoming regional disparities in services. Nationalisation would enable effective planning of the economy which would ensure greater efficiency and, as Attlee had spelt out, the equalisation of wealth and industrial democracy under a socialist government.

For labour activists, as suggested by the reception of *The Ragged Trousered Philanthropists* during this period and into the war years, the novel's vision of a classless society in a state-controlled economy remained the shared ideal of the movement. They were wedded to the idea of an immediate and substantial public ownership of industry and redistribution of wealth. The leadership, on the other hand, had moved in a more conservative direction, subordinating the idea of nationalisation to proposals for managing the economy without fundamental structural change. In his exposition of the party leadership's policies, Attlee found it necessary to reassure his rank and file audience that the remedy for the evils of capitalism remained public ownership, quoting Bertrand Russell to the effect that the meaning of socialism was 'the common ownership of land and capital ... production for use not profit, and distribution of the product either equally to all or, at any rate, with only such inequalities as are definitely in the public interest.'[77]

Despite the discrepancies between the party's immediate programme and full socialism, the unity of the party was maintained by the dualism inherent in the socialist ideal: 'the idea that Labour had a distinctively socialist commitment remained vital. It is this ambiguity, then largely concealed, that is at the heart of the social democratic perspective.'[78]

What I have demonstrated in this chapter is the that the ideas of orthodox socialism continued to dominate Labour Party discourse. At the same time, the leadership were exploring immediate solutions to unemployment within the structure of the existing state, which attracted them to Keynesian concepts of macroeconomic management that created full employment without the need for nationalisation. The party was held together ideologically by the idea of taking 'practical steps' to end unemployment and poverty in the short term, but understood as a means of paving the way for the ultimate goal of a socialist commonwealth. What the next chapter will address is how the fundamental social and political changes that took place during the Second World War altered the public perception of the party as a sectional movement tied to the unions, and universalised a 'Labour' political culture among the working class as a whole, even that large part of it that had voted Tory in the 1930s.[79] Throughout the war years, write the historians Steven Fielding, Peter Thompson and Nick Tiratsoo, Labour discourse 'would have been familiar to members of the turn-of-the-century ILP. The pioneer Robert Blatchford would have felt very much at home with most of the sentiments expressed during the decade.'[80] In other words, the membership's conception of socialism as a complete reconstruction of society had not changed, despite the party leaders' participation in the war coalition.

Chapter Two

The Changing Political Status of Organised Labour

'*When one came to work out solutions [in the War Cabinet] they were often socialist ones, because one had to have organisation, and planning, and disregard private interests. But there was no opposition from Conservative ministers. They accepted the practical solution whatever it was.*'[81] Clement Attlee, 1959

Labour in the wartime coalition

The Second World War brought about an important change in the relation of the labour movement to the state. In order to wage total war, the state had to rationalise industrial production and seek the cooperation of the organised working class. Labour was incorporated into the government, and insisted on trade union recognition in the factories; for the Labour leadership, state direction of industry appeared to coincide with the economic ideas of orthodox socialism. The idea of shared sacrifice that cut across classes was an expression of a radical egalitarian mood that was embodied in the proposals of the Beveridge Report for universal social security. Its popular reception and Labour's adoption of the report was a major factor in the party's election victory in 1945.

Despite the misgivings of its constituency parties, Labour supported Chamberlain's declaration of war on Germany after the Nazi invasion of Poland in September 1939. As acting leader of the parliamentary opposition while Attlee was ill, Arthur Greenwood broadcast to the nation: 'If we do not overthrow the forces of dictatorship now, our turn will come sooner or later.'[82] But the government's lacklustre prosecution of the war led to a military debacle in May 1940, when British forces had to be hastily withdrawn from Norway. The military escalation of the war coincided with a crisis of leadership in the government, which could only be resolved by ending Labour's pre-war marginalisation: if all-out war was to be fought, an accelerated programme of rearmament was essential, and, Ross McKibbin argues, 'it was almost impossible to devise any way of rearming which did not enormously increase the claims of the organised working class on society. The policy of appeasement must always be seen in that light; and the phoney war was an attempt to prolong the pre-war order into the war itself.'[83]

In this chapter I will show how the experience of war generated popular acceptance of the idea of state responsibility for social welfare, which drove Labour's social policy from below through its adoption of the Beveridge Report. The Labour leadership faced demands from the membership for an extensive programme of nationalisation, but was able to maintain party unity by combining its pragmatic drift to Keynesian methods of economic management with orthodox socialist rhetoric in its post-war election manifesto. Activists understood the party programme to be the sign of a 'first step' to a full socialist reconstruction of society, while the leadership cautiously foresaw, in Attlee's words, 'steady progress towards greater equalisation of wealth' in a mixed economy.

The fall of Chamberlain opened the way for Attlee and his parliamentary colleagues to join a coalition government under Churchill, changing the political complexion of the war from a big-power conflict to a fight against fascism. The course of the war itself had not only revealed the incompetence of the military establishment but also the authorities' inadequate preparation for the population's welfare, and it changed public expectations of the role of the state. People could not be expected to rehouse or feed themselves after being made homeless by bombing; food rationing had to be enforced, and emergency medical help had to be organised. *Daily Herald* journalist Ritchie Calder wrote a series of campaigning articles describing the plight of bombed-out families who were forced to navigate the bureaucratic jurisdictions of various ministries and local authorities in order to get shelter. They bore fruit when Herbert Morrison was promoted to Home Secretary and given overriding authority for welfare in London.[84] The demands of wartime administration merged local government health and welfare services into centrally directed institutions, and in effect the new bureaucracies this created began to change the character of the state.

1940 saw an important realignment of class forces, as the surge of production in the highly unionised but economically depressed heavy industries bolstered the self-confidence of the organised working class and legitimised its political aspirations and bargaining practices. Ernest Bevin used his position as Minister for Labour and National Service to advance the recognition of unions and improve working conditions in the factories essential for war production, cutting hours in munitions factories, and instituting workplace canteens and medical services. Even though the unions made major concessions over working practices as they redefined priorities, their bargaining power was greatly enhanced. Lewis Minkin notes: 'In these new conditions of production, local trade unionism thrived. Compulsory arbitration meant that employers were forced to negotiate.' The employers' 'right to manage' could now be challenged in the light of the need for maximum wartime production.[85]

The transformation of organised labour's political significance is affirmed by Jim Tomlinson, who describes how labour 'became *the* constraining factor in the war economy, the ultimate resource by which the war effort was planned.'[86] McKibbin comments: 'The political conception of the working class did not change; but the numbers of working people who thought they had an interest in embracing or perpetuating it increased rapidly.'[87] By the end of the war, the leaders of organised labour were incorporated into government policy-making on the same level as the representatives of big business.

Coinciding with Labour's entry into the coalition, the evacuation of the British army at Dunkirk created a sense of national unity, together with anger at the unpreparedness of the authorities, and with the Blitz fostered a new public mood which changed expectations of the state's responsibility for its citizens.[88] State direction and intervention were understood to guarantee equality of sacrifice, epitomised in the sentiment that 'we're all in it together', an idea that was crucial in motivating public effort. The collapse of pre-war Tory cultural hegemony facilitated this egalitarian attitude, even though the class divide remained intact and workers continued to resent the privileges of the middle class. Patriotism was redefined in terms of loyalty to the needs of ordinary people rather than support for military success. Practical considerations such as the need to reduce private consumption through rationing of essential commodities meant that the wealthy lost some of their privileges. 'Fair shares' were the order of the day.[89]

The substitution of the 'nation' for the 'community' in Labour's rhetoric during the 1930s facilitated a social patriotic outlook that was carried over into the coalition, and Labour ministers' participation in government administration allowed them to become acquainted with centralised state control of industry and manpower. This presented the leadership with an opportunity to implement reforms they had been advocating before the war, when they had no clear idea of how the measures were to be achieved, and it confirmed their belief that the existing state could be used to transform society through rational planning. Shortly before entering the coalition,

Attlee wrote to Grant McKenzie, secretary of Labour's subcommittee on local government, that 'It is abundantly clear that in order to win the war it will be necessary to utilise to the full the resources of the nation and that this cannot be done without direction and control ... While planning for war the government must plan for peace and a new society. Instead of regarding each piece of state control as a temporary infringement of the normal, the occasion should be seized to lay the foundations of a planned economic system.'[90]

The unions were established as an important part of state legitimacy. Leaders of the TUC were brought into government bodies alongside representatives of employers. Substantive concessions in economic and social welfare through existing administrative institutions rewarded unions' acceptance of the suspension of traditional industrial practices. However, from the left, Bevan bitterly criticised this integration for making union officials into agents of government policy. The experience reinforced the idea that tripartite collaboration between state, employers and unions was a model for peacetime planning, but, as Howell observes, 'The coalition measures labelled by Attlee as socialist involved the control of private industry by government agencies, and not the takeover of industries by the state.'[91]

In fact, Attlee identified the government's war measures with the general line of Labour's policy. The social changes that had been secured in the three years since 1940 would not have been believed possible before that time, he told a Labour Party rally: 'I spent many years of my life in a dock area where we suffered from the evils of casual labour. Over wide areas of industry today we have established the guaranteed week and the guaranteed weekly wage. In dock work, the build trade and many others, this is an immense advance.' Looking back 36 years to when he joined the movement, 'the most striking thing is the contrast between current conceptions of society then and today'. The socialist ideas which had been derided in the days of Keir Hardie and Bruce Glasier were now accepted by people of all kinds, he said, adding that 'In the midst of a world war, which seems to be the negation of ideals of human brotherhood, we can discern arising a greater acceptance of the Socialist ideal'.[92]

Labour's vision of the Socialist Commonwealth was strengthened by the party's new-found popularity. It was thought that this had happened not because of the party popularising its message, but that there had been a movement of the people towards the party.[93] The rhetoric of a Socialist or Co-operative Commonwealth remained in the party's wartime propaganda, alongside the commitment to nationalisation of basic industries.[94] It seemed also that orthodox socialism had been validated by the experience of war. Herbert Morrison was convinced that society had changed: he thought that a 'genuine social idealism' had been created, reflecting the 'altered sense of the community', and therefore Britain was 'moving into an altogether different form of society, working in an altogether different atmosphere of ideas,' shifting from the values of private enterprise to the values of socialism.[95]

Wartime radicalisation

The shift in the balance of economic power, together with the public's greater engagement with the war effort after the fall of Chamberlain, created a popular radicalisation that was not tied to any political party but was hostile to pre-war Conservatism. The dislocation and increased mobility of the population, together with the way wartime dangers overrode class differences, 'acted as a solvent on pre-war society, increasing the expectations of the disadvantaged, and perhaps in some cases chastening the consciences of the privileged. In this context, a vague popular radicalism developed; it was not for the most part explicitly socialist, but it centred around an instinctive rejection of the old order.'[96]

One of the early left critics of the 1945 government, Ralph Miliband, drew attention to the ideological message of a war against fascism as a factor in popular radicalisation but, drawing heavily on Mass-Observation reports, Fielding et al maintain that the public was not radicalised in the sense of wanting to change relations of power, being more concerned to prevent a return to pre-war unemployment and poverty. Its discontent, they claim, was diffuse and unfocused and had no coherent view of the future organisation of society; however, as McKibbin observes: 'The fact that people had real grievances is more significant than that the grievances were "vague".'[97]

Despite historians' disagreements about the political content of the radical mood, there is a general recognition that it was a rejection of specific aspects of the conditions of life in the 1930s. Most people wanted to return to the familiarity of the pre-war world, but 'with its blemishes – unemployment, slums and insecurity – removed.'[98] David Kynaston cites a survey of 200 working-class soldiers conducted between 1943 and 1946, which found that most feared a return to unemployment after the war. 'Some have experienced it themselves; others remember its effect on their own childhood; and for still others it exists as a malignant bogy that must dog the steps of every working man. Again and again a preference is expressed for the "steady job" as opposed to high wages, more especially by the older men. It is not likely that the lesson that England learned from the years of the trade depression will ever be forgotten.'[99]

There is, of course, a distinction to be made between the political orientation of labour activists and the extent of popular radicalisation, but the two are not disconnected. Fielding et al question the idea of radicalisation in industry, since 'rank-and-file demands had little to do with challenging control. Political considerations came a poor second to bread and butter issues. ... As in the army, radicalism was confined to the few and disregarded by the many.'[100] The authors discount the significance of the increase in the number of strikes, from 922 in 1940 to 2,194 as victory approached in 1944, because of their generally short duration and the fact that the most common cause of disputes was over wages. However, the readiness of workers to challenge management over wages when striking was officially illegal reflects an assertiveness built up over many smaller confrontations. There was at the very least a pervasive class hostility to management, sustained by conflicts over workplace discipline and working conditions. The authors' very narrow conception of radicalism excludes the covert but intense pattern of industrial conflict that Minkin considers reflected 'both an increased confidence of working people and the growth of a more vigorous industrial Left – all part and parcel of the new radical mood but not itself a significant cause of it.' Military and national political developments were a much greater influence on radical political opinion in wartime than disputes in industry.[101]

Mason and Thompson found other evidence of political radicalisation, especially the substantial increases in membership that all parties on the left experienced. The Common Wealth party and a number of independents inflicted several humiliating defeats on Conservative candidates in by-elections, while individual membership of the Labour Party rose from a low of 218,783 in 1942 to 265,916 in 1944 and 487,047 in 1945. The Communist Party increased its membership to between 50,000 and 60,000, three times its pre-war peak, and the orbit of Labour politics expanded by the increase in affiliated trade union membership from 2,663,000 in 1939 to 3,039,000 in 1945, despite wartime population movements and conscription.[102] Constituency activists were frustrated by the wartime electoral truce and were not deterred by the party leadership from campaigning for independent candidates. Tom Driberg stood in the Maldon by-election in June 1942 on a platform of common ownership of industries, the establishment of works councils, and improved pensions. Labour members in the local Braintree party protested the leadership's support for the Tory coalition candidate and unofficially worked for Driberg, who won the seat by 1,476 votes.[103]

The ramping up of war production effectively ended unemployment by the second year of the war, and workers began to reorganise trade union structures in the factories, becoming more militant in their struggles against factory management. The inefficiency of private industries necessitated state intervention through the building of 'shadow factories' with the most modern semi-automated equipment to utilise all available labour, including women workers, who were conscripted into factory production in 1941. The employers tried to take advantage of this by categorising women as semi-skilled, and not entitled to be paid at the skilled men's rate.

When Guest, Keen and Nettlefold in Smethwick attempted to do this in 1941 they provoked a strike in which skilled men supported the women but union officials sided with management. Similar strikes broke out in other factories where Amalgamated Engineering Union (AEU) officials failed to respond to women's grievances.[104] Bill Hunter, a Trotskyist, militant trade unionist and an acute observer of shifts in mood in the working class, was union convenor at the Chrysler factory in West London. In his autobiography, he writes that many of the large number of women workers 'had been conscripted from jobs in offices and shops; many had husbands or boyfriends in the Forces. They had been compelled to come into dirty conditions, with long hours of work, noise and smell. A remark made by one of the older working women sticks in my mind. She said: "If I don't fight for conditions and wages or let them get worse, my husband will kill me when he comes home." In this and other factories the women were a most militant force.'[105]

Conflicts with management over work practices were channelled by the newly strengthened shop stewards' movement into reorganising and increasing production through the newly-created Joint Production Committees (JPCs). Collaboration on production cut across the class-war outlook of militant trade unionists, but, in the Coventry engineering industry (critical for aircraft production), the majority of union activists in late 1941 embraced the JPCs because it enhanced trade union organisation across the industry, and also because they witnessed managements openly resisting the idea. 'The committees were only obtained after real struggles in the course of which large numbers of workers saw for the first time that it was possible to force their managements into taking unpalatable decisions.' The Communist Party's influence in the factories increased after the Soviet Union entered the war, becoming associated with the idea of sweeping away 'red tape', inefficient bureaucracy and management who defended the status quo. There was a public demand for greater efficiency in production regardless of whose authority might be diminished.[106]

In his study of the Coventry shop stewards' movement in wartime, Richard Croucher judges that the more left-wing shop stewards 'reflected and reinforced an increasing willingness on the part of workers in manufacturing industry to challenge the "managerial prerogatives" which employers had long claimed were necessary for the running of their enterprises.' However, now these attitudes were extended to a much wider stratum of engineering workers who had little connection with the craft union tradition. As well as JPCs giving workers a new forum to voice their opinions on work issues, wider social issues could also be raised; they encouraged a socialist patriotism that matched Labour's rhetoric of acting on behalf of the nation rather than for class interests, and of restoring the economy as a way to unite the country, independent of class power.[107] The expansion of the trade union and Labour Party affiliated memberships created 'reasonable expectations that a post-war government, whatever its political complexion, would pay due heed to the pressure from organised workers'.[108]

The Beveridge Report

Despite the fact that public radicalisation was not expressed in direct support for a political programme, it found an immediate focus in the Beveridge Report's advocacy of universal social insurance. The report was published by the government as a White Paper on 1 December 1942 and created an immediate sensation. 'It was received rapturously by the press and public,' writes Noel Whiteside, 'queues at the government bookshop signalled the eventual sale of half a million copies.' The report 'was initially seized by public officials as the means to raise depressed public morale. An abbreviated version was drawn up by the Ministry of Information and circulated to the troops; the full publication became the best-selling British government document of the twentieth century.'[109]

Bill Hunter wrote at the time that an official's mention of the Beveridge report in the Chrysler works canteen created a stir – to the chagrin of the management. 'In the canteen at dinner-time there was a propagandist for the Home Nursing Scheme. He was explaining its value and somehow managed to link it with social security and the Beveridge Report. "We are going to have our Beveridge," he said. There was a loud burst of clapping and banging of tables at this. A director was seen to take the personnel manager aside and agitatedly talk to him. It seemed he was chastising him for allowing "propaganda" in the canteen!'[110] The Chrysler management's dismay was matched by that of the Treasury, which had intended to keep the report secret. The report's publication had been delayed because, Cripps told Beatrice Webb in October 1942, 'some in the Cabinet object to it as too revolutionary.'[111]

The committee investigating social security that Sir William Beveridge headed had originally been set up in response to TUC pressure over the bewildering variety of sickness and disability schemes then in operation. The government conceded a small increase in benefits which the unions only accepted with the promise of a full inquiry, despite Bevin's grudging insistence it should not be a 'policy enquiry'. The Treasury especially was anxious that the committee should be secret, 'fearing that its inquiries would be interpreted as an indication of future policy'.[112] The government intended it to be a harmless exercise in administrative rationalisation, but Beveridge seized the opportunity to propose a comprehensive plan that would replace all the separate pre-war schemes with a single system of social security covering the whole community and financed by compulsory contributory insurance. He was convinced that poverty could be abolished by redistribution of income within the working class itself, without touching any of the wealthier classes – he argued that poverty in the 1930s was not the result of low earnings, but of unemployment, sickness, old age, or the death of a breadwinner.[113] Although no socialist, Beveridge leveraged the disruption and sense of social unity created by the war, as well as the opportunities provided by the enhanced political status of organised labour, to promote a bold scheme of liberal reform.

He prepared the ground carefully: throughout 1942 in speeches and articles he had referred to the need for 'equality of sacrifice' and the possibility of the abolition of poverty – creating the expectation that his report would be far-reaching and radical. Many witnesses to the inquiry already supported aspects of his reforms, 'a measure of the extent to which Beveridge himself was interpreting and responding to, rather than creating, the spirit of the times,' writes his biographer. Witnesses called to his committee spontaneously pressed for the same proposals as his main policy ideas: family allowances, full employment, a universal health service, a uniform system of contributory insurance, subsistence-level benefit at a flat rate, and the reduction or abolition of public assistance.[114]

Beveridge spent a considerable amount of time negotiating with the TUC over his plan to integrate workmen's compensation into social insurance. Industrial injury payments were earnings-related and therefore much higher than the subsistence level, and the unions also believed it gave employers an incentive to make workplaces safer. He compromised by distinguishing short-term injury – to be compensated at the flat rate – from longer-term injury where benefits should be earnings-related. He was able to tell a meeting of the TUC soon after the report was published that there was little difference between its proposals and those of the unions, with the exception of their disagreement over disability benefit.[115]

Beveridge's plan to defeat the 'five giants on the road to reconstruction' – Want, Disease, Ignorance, Squalor, and Idleness – rested on three main assumptions: family allowances, a health system free to all in need of medical care, and government-engineered full employment. In return for a single weekly flat rate contribution, shared between employers, the insured, and the state, every contributor would receive unemployment or sickness benefit sufficient for a minimum subsistence, except in the case of pensions, which were to be raised gradually over twenty years. The most controversial issue was family allowances, which would supplement subsistence level benefits for families with more than one child. A free health service would prevent medical bills wiping out the benefit, and full employment would ensure that all contributed.

The report itself was not exactly generous to claimants. It was a conservative document, setting benefits at the minimum necessary for subsistence – just below the wages of the lowest-paid worker – and restricting benefit to those both available and willing to work. Applicants in fact had to supplement national insurance with a more generous but means-tested national assistance. However, it contained the premise that the state would guarantee the security of a basic income, removing the fear of poverty from all sections of society. His assumption of full employment directly addressed the anxiety of returning to 1930s unemployment lines after the war ended. However, it also assumed a conventional family unit with the man as the main breadwinner and the woman having primarily domestic responsibilities.

What most resonated with the public was the principle of universality embodied in its promise of benefits 'as of right and without means test', as Beveridge summarised his plan. The context of full employment, conscription and mass mobilisation engendered by the war enabled him to define social insurance as an attribute of citizenship – although this contradicted his emphasis on a 'contractual' entitlement gained through contributions.[116] The abolition of the means test was particularly welcomed by the labour movement; when unemployment rose in the 1930s, skilled workers in traditional industries like shipbuilding, the mines and engineering did not have the requisite 15 weeks of contributions and had found themselves treated like paupers.

The war itself was sweeping away 'sectional interests' – it was a 'revolutionary moment in the world's history,' Beveridge wrote. But the individual had to take responsibility as well as the state to provide for the family. The plan was based on 'benefit in return for contributions, rather than free allowances from the state'. Moreover, '[to] give by compulsory insurance more than is needed for subsistence is an unnecessary interference with individual responsibilities'. Citizens 'should not be taught to regard the state as the dispenser of gifts for which no one needs pay'. The report even contained an element of coercion: 'The correlative of the state's undertaking to ensure adequate benefit … is enforcement of the citizen's obligation to seek and accept all reasonable opportunities for work.'[117]

Beveridge combined these stern admonishments with radical language that rejected 'the scandal of physical want' and redefined the object of government, in line with the Atlantic Charter, as 'the happiness of the common man'. In stirring language that appealed to egalitarian objections to privilege, he declared that winning freedom from want requires 'faith in our future and the ideals of fair-play and freedom' as well as 'a sense of national unity overriding the interests of any class or section'. His tone matched exactly the popular mood, while his assumptions of full employment and a national health service placed social reform squarely on the agenda of national war aims.[118]

As Beveridge hoped and the Treasury feared, the report 'was interpreted in many quarters as a token of the government's commitment to post-war social reform … in industrial areas like Clydeside, meeting after meeting of workers passed resolutions of support'.[119] Trades unionists across the country welcomed the plan and urged the government to stop delaying the setting up of a Ministry of Social Security. At a meeting of the Midlands Federation of Trades Councils held on 16 January 1943, Mr. E.W. Bussey told delegates that 'though the plan envisaged no fundamental change in the capitalist system, it should be the aim of the trade union movement to lead the fight for its adoption.'[120] However, this sentiment was not universal: for the ILP, which had maintained its separate organisation during the war, Campbell Stephen wrote that without socialism, 'we shall have to face the possibility, nay, probability, of mass unemployment in the post-war years as formerly. Then the finances of the scheme will break down.'[121] Jack Rogers, a rank-and-file member of the Fire Brigades Union, urged the TUC to reject the report. He was certain 'that it is the alternative of the Tory party to a Socialist Government and a planned economy. … It is a typical Tory move to secure class collaboration and to return to pre-war conditions.'[122]

Beveridge had been convinced by the war that planning could be made compatible with democracy, that extension of central regulation would be accepted and could be used to maintain full employment after the war. But far from assuring a minimum standard of life as of right for every citizen, as the National Council of Labour had assumed, describing it as a 'Charter for Security', Beveridge had argued that people were not entitled to welfare by virtue of being members of a community, but only as contributors to the system. Eligibility for welfare depended on participating in the labour market – but by the same token, it was not dependent on a means test or social conformity. The report thus recognised workers' legitimate claims on state support, and, for Labour, the universality of the system meant that entitlement to benefits was equated with social citizenship.

McKibbin judges that '[w]hat Beveridge did was to give [public] opinion something around which to organise and a new political mood coherence and detail'. He adds: 'most contemporary surveys of opinion detected four fundamental themes: support for the expansion of social services; a conviction that the state could and should maintain full employment; a growing faith in "planning" (partly a result of admiration for the Soviet Union); the development of a language of social citizenship. The extraordinary support for Beveridge must be seen in terms of these expectations: it seemed to embody all of them. ... It spoke to a population ready to listen, which is one reason why it was so widely publicised.'[123]

Comprehensive national insurance had never been part of Labour's pre-war perspective, but the popular enthusiasm for Beveridge led the party to claim it for itself, in place of any coherent plan of its own. Labour intellectuals had paid little attention to social insurance, instead focusing on the economic transition they believed should precede and underpin measures of social amelioration. 'Although proposals for extending welfare were included [in Labour's 1937 *Immediate Programme*], these were regarded as secondary measures intended for implementation in the wake of economic reconstruction.' The egalitarian mood created by the war 'did not necessarily alter Labour's understanding of the kind of measures needed for reconstruction, but it forced a rethinking of the order in which they might be implemented. Social reform moved up the agenda.'[124]

Working-class enthusiasm for social insurance during the 1930s had surprised the left in the Labour Party, which held a largely hostile attitude to the state as a vehicle for capitalist domination. But the 1934 party programme committed to the principle of a state health service, and in 1937 to pension and social security reform. 'This growing priority given to social welfare schemes received a great reinforcement from the outbreak of war and particularly from Labour's entry into the Churchill coalition. ... The "price" of Labour's support for the war was to be the implementation of social justice and the "making of a more equal society", wrote Harold

Laski.'[125] The document on reconstruction produced by Laski and Shinwell for the 1942 party conference, *The Old World and the New Society*, repeated orthodox socialist ideas about the bankruptcy of the capitalist system, but its general conclusions were in line with wartime public attitudes: 'We must organise now to provide full employment; to rebuild a better Britain; to provide social services to secure adequate health, nutrition and care in old age, for everybody; to provide full educational opportunities for all.'[126]

The 1942 conference in fact saw an important shift in the attitude of the unions to family allowances. Since 1930 the TUC had opposed them on the grounds that collective bargaining for a high standard wage would be sufficient to allow a worker to support his (*sic*) family, while cash payments to mothers would undermine unions' bargaining power and upset the wages structure. The unions were now divided over the proposal to include them in a comprehensive scheme of social security, with Arthur Deakin of the T&GWU backing an amendment that would have removed mention of family allowances from the main resolution. Supporters of the amendment argued that until social reconstruction had removed the root causes of poverty, allowances should be rejected, despite the immediate needs of children whose fathers were missing or killed in the war. The ASLEF delegate, moving the amendment (which was overwhelmingly defeated in a card vote), declared: 'Once you have socialised the main industries of the country, once you have taken control of the railways and the mines and the factories, and have removed the profit motive from industry, [then] there might be a case for family allowances ....'[127]

After the publication of the Beveridge Report, however, Labour's hostility to the state as an oppressive force was muted and it gained a more positive role in party discourse. The left took up the report's proposals as their own special mission and demanded their immediate implementation. 'When voices were raised at the party conference in 1943 against Beveridge's advocacy of direction of manpower they were drowned by an extraordinary outburst of enthusiasm for what had always in the past been one of Labour's sacred nightmares. "So far from protesting, I, who have just received a direction, rejoice in it," declared a delegate from England's largest coalface. "I am glad that the government has got both the guts and the intelligence to tell me what I have got to do".' The party leadership was cautious about how quickly the proposals could be implemented, but did not disagree with their underlying philosophy. Attlee declared that the Beveridge plan marked the transition from the 'conception of the police state' to the 'conception of the social service state'.[128]

Churchill, the Treasury, Cabinet members and the Tories all had grave misgivings about the financial commitment being entered into, but for the left Bevan claimed that Beveridge had elevated social security above the claims of property, thereby unconsciously threatening capitalism. In a parliamentary debate on the report in February 1943, virtually all Labour backbenchers voted in favour of a motion condemning the government position of avoiding any commitment to implementing Beveridge. They were joined by enough other MPs to endanger the basis of the coalition; only two Labour backbenchers supported the government.

Widespread support for social reform could not quell a general anxiety that the welfare plan would be watered down or shelved because of 'vested interests', a term associated with the Tories. In response to Churchill's attempts to defer legislation until after the war, Attlee wrote to him: 'decisions must be taken and implemented in the field of post war reconstruction before the end of the war. It is not that persons of particular political views are seeking to make vast changes. These changes have already taken place ....'[129] Attlee's comment is another indication that Labour's social policy was being driven by events, rather than by the socialist commitment of the party, although such a commitment certainly existed.

According to Addison, Home Intelligence inquiries between August and October 1942 found that the majority of the population were not thinking much about the future. But there was a 'thinking minority' of people, between 5 per cent and 20 per cent of the population, which believed that 'i) there must be work at a living wage for everyone who is capable of doing it; ii) private profit must cease to be the major incentive to work, everyone must work primarily for the good of the community; iii) there must be financial security for everyone who is unable to work; iv) there must be decent homes for everyone at a cost which will not reduce people to poverty; the same education must be available to everyone so that all will have an equal chance. ... The level of war expenditure had led the majority to believe that finance could not in future be regarded as a barrier to its [social security's] achievement.'[130]

The debate over nationalisation

While the foremost ideas among the 'thinking minority' discovered by the Home Office were the security of work at a living wage, affordable homes, and the end of an economy based on profit, Labour's activists were insistent on realising these aims through the socialist ideal of nationalisation. The Labour leadership was working within the coalition's parliamentary discipline, but from the back benches Aneurin Bevan demanded that property had to be conscripted as well as labour, and people should be given arms for defence in a 'people's army'. He linked the war for liberation in Europe to colonial freedom, especially the independence of India. His own plan for post-war reconstruction relied on radical economic centralism and ultimate control by the House of Commons as an expression of the popular will.

In a 1943 Fabian pamphlet, he 'envisaged the immediate nationalisation of all the basic industries of the country and their administration by a Supreme Economic Council of "able men" ... under the general but not the detailed control of the House of Commons; distribution of certain goods like milk and public transport should be free, the price of all other economic essentials fixed ... and the free market left to operate only in minor areas of economic activity.' Bevan rejected the coalition's 1944 White Paper pledging full employment through the use of Keynesian demand management. 'If a progressive society and an expanding standard of life can be achieved by this document and unemployment can be avoided, then there is no justification for public ownership and there is no argument for it. ... This party believes in public ownership of industry because it thinks that only in that way can society be progressively and intelligently organised.' Public ownership for Bevan was a sign of a commitment to reorganise society on socialist lines.[131]

While the parliamentary leadership had been confirmed in its confidence that a consensus between the state, management and the unions would provide a solution to the pre-war problems of unemployment and poverty, the party membership remained committed to a socialist policy of full nationalisation and redistribution of wealth. At the Labour Party conference in December 1944, rank-and-file delegates demanded a much more rigorous programme of nationalisation than the leadership would contemplate: 'The main economic resolution which the Executive presented to the Conference ... made no mention whatever of public ownership ... the activists, both in the constituencies and in the trade unions, had very different ideas. Resolution after resolution on the agenda of the Conference demanded an extensive programme of common ownership.'[132]

The NEC's resolution avoided any specific commitment to nationalisation by referring to 'the transfer to the State of power to direct the policy of our main industries, services and financial institutions'. But most of the participants in the conference debate argued that unemployment was inseparable from capitalism and called for substantial plans for nationalisation. The delegate from Reading Labour Party was Ian Mikardo, who successfully moved a counter-resolution for a commitment to 'the transfer to public ownership of the land, large-scale building, heavy industry, and all forms of banking, transport and fuel and power ...' The Reading CLP's resolution was seconded by Mrs E. Denington of the South-West St. Pancras Labour Party, who clarified: 'Everybody now can see that anarchic capitalism means unemployment, degradation, malnutrition, and misery, and that any form of capitalism means inevitable war. Sir William Beveridge in trying to put forward a new solution dressed the old wolf in sheep's clothing, but the wolf is still there, and the only way of getting rid of it is to kill it stone dead.' Mrs. Denington's remarks expressed the continuing tension in party discourse about the relation of social welfare to the aim of complete socialism.[133]

While the party membership adhered to these orthodox positions, Attlee and the labour leadership believed that the consensus that had emerged in the war meant that society had already changed in a socialist direction. After Harold Laski had written to Attlee in 1944 to urge a rapid transition to socialism, Attlee replied: 'Although you are a theorist and I am only a working politician I think that I give more and you give less attention to changes of conception than to legislative achievements. For instance, I have witnessed now the acceptance by all the leading politicians in this country and all the economists of any account of the conception of the utilisation of abundance. ... There follows from this the doctrine of full employment. The acceptance of this again colours our whole conception of the post-war set-up in this country. ... I count our progress much more by the extent to which what we cried in the wilderness five and thirty years ago has now become part of the assumptions of the ordinary man and woman.'[134]

While some politicians, such as the Tories Harold Macmillan and Quintin Hogg, as well as the economist J.M. Keynes, had indeed accepted the need for social reform, their disagreement with orthodox socialism was over the question of nationalisation. Attlee had prefaced his remarks to Laski with the observation that, whatever the complexion of the post-war government, it would 'have to work [with] a mixed economy'; and if it was a Labour government, 'a mixed economy developing towards socialism'. This somewhat ambiguous formulation reflected Morrison's argument in 1943 that Labour should no longer seek to nationalise the whole of private industry, but instead opt for 'a practical mixture of genuine socialism and genuinely free enterprise', that would support policies of social and industrial welfare.[135] What this implied was that state-owned industry would support, rather than replace, private corporations in a mixed economy, contrary to the membership's understanding of Labour's aims.

The 1945 election

In 1945 the Labour Party leaders were prepared to continue the social arrangements achieved under the coalition, but were nevertheless cautious about the policies to be followed. Attlee argued that the majority of people had acquired some form of property through pension schemes, savings deposits, and social security rights. Remembering the 1931 election, he wrote: 'In face of this it is time that the Labour Party ceased to mouth Marxian shibboleths about the proletariat having nothing to lose but their chains. It is just not true.'[136] Labour stood squarely for the corporate form of economic direction that had been established during wartime. The apparatus of wartime planning buttressed their predisposition to control industry through means other than public ownership.[137]

This approach was reflected in the party's election campaigning. Both Attlee and Morrison downplayed the extent of nationalisation envisaged by Labour. Not everything would be nationalised, Attlee told supporters: only those industries that would enable a Labour government to build 'the kind of Britain they wanted to see'. Likewise, Morrison made clear that 'The Labour party offers a short-term programme of socialisation of a limited number of industries and in each of these industries it rests its case on the practical facts of the situation'.[138] The collapse of Toryism meant that an unprecedented portion of the middle class had moved away from Churchill and his party, but the most significant shift of opinion had taken place in the manual working class. While not necessarily enthusiastic about the prospect of socialism or nationalisation, 'they did hope – manual working class and middle class alike – that Labour's support for welfare reform was genuine. By implementing Beveridge and building houses they trusted that Labour would stand a good chance of preventing Britain returning to pre-war poverty and misery.'[139]

Labour's 1945 election manifesto, *Let Us Face the Future*, contained a commitment to implement the main features of the Beveridge report, adding to them a national health service and a major effort to build new housing. It contained a mixture of Keynesian and socialist ideas, with proposals to continue the kind of economic management that had been carried out under the coalition. The government would take responsibility for maintaining full employment through stimulating production. The party's membership saw the reforms outlined in the manifesto 'as only a preliminary step towards the [Socialist] Commonwealth. Few in the Party believed that in themselves nationalisation and the welfare state constituted socialism. ... The definition of socialism and the strategy of gradual reform outlined in the document were accepted with little dispute [at the 1945 conference].'[140]

The manifesto promised a complete overhaul of the nation, evoking 'the Dunkirk spirit' to make the effort involved in 'a great programme of modernisation and re-equipment of its homes, its factories and machinery, its schools, its social services'. As well as government-planned investment in essential industries and infrastructure, 'production must be raised to the highest level'. Private monopoly of basic industries should be overturned by public ownership in order to advance industrial efficiency. The 1930s depression was blamed unequivocally on under-consumption; an expanded economy depends on 'our ability to produce and organise a generous distribution of the product' that will maintain 'a high and constant purchasing power'. The themes of increasing demand and full employment were unmistakably Keynesian, but the presence of Ian Mikardo on the drafting committee had ensured the inclusion of the calls for nationalisation.

Labour would introduce social security for all, but 'only an efficient and prosperous nation' can afford 'great national programmes of education, health and social services', it declared. 'There is no good reason Britain should not afford such programmes, but she will need full employment and the highest possible industrial efficiency in order to do so.' The stern homilies of the manifesto gave voice to the planners and experts at the centre of the existing administration. Its promise to give industry any help needed 'to get our export trade on its feet' on the condition that 'industry is efficient' advanced a prototype of industrial corporatism, extended from the wartime planning measures of the coalition government, in order that Britain should 'keep her place as a Great Power'. But the manifesto also proclaimed that 'The Labour Party is a Socialist Party, and proud of it. Its ultimate purpose at home is the establishment of the Socialist Commonwealth of Great Britain – free, democratic, efficient, progressive, public-spirited, its material resources organised in the service of the British people.'[141]

While social surveys did not show much excitement about the politics of the 1945 election – most thought that not much would change and feared a return to 1930s unemployment – in general Labour convinced voters that it could deliver on two major issues: security of work and a crash programme of house-building. However, there was intense interest from organised workers. The possibility of full employment, of the nationalisation of private industries, depended on which party was in government. 'The move away from the Conservatives was particularly striking in the larger industrial towns, reflecting the strong reformist spirit reigning in these areas. ... The election campaign [had] the deep involvement of many trade-unionists at all levels ....'[142]

This was typical of most industrial centres, including Luton, home of the Vauxhall car factory. 'Electors Losing Apathy: Political Warming Up Beginning in Luton: First Assembly Hall Meeting Draws 2,000 Audience' ran the headline in the local paper as the Labour candidate, William Warbey visited the Vauxhall works. However, his most enthusiastic reception was in the heavy-machine shop of Hayward-Taylor & Co. as workers 'banged out a welcome with hammers and other tools'.[143] It was not just the industrial centres, either. As a returned soldier in 1945, E.P. Thompson witnessed several election meetings in rural Buckinghamshire. 'Packed meetings of suddenly undeferential villagers applauded every expression of hope for a socialist Europe and every reference to the heroism of the European Resistance movements or the feats of the Red Army (which everyone knew had saved what small ration was left of British bacon).'[144]

In London's East End, Lord Elwyn-Jones recalled the packed eve-of-poll meeting in Canning Town Public Hall. 'None of us who took part will ever forget it – the rows of intent, uplifted faces – dockers in their caps and white mufflers, the wives and children and old men and workmen who had been through so much.' Barbara Castle, likewise, remembered the eve-of-poll meeting in St. George's Hall, Blackburn, which had 'a sort of unbelievable buoyancy in the atmosphere, as though people who had had all the textile depression years, the men and women who had suffered in the forces and the women who had been working double shifts, making munitions and the rest of it, suddenly thought, my heavens, we can win the peace for people like us.'[145]

Wartime social patriotism enhanced the idea that people were entitled to the spoils of victory. Philip Masheder explained his reason for voting Labour with the belief that if the war had been lost, 'all the landowners in Great Britain would have lost their land, it would have gone to Germany. Now here you've got millions of lads coming out of the forces, literally hundreds of thousands of them getting married, they go into a house. That house is costing them extra money because somewhere along the line someone had to pay for that land. Now that ground that those houses were built on belonged to me and you, shouldn't really belong to the landowners. We'd just fought for England, and Scotland, hadn't we?'[146]

The election of a Labour government did not change the class system – but the leadership of the organised working class had become part of governmental legitimacy, dislodging the identification of the state with an exclusive social elite. Arthur Marwick argues that society had changed 'not in basic structure, but in ideas and social attitudes and relationships in how people and classes saw each other and, more important, in how they saw themselves'.[147] The right-wing but socially conscious journalist Peregrine Worsthorne (later editor of the *Sunday Telegraph*), noted that what changed in 1945 was not an ending of the privileges of the social elite; what had ended was 'the ethos of hierarchy that made sense of those privileges. Everything about the class system was left intact except its *raison d'être*.'[148] An anecdote cited by Kynaston illustrates this: '"My man," called out a blazered, straw-hatted 14-year-old public schoolboy, John Rae, as he stood on Bishop's Stortford station with his trunk that late July. "No," came the porter's quiet but firm reply, "that sort of thing is all over now".'[149]

The effect of these changing social attitudes had been to bolster Labour's support. The war had restored the communities in the North that were the foundation of the labour movement and had 'tended to universalise a "Labour" political culture among the working class as a whole, something deliberately promoted by those Labour members of the coalition government disproportionately represented in its domestic portfolios ... The result of such universalising was to sweep into the Labour party much of the working class that had hitherto stood outside it, most notably in the West Midlands.'[150]

McKibbin concludes that society's shift to the left in 1940 was primarily 'an ideological change; a shift in perception rather than a "structural" shift'. This was the outcome of the resolution of a political crisis largely confined to a political elite, but which almost inevitably radicalised much of the population to Labour's benefit. Moreover, 'radicalisation was genuine; people were not apolitical or cynical. Nor did they vote Labour because they could think of nothing else to do. ... people seem to have had a reasonable idea of what they wanted, and the Beveridge Report gave that idea coherence.' People voted Labour in 1945 because it was identified with Beveridge and because the Tories were identified with the unemployment and misery of the 1930s.[151]

Going into the election, voters proved to be in a remarkable accord with Labour's conception of the common good. The population had endured privation and collective sacrifice and its expectation was that full employment, at the very least, would be restored. Labour better expressed this mood, to which it had responded in the reorganisation of its priorities. From the standpoint of the party rank and file, the implementation of welfare reforms could only be a temporary solution to the problems of capitalism. They believed public ownership of industry was imperative in order to prepare for a future socialist society. However, the public was less inspired by Labour's nationalisation programme than by an understanding that, as the Beveridge Report put it, victory in war would reward them with 'a better world than the old world'.[152]

In this chapter I have shown how the incorporation of the Labour Party into the wartime coalition reinforced the leadership's belief in a gradualist approach to nationalisation, wealth redistribution and social reform, and undermined their left critics' calls for an immediate transition to socialism through wholesale public ownership. Labour activists were still strongly committed to the ideal of a Socialist Commonwealth, but Attlee was probably closer to the public mood in his reluctance to initiate more economic disruption instead of first ensuring full employment and a social safety net. The public exerted its own agency in its reception of, and demand for the implementation of, the Beveridge report. The report was also backed by the TUC and, more reluctantly, by the party leadership. This circumstance marked an important shift in the Labour left's attitude to the state, from conceiving it as a repressive force, to envisaging it as a vehicle for undermining private property. However, activists' assumptions continued to be shaped by the orthodox socialist idea that the government should replace all capitalists with state ownership.

Three major categories of analysis that conceptualise historical agency in this period can be discerned: firstly, political discourse within the Labour Party itself, revolving around the policy of nationalisation; secondly, the independent role of public opinion, unequivocally supporting the egalitarian message of the Beveridge report; and finally, social change achieved through the wartime accommodation to labour's prerogatives, augmenting the egalitarian trend through the idea of equal sacrifice for the war effort. In the next chapter I will address how the Labour government approached the management of the capitalist state with an initial reforming zeal, which ran out of steam after wartime discipline began to evaporate. However, its implementation of Beveridge's proposals and the establishment of the welfare state reacted back on society to consolidate a collectivist consensus, and for the left created a new understanding of what a socialist society should look like.

Chapter Three
Labour in Power

'If the faith in economic planning, as Socialists conceived it, could be undermined, the case for nationalisation would lose a major support in Labour's ideology. That, in a nutshell, is what happened as a result of the experience of Attlee's Governments.'[153] Samuel Beer, 1965

The 1945 Labour government

When Harry Leslie Smith, then an RAF serviceman stationed in Hamburg, cast his ballot in the 1945 general election, he understood it as giving him a chance of changing his future for the better. He voted for 'all those who had died, like my sister, in the workhouse; for men like my father who had been broken beyond repair by the Great Depression; and for women like my mum who had been tortured by grief over a child lost through unjust poverty. And I voted for myself and my right to a fair and decent life. I voted for Labour and the creation of the welfare state and the NHS, free for all its users.'[154]

In this chapter I shall show that many of those, like Harry Leslie Smith, who voted for a brighter future and a better world, found that the government they elected was constrained by the capitalist foundations of the economy. It depended on US loans to avoid immediate bankruptcy, and adopted Keynesian methods of economic management that made the idea of a fully socialised economy redundant. It created a welfare state on the foundation of a mixed economy in the conditions of a post-war economic boom that allowed full employment to be maintained. It was the first time that the idea of nationalisation was put into practice on an industry-wide scale – with the result of making explicit the divergence between orthodox socialist ideas of public ownership and the government's subordination of production to the needs of rebuilding industrial capital. The left's idea of socialism shifted to an emphasis on the government's achievement of full employment and social welfare, with further nationalisations postponed to a future date.

Labour won the election with a commanding parliamentary majority. Sustained by popular expectations, it placed major industries in public ownership and legislated welfare reforms which materially improved the living standards of the working class, despite the challenge of restoring an economy bankrupted by war. Social reconstruction in Britain had a special significance because of the way the idea of the welfare state had become identified with the country's war aims. In addition, the government's actions were understood by the labour movement as the realisation of the programme it had campaigned for since 1918: nationalisation, social welfare, pensions, and an end to endemic unemployment.

The government did not bring about the socialist commonwealth, but instead fought for the survival of British capitalism, to which workers were bound by the chains of work discipline and their orientation to the state. However, its rescue had the effect of perpetuating the country's industrial backwardness. Unlike European nations that had experienced occupation and defeat, there was little thought about the need for industrial restructuring. The Attlee government continued a social consensus that maintained full employment, but that left intact the hegemony of private property; it was the change in the labour movement's understanding of the class nature of the state – from an instrument of class repression to an agent for reform – that enabled this corporatist approach to be portrayed as socialist.

The government continued and consolidated the social gains made by the working class during the war, implementing Beveridge's proposals and instituting a national health service, extending free education, and building council homes. Together with full employment, these were 'facts on the ground' that engendered a fierce loyalty from the industrial working class.[155] At the same time, the party's political discourse was re-configured: the government's legislative achievements undermined the left's argument for the necessity of a swift transition to 'complete socialism', which gave way to the idea that the reforms were 'the first step' towards a socialist society. Ralph Miliband remarks: 'The activist saw the Welfare State and the nationalisation measures of 1945-8 as the beginning of the social revolution to which he believed the Labour Party was dedicated; while his leaders took these achievements to *be* the social revolution.'[156]

Labour's cohesiveness was ensured by framing the government's actions within the shared socialist ideal. The material and moral changes brought about by the war meant that 'party members thought it realistic to expect that a Labour Government could move purposefully and, given the constraints of parliamentary democracy, swiftly towards the Socialist

Commonwealth. ... That Labour stood for something less than socialism was unthinkable.'[157] Even the attempts by the government to combat inflation through wage controls, or its prosecution of industrial militants in the 1950s under the wartime Order 1305 – provoking a strong reaction from the party and unions – did not shake this conviction.[158] However, after 1947 the government shifted away from its commitment to the socialist commonwealth and towards a Keynesian managed economy, subordinating the socialist aspects of Labour's ideology to considerations of efficiency and economic survival.

The close relation between the unions and government was consolidated and strengthened after the electoral victory. It established the framework of 'economic success, political moderation, industrial accommodation and access to government by the unions' that Minkin identifies as the basis of the post-war settlement, buttressing the dominance of the right in the party and the unions. At the same time, the separation of industrial strength from political power was reinforced by a Labourist ideology that was 'deeply rooted in the commitment to Parliamentary democracy and in the perception of the state as a neutral and potentially beneficial instrument of the community'.[159] In other words, the social rapprochement arrived at in 1945 was institutionalised as part of the foundation of government legitimacy, validating the role of trade union leaders as participants in government.

As John Saville points out, Ernest Bevin 'was to look to the State as the third partner in a new tripartite grouping that would regulate industry and eliminate the injustices that he had been born into. ... For Bevin, the experience of the wartime Coalition Government confirmed the central proposition of labourism: the achievement of national recognition for the workers' movement and their acceptance within the national interest.'[160] Like Bevin's, the perspective of union leaders was to achieve recognition of the importance of labour, not to change power relations within industry. What distinguished the ministers of Attlee's government from other European government leaders, according to Eric Shaw, was 'less their collectivism than their traditionalism, that is the extent to which, in making key choices, their calculations were influenced by principles derived from the established and highly traditional national culture'.[161] The government had no desire to continue wartime economic planning into the post-war economy, and were averse to new forms of administrative control that might undermine the familiar parliamentary system. Bevin and the trade union leadership, in particular, were deeply opposed to outside interference in wage bargaining or the compulsory direction of labour.[162]

Labour claimed a national victory over the Axis powers, but it was a military and economic victory for the US and Soviet Union – although Labour's leaders took it for granted that Britain was still a great power, and their decision to build an atomic weapon reflected that belief. After 1945, however, the US drove home Britain's subordinate status by insisting it agree to the full convertibility of sterling into dollars as the condition for receiving a $3.75 billion loan, which launched a dollar crisis that was stemmed only by the reimposition of worse austerity than during the war. Much of the financial shortfall resulted from the expense of maintaining imperial commitments to a strong navy and military bases throughout the world.

Economically, the government was entirely dependent on US loans for its survival. After the abrupt ending of Lend-Lease following the fall of Japan, the economy was at a standstill. Without the loans, the welfare state would have been an impossibility. However, it was apparent that the initial loan would quickly run out, and disaster was only averted by the launch of Marshall Aid in 1947. The US government had recognised that the economic recovery of Europe and Japan was crucial for restoring capital circulation and markets for US exports; its rationale was also the perceived potential for revolutionary upheaval in Europe and the need to shore up the social discipline of the state system. When Cripps became Chancellor of the Exchequer in 1947, replacing Dalton, he squeezed personal consumption and rigorously controlled imports to direct resources into the export industry to alleviate the acute dollar shortage and the growing gap between the cost of imports and exports.

By 1948 the balance of payments was in surplus, but in 1949 the US economy entered recession, and the British government was forced to devalue the pound. The Treasury urged major cuts in public spending and deflation to accompany devaluation, but ministers resisted, and by the end of the year the economy had recovered. The government's determination to maintain full employment and enhanced social welfare, resisting official advice and challenging the assumptions underlying that advice, was a singular feature of the Attlee government. Shaw points out that 'the post-war Government exhibited a radicalism and strength of purpose that were not to be emulated by its successors'. Even so, devaluation was treated as a national humiliation, even though its effects were entirely positive.[163]

What should not be underestimated, writes Kenneth Morgan, were 'the overwhelming financial and economic pressures resulting from the loss of overseas assets, the imbalance of trade, the loss of markets, the shortage of raw materials, and the vast dollar deficit,' the result both of the war and the pre-war heritage of industrial decay. The government was fully preoccupied with restoring the circulation of capital, with transitioning war industries to export production rather than furnishing new commodities for the domestic market. Even though opinion polls showed that new housing was the highest priority for the public, the government allocated resources preferentially to industrial reconstruction. Cripps told the 1949 party conference that the government's first priority was 'exports … second is capital investment in industry, and last are the needs, comforts and amenities of the family'.

After the destruction by bombing of thousands of homes, combined with the shoddy state of much housing before the war, the demand for new homes was acute. Shortages of materials and labour slowed down Bevan's council house building programme, and by August 1946 there was a 7-8 year waiting list in London and elsewhere. Taking matters into their own hands, tens of thousands of people took over disused army camps around Britain. They enjoyed much public sympathy because of the perceived need for fairness 'and a frustration that the promised "New Jerusalem" of the post-1945 world seemed slow in arriving'.[164]

Initially the government was content to leave the squatters alone, but after the takeover of empty luxury flats in Kensington, it decided to prosecute the leaders of that occupation on the grounds that it had to uphold its policy of 'fair shares' with no queue jumping.[165] In the end a potentially embarrassing confrontation was averted once the occupation of the London flats was ended, and thousands of squatters stayed on in the camps for years afterwards.

The implementation of nationalisation

Nationalisation appeared to correspond to the socialist principle of public ownership of industry, originally conceived as a means of making ethical decisions about production and distribution of wealth. Now, however, Labour's policy-makers shifted party discourse away from the ideal of controlling industrial production for the benefit of society, towards the justification that industrial efficiency would be increased so as to generate a greater economic surplus as a foundation for welfare expenditure. Only those industries were nationalised that were 'failing the nation' such as ageing industries like coal or railways. Morgan notes that as early as 1945, 'most advocates of public ownership were drawing a line between the method of nationalisation, and the objective of socialism. The one was short-term, instrumental, and probably finite. The other was long-term, ideological, and perhaps postponed to an indefinite future.'[166]

The term 'nationalisation' itself signified a shift away from the idea of socialisation of the economy. 'National criteria, national interests, national requirements and national priorities were the considerations which enveloped the nationalised industries.' Industries that were fundamental to the national economy but that private ownership had failed to modernise were taken into public ownership in order to ensure their economic viability through the injection of public capital.[167] From an economic perspective, public ownership did little to improve the underinvestment in basic engineering technology and the low level of productivity. If anything, it preserved the imbalance in the economy. In the nationalised industries, 'the labour movement in this period never succeeded in evolving a consensual theory of the reconciliation of the public interest, the management function, industrial democracy and trade unionism. Nationalisation, on which so much visionary hope rested, was experienced by both workers and consumers as something far short of the transformation that had been expected.'[168]

Its significance was symbolic rather than a precondition for economic planning. Nationalisation had been the government's main evidence of a socialist commitment within an otherwise moderate economic programme. There was little appreciation of the outdated structure of British capital compared to that of other European nations which at the time were heavily investing in rebuilding infrastructure and replacing machinery. 'It was the demons at home that Labour wished to exorcize in 1945. ... Without nationalisation above all, the morale and impetus of the 1945 Labour government could not have been sustained. For most members of the party and the movement, that was its ultimate justification.'[169]

David Howell comments: 'The content of Labour's public ownership proposals had been determined to a considerable extent by the interests of influential trade unions. ... Since the industries chosen were those for which it was hoped public ownership would mean an increase in efficiency, it followed that they tended to be industries which had acted as a brake on economic growth, and whose condition was unsatisfactory. ... Accordingly, public ownership became widely associated with obsolescence.' Moreover, it represented an implicit subsidy for the private sector through public investment in basic industries necessary for production.[170]

The ambiguity of the concept became apparent with the incompatibility of the many hopes placed in it by party members. Some saw it as a means to redistribute wealth and introduce workers' control of industry, others as providing the basis for economic planning. The left believed that public ownership would make possible production for social need rather than profit. However, commercial considerations triumphed over political criteria for decision-making in public enterprises.[171] The government's failure to use state power more effectively for planning stemmed both from the instinctive resistance of the Treasury to interventionist policies, and the conservatism of the cabinet in relation to state institutions. As former members of the coalition, ministers 'knew the wartime machine personally, and liked what they saw', allowing the civil service to retain its monopoly of expertise and advice.[172]

The historical experience of this corporate form of nationalisation is contradictory, however: conditions *did* improve because the unions were incorporated as a legitimate factor in industrial relations, preserving the tripartite arrangement arrived at by the coalition government; on the other hand, heavy industry necessary for production was subsidised for the benefit of private enterprise, facilitating continued capital accumulation. 'Whatever the admitted inadequacies of the system of labour relations devised under nationalisation, it would be impossible to dispute the enormous improvement in the climate of industrial relations – and of growing prosperity for the workforce – in the new age of public ownership. In large measure, this was simply because of the symbolic fact of nationalisation itself,' notes Morgan. He adds: 'On Vesting Day, 1 January 1947, there were mass demonstrations of rejoicing in mining communities from South Wales to Nottingham, Yorkshire, Durham, and Fife, as the flag of the NCB replaced the ensign of the old, discredited private coal-owners.'[173]

Bill Hunter writes in his autobiography: 'For decades the miners and railwaymen had fought for nationalisation, and the Labour government's measures were seen as a great victory and one which many older workers had begun to feel was unobtainable.' He recounts the story of a Wigan miner who found, when he first went down the pits in 1949, 'there was a great deal of pride of having come through the thirties and come back from the war to win these conditions: pit head baths for instance, with the coal owners gone and that blue flag of the NCB flying on top of the pit-head gear and the notice that used to say the mine "belonged to the people".'[174]

Initially miners, especially those on the new Colliery Consultative Committees, had not been overly enthusiastic, complaining of the same owners and managers remaining in charge. The statutory consultative machinery itself created friction between working miners and union branch leaders who were coopted into the management drive for higher production.[175] Nevertheless, Roy Mason, a Yorkshire miner who later became a Labour minister, recalled that in 1947-8, 'Working conditions improved markedly almost from the beginning. Training was introduced for newcomers before ever they went down to the coalface. A ban was introduced on young boys going underground before they were sixteen. We had a national safety scheme, with proper standards at every colliery. And for the first time, pithead baths became a standard facility.' Despite ministerial and managerial misgivings, the five-day week was introduced.[176]

Unlike the miners, railway workers found that the economic problems of the industry and their conditions had not improved. Wages remained low and managerial hierarchies stayed much the same. But, now a cabinet minister, Bevan had little tolerance for those who criticised nationalisation because not enough had changed. He insisted that the government had made a tremendous start which was in itself a great achievement: 'I speak as a trade unionist who has been fighting for this all my life, and I do not want to see it spoiled now because there are some people who cannot see the wood for the trees.'[177] The failure of public ownership to change the terms of working relations, however, marked the abandonment of any attempt to seriously challenge the private ownership of the rest of industry. Socialist ideals and government practice more clearly diverged: when in 1948 Michael Young wrote a party pamphlet on 'industrial democracy', privileging the rank-and-file worker above the union leadership and even flirting with the idea of workers' control, the first edition had to be withdrawn after objections from both Bevan and Morrison. Bevan wanted ministerial control of nationalised industries, not workers' control.[178]

Morgan observes: 'There was no attempt either to democratise industry on the basis of workers' control, co-partnership or any other method. Nor, it must be said, did the unions show any particular enthusiasm for this.' He is correct in the case of the TUC leaders, who opposed any measures that would interfere with collective bargaining, including representation on the boards of nationalised industries. But among the rank and file, an increasing demand for workplace democracy had become a criticism of the Morrisonian form of nationalisation. Railwaymen in particular were dismayed both by the management structure of the nationalised industries and the excessive sums paid in compensation. Detailed discussions of forms of workers control were published in their union journal, the *Railway Review*, debating regional or works councils as the basis of shopfloor democracy. A signalman from Solihull stated at the NUR's 1947 conference that 'it is essential from the point of view of the workers coming into control that they have representation and relationships from the top to the bottom. That is the theory and, I believe, the spirit of nationalisation as the rank and file understand it.'[179]

Chemical workers produced the most creative and detailed plans for workers control. Bob Edwards of the Chemical Workers Union rejected the approach for elected representatives on a board of management, settling on the structure of local government as a model. He told the TUC in 1950 that 'we want industrial parliaments based on the voluntary efforts that you have in local government, attached to our nationalised industries, where the workers, the consumers, the technicians and other interested elements in our community can participate in these great economic investments'. Ministers would meet in public with a small national council and a clear chain of responsibility established down to the individual operatives. The system would be based on 'two inseparable principles ... centralisation of policy making and decentralisation of executive responsibility'. In 1947 the TUC had unanimously passed a resolution calling for increased workers' participation in control of nationalised industries. But as the cold war ramped up, advocates of workers control were marginalised and Edwards' resolution demanding democratisation of the workplace was defeated overwhelmingly.[180]

The first signs of a division in the cabinet between pragmatic possibilities and socialist principles came in 1947 over the issue of nationalisation of steel. As a manufacturing industry, rather than a monopoly utility, that impinged on numerous other industries, it was a clear example of a 'commanding height.' Dalton summarised: 'We weren't really beginning our Socialist programme until we had gone past all the utility junk – such as transport and electricity – which were publicly owned in every capitalist country in the world. Practical Socialism ... only really began with Coal and Iron and Steel, and there was a strong political argument for breaking the power of a most dangerous body of capitalists.' Bevan saw the issue as a test of the government's socialist intentions. However, the balance of payments crisis convinced Attlee the timing was unpropitious, and it was postponed.

After its initial success in fulfilling the promises of *Let Us Face the Future*, the government now abandoned physical economic controls and attempted to manage the economy by securing the cooperation of the unions in controlling wage increases. The TUC urged the government to enact comprehensive planning of investment as a condition for its cooperation, advocating the continuation of rationing, utility goods schemes and price and profit controls. The government, however, was reluctant to restrict capital accumulation by private industry on the grounds that investment was necessary to increase production for exports. In August of 1947 it made a partial return to the direction of labour; Attlee made a formal statement appealing to workers not to press for wage increases, and in 1948 declared a national emergency and mobilised troops during a dock strike. The government's pragmatic acceptance of the profit motive as the mainspring of the economy dashed the remaining hopes of organised labour for the creation of a cooperative society that would enable the state to plan the economy without conflict.[181]

At the 1948 party conference, Morrison rejected the further extension of nationalisation and called for 'consolidation' of what had been achieved so far, representing the party as appealing to a national rather than a class constituency. He was opposed by Hugh Lawson, the delegate who followed Morrison in the debate, who rejected his argument and called for taking further industries into public ownership: 'the programme will be attractive to the public, not if it is something very wishy-washy and watered down but if it is bold and challenging. I want to see in the forefront of our General Election programme a declaration of faith in Socialism ... that the large resources of production in this country ought to belong to the common people. .... I would say that there are two ideas as to the next step. One is to increase the degree of public control, the other is to extend the area of publicly-owned industry. ... I want it to be made quite clear in our programme that we stand for control through common ownership.'[182]

Although Morrison had boldly introduced the issue that was to divide left and right in the party over the following decade, Bevan avoided any public criticism for the sake of party unity. However, at the following year's conference he formulated a compromise between the wings of the party by conceding that 'the kind of society which we envisage, and which we shall have to live in, will be a mixed society, a mixed economy, in which all the essential instruments of planning are in the hands of the State ... but where we shall have for a very long time the light cavalry of private competitive industry.'[183] Although he had restated his faith in state planning as key to the relationship between public and private sector, his speech had no clear programme for the next steps – his biographer John Campbell comments that he 'was happy so long as he thought the *direction* was right and was satisfied socialist *principles* were still intact.' The ideological struggle within the party over the next few years was not so much about practical issues than about 'symbols of priorities'.[184]

Despite the prominence of the idea of planning in the party's rhetoric, it played little part in the government's economic strategy: it had abandoned wartime economic controls, and, as Treasury official Otto Clarke wrote in his diary, 'there was no known plan and no known means of implementing a plan even if there had been a plan ... Not a single one of them [the cabinet] with the shadowiest concept of what they meant by planning.' Bevin was heard to comment on the substantial post-war planning being carried out in France: 'We don't do things like that in our country; we don't *have* plans, we work things out practically.'[185]

The export drive was based on a small range of traditional heavy industries and avoided the problem of long-term capital investment. Its success in restoring production to 1938 levels concealed the pre-war legacy of industrial backwardness and the government had no conception of a state-driven, planned re-tooling of industry and rebuilding of physical infrastructure. Significantly, 'No real effort was made to eliminate, or even partially modify, the maldistribution of wealth and property which remained very pronounced in Britain even after six years of supposedly socialist government. In the early fifties, 1 per cent of the population owned 50 per cent of the private capital in England and Wales.'[186]

The welfare state and the socialist ideal

By making social welfare and full employment the responsibility of government, universal welfare and health care became identified with Labour, and public support for it remained strong. The government's achievement on the domestic front had enabled it to avoid clarifying whether its direction was towards fundamental social reform, or greater efficiency of industry within a mixed economy. In effect, the Labour leadership identified socialism with the welfare state, while leaving the bulk of the economy in private hands.

Bill Hunter writes that workers 'were prepared to give the government a great deal of credit in the early years. It was not cynicism and apathy. There was no "return to the 1930s", as there had been a return to old conditions after 1918. More houses were being built; there was a National Health Service; the Beveridge report was being implemented; and the millions of unemployed had gone ... the rise in employment had increased the workers' militancy, not made them more apathetic.'[187] The concept of a universal social safety net, especially a nationalised health service, became incorporated into the labour movement's understanding of the socialist ideal. 'Full employment, an abiding priority for the government, involved an immense economic and social shift from the defeatism and stagnation of the twenties and thirties,' writes Morgan. The social egalitarianism of the war years had been strengthened by the construction of the welfare state. 'The Attlee government ... actually kept the momentum [of wartime radicalism] going, and added new elements (notably in health) drawn from Labour's own programme of the thirties.'[188]

A compulsory national insurance scheme had not been part of the pre-war socialist narrative, since it was assumed that once the state had ended unemployment through its ownership of industry, an egalitarian commonwealth would take care of all people's basic needs. Plans for social welfare had been a low priority for the party in the 1930s; it was the popular radicalisation of the 1940s that made it a political imperative. George Orwell noted in August 1948 that the public were more interested in welfare than socialism: 'The change-over to national ownership is not in itself an inspiring process, and in the popular regard the Labour party is the party that stands for shorter working hours, a free health service, day nurseries, free milk for school children, and the like, rather than the party that stands for Socialism.'[189]

Little of what the government had done diverged far from the plans that liberal reformers had put forward in the 1930s and 1940s, except when the left of the party was able to successfully exert its influence. For example, the Minister for National Insurance, Jim Griffiths, insisted that pensions be paid at once, rather than follow Beveridge's recommendation that they be phased in over a 20-year period. Harvard academic Harry Eckstein, summing up the government's reforms, wrote: 'Whatever aspect of the Labour programme one considers, one always returns to the same theme: a similar policy was advocated, perhaps even before Labour advocated it, by nonsocialists. ... one of the most remarkable things about Labour's nationalisation measures is that most of them were enacted in response to the reports of Conservative-dominated investigating committees.'[190]

The difference was that Labour actually realised these plans, which the Tories would have diluted and hedged around with multiple concessions to private interests, and was ready to commit the huge sums of public spending required. In its historical context, Attlee's government was in fact extremely partisan; while the Tories later adapted to the welfare state, continuing this rate of spending was the most challenging decision their party had to make.[191] Despite its limitations, the social legislation that was enacted made a vast difference in the wellbeing of the working class, primarily because its condition had been so miserable before the war. The driving force for the implementation of social welfare had not been Labour's socialist beliefs, but the popular pressure for change; it was Labour that more adequately responded to this pressure.

The National Health Service

The signature achievement of the Attlee government was the establishment of the National Health Service in July 1948. This went far beyond the wartime coalition's recommendations for a national medical service – Bevan refused to begin from where the 1944 Willink committee's White Paper left off, literally throwing it into his ministry wastebasket, and devised his own approach. 'The establishment of a universal, free health service where treatment would be determined by need rather than ability to pay enshrined fundamental socialist values. It was difficult to believe that a Conservative government would have mustered the determination – borne out of his deep, philosophical commitment to the idea – displayed by Bevan to overcome the vehement objections of much of the medical profession.'[192]

Bevan's conviction of his rightness was based on both pragmatic considerations – the experience of the wartime health services – and his socialist belief that the state could channel the community's need for social solidarity. His ethics embodied his appreciation and respect for ordinary workers, crystallising the collectivism of the immediate post-war period. 'Bevan saw medicine, at least as it was structured in Britain, as a profession in which individual commercialism ran counter to the most appropriate social values. To him the NHS would be "opposed to the hedonism of capitalist society". His determined opposition to the custom of purchasing and selling patient goodwill originated in his firm belief that the custom was inherently evil. This belief was distinctive, and perhaps even unique, among the British political elite in 1945.'[193]

His greatest single accomplishment was to nationalise the hospitals, thereby bypassing the dual system of voluntary charity hospitals and local authorities. Rather than adopting the Socialist Medical Association's plan for an integrated service based on health centres, with doctors employed by local authorities, instead 'buying the top doctors in on their own terms, Bevan secured an alternative socialist objective much more in tune with the instinct of the Labour Party and the mood of the time, a universal NHS to which all were equally entitled and of which even the wealthiest were happy to make use for everyday complaints.'[194] Bevan's friend Lord Moran, president of the Royal College of Physicians, had been put in charge of emergency plans for medical care in 1939, and had therefore experienced first-hand the regional disparities and bureaucracy of the patchwork of municipal welfare services. This put him firmly in favour of centralised medical administration, and he was an influence on Bevan's decision to nationalise hospitals as a solution to the problem of eliminating the major regional differences in quality of health care.[195]

In order to establish the NHS, Bevan had to confront the actual character of the British state as an ongoing compromise between conflicting claims of property ownership, in this case the ownership of medical practices. Despite the egalitarian legacy of the war years, the government still had to fight against diehard Tory supporters of the existing system, where medical practices were run as small businesses; Churchill strongly opposed Bevan's plan and the Conservatives voted against the legislation that created the NHS more than 20 times, including its second and third readings and the implementation of the Act in 1948.[196] Bevan's achievement in setting it up was to reconcile the private ownership of these practices with a state-funded system; nationalisation of hospitals was relatively unproblematic, since they were either already municipally controlled or in dire need of funding. The actual implementation of the NHS, however, abandoned the socialist aspiration of health centres – included in Bevan's Act but with no provision for the direct employment of doctors by local authorities, reflecting concerted opposition to the idea of a full-time salaried service for general practitioners.[197]

No Tory government would have nationalised municipal and voluntary hospitals, and even within the Labour Party opinion was closer to those who, like Morrison, favoured keeping hospitals under local authority control. As far as Bevan was concerned, however, 'the only part of that public [opinion] that mattered to him were the working classes, which he clearly distinguished from their institutional expression in the Labour Party'. Bevan established the basis for a new system of medical care 'with remarkable speed and with generous Treasury funding. ... In and outside Cabinet and Parliament he overcame opposition which would have deterred an administrator seeking consensus.' Bevan's socialism clearly guided his practices in driving through the compromises necessary to get the NHS established. It is arguable whether or not his youthful experience of the Tredegar Medical Aid Society influenced his insistence on the principles of universality and free treatment – Rintala asserts that 'the NHS bore no significant resemblance' to the Tredegar institution, and considers giving priority to the need for equal access to quality medical treatment 'was his personal achievement'. It should be remembered, however, that even while enforcing public austerity, Cripps made sure that Bevan's plans were fully funded.[198]

Bevan skilfully exploited the disagreements between hospital consultants and general practitioners in the often-fraught negotiations with the British Medical Association, in order to push through acceptance of the new arrangements within the medical profession. Once accepted, however, the existence of a functioning NHS changed doctors' expectations and behaviour to the extent that the most enthusiastic defenders of the service against threats of defunding by governments from the 1980s onwards were the general practitioners in the BMA. Bevan's assumption had been that, once it got into its stride, the health service 'would naturally provide a *better* standard of service than private enterprise could hope to offer ... collective organisation must inevitably by the natural process of evolution come to predominate over individualism'.[199]

Part of Bevan's conception was a redistribution of national income by a special method of financing the health service, as he explained to the House of Commons in 1958. He had rejected the insurance principle because it led to an unequal distribution of benefits, and decided that 'the best way to finance the scheme, the fairest and most equitable way, would be to obtain the finance from the Exchequer funds by general taxation, and those who had the most would pay the most. It is a very good principle. What more pleasure can a millionaire have than to know that his taxes will help the sick? ... The redistributive aspect of the scheme was one which attracted me almost as much as the therapeutical.'[200]

When the service was inaugurated, there was a huge, pent-up demand for medicines, spectacles and false teeth. Their availability under the NHS greatly improved the quality of life for a large part of the population, especially the elderly. One general practitioner noted that many women came to him suffering from severe gynaecological conditions that had gone untreated for years because his patients had not been able to afford the expense of a doctor's visit.[201] Local authorities were able to undertake mass screenings for tuberculosis, establish maternity and child welfare clinics, and modernise the ambulance service. Despite economic austerity, regional hospitals were successfully modernised and a comprehensive system of specialist services was set up.[202] According to Dr. Peter Estcourt of East Sussex, writing to the *Guardian* in 2018, among the many medical innovations pioneered by the NHS were CT, MRI* and ultrasound scanners, joint surgery, cataract surgery, and chemotherapy. In the field of public health, it established the health risks of smoking and produced true health statistics for an entire population. 'All this,' he adds, 'was achieved in the public sector with public money, and with no thought of monetary gain or profit – a fact missed by the privatisation free-marketeers.'[203]

Labour's collectivist ideology

Attlee's government had a collectivist orientation that rationalised its combination of central control of the economy through wage and price controls with the continuation of private property and profit. It applied a moral earnestness in economic matters. 'Obedience to controls was publicly proclaimed as necessary to promote social welfare, full employment, and economic recovery. The new concentration on exports was given a moral aura.'[204] However, the government's attempts to guilt people into working

---

* Computed Technology; Magnetic Resonance Imaging.

harder fell on deaf ears. The idea that the public should cooperate in restoring capital circulation did not address the fact of the accumulation of wealth at the top. Trade unionists resented the exhortations for increased productivity. 'We are told that our job now is to recapture the spirit which was displayed after Dunkirk, work harder and produce more so that we might expand our export trade especially to America,' wrote a tobacco worker in his union journal in 1949. He would have no objection to making sacrifices if they were truly necessary, however, provided that 'the increased profits ... will be shared by the workers whose efforts make them possible'.[205]

The gap between the government's moralistic interpretation of socialism and the mood of the working class was underlined by the failure of Labour's 'socialist policy for leisure'. Party memos in 1946-7 'lamented the 'failure of the majority of Britain's citizens to enjoy a full life through their leisure pursuits'; labelled the cinema and gambling as two prime examples of regrettably 'passive' and superficial leisure pursuits; and drew the rather defeatist conclusion that 'all forms of escapist entertainment or recreation are encouraged by the drabness, insecurity and hopelessness of daily life'. Efforts to encourage collective cultural activities were largely ineffectual; housing plans aimed at encouraging the formation of community foundered on the lack of financial resources committed. What worked in Scandinavia – with access to ample social resources – was an abject failure in penny-pinching England.[206]

Morrison doubled down on his efforts to harness Labour to the national interest. He told delegates at the 1948 party conference: 'We must have an active, living democracy in our country and we must whip up our citizens to their responsibilities just as we canvass them in elections or just as the air-raid wardens did in the war.' Party members were expected to 'shoulder personal responsibility' to increase productivity during the government's export drive. Their personal example was considered to be vital to generate enthusiasm amongst the wider workforce. The war, thought Morrison, had united the working-class majority with management professionals and even industrialists in a common objective. 'Thus, as it embodied a commitment to maximise production, socialism was considered to be in the interest of all but a small minority of people. ... Union influence was increasingly seen to be debilitating by those wanting Labour to become a genuinely mass party.'[207]

This corporatist orientation had little appeal to the party's supporters. A significant feature of the government's difficulties over policy was public apathy, not just lack of resources or Tory opposition; it became clear that many people were not really in sympathy with what Labour's leaders were trying to achieve. The priority of economic survival meant keeping existing economic arrangements intact. 'Cripps spelt out his blunt belief that further redistribution was dependent on the creation of further wealth. This was a rejection of the traditional socialist belief that the problem of production had been solved.'[208] Appealing to east London dockers to return to work in 1948, Attlee described their strike as being 'against your mates, a strike against the housewife, a strike against the ordinary common people who have difficulties enough now to manage on their shilling's worth of meat and other rationed commodities.'[209]

The conservatism of Attlee's approach to socialism became even clearer in the 1950 election campaign. He had always subscribed to the overlapping ideals of citizenship, patriotism and ethical socialism, which for him had found its highest expression in the social patriotism engendered by the war. 'For the first four years of his government, the same core convictions had crystallised in the form of a new system of social insurance and healthcare which was beyond anything that Attlee could have dreamed of forty years before. When the battle was won, but other problems had to be confronted, the prime minister fell back upon the old script. ... As the sense of solidarity and shared sacrifice that had been so profound during the war faded, these words began to seem hollow.'[210] The increasingly moralistic tone of Attlee's message towards the end of his period as prime minister derived from the economic difficulties of the government, when he exhorted the country to continue with its wartime self-sacrifice. He resisted critics who believed he was evading a commitment to further socialist advance with the argument that socialism demanded 'a higher standard of civic virtue than capitalism ... We need to stress duties as well as rights.'[211]

The Labour government's legacy

Historians of the period are divided on how instrumental the Attlee government was in implementing social reform. To what extent, as Paul Addison has argued, did Attlee merely continue the egalitarian consensus of wartime into legislation, or did the government actively pursue 'the most radical available options' to add new elements to that consensus, as Kenneth Morgan surmises? The government was clearly responding to public pressure in its welfare legislation, building large numbers of council houses, and maintaining full employment. But there were competing pressures – from the US administration, on whom the government depended for loans, from the Treasury and from the Tories. While resisting these forces, the government's options were constrained by remaining within the framework of parliamentary constitutionalism and the preservation of private property.

Labour's crowning achievement was the establishment of the health service free at the point of use; but in the field of education it retained independent public schools, acknowledged bastions of class privilege. The industries that were nationalised were the old and failing heavy industries like railways and coal, where government ownership represented a subsidy to private industry, not only because of the over-generous compensation paid to the former shareholders, but also by the provision of basic materials to manufacturers at a low cost. Government economic planning – held to be the answer to capitalist crisis – remained only a theoretical possibility since the coercive measures needed for a state-enforced plan were avoided in favour of voluntary cooperation. The state continued its tradition of appeasing manifold private interests.

Labour's real achievement was to consolidate the collectivist advances achieved during the war in a social democratic consensus that constrained subsequent Tory governments to act 'in a field of force, created by Labour', as Addison described Tory efforts to block social policy reform during the coalition government.[212] The overturn of the inter-war political isolation of the labour movement was sustained by the framework of this consensus, which, since it was compatible with the hegemony of private property, was contained but not reversed by the Churchill government after 1951. Harriet Jones and Michael Kandiah, who argue against the notion of political consensus, point out that the Tories were by no means reconciled to the egalitarianism implied by the welfare state, instead mounting a propaganda offensive championing individual property ownership and the demand to end wartime economic controls.[213] Minkin also questions this notion: 'The post-war "settlement" was more an acceptance of a new balance of power forged during the Labour Government than a conscious all-party agreement which predated it,' he argues. While the Tory party moved to the political centre, manufacturers, particularly the engineering employers, remained hawkish against union power.[214] Nevertheless, while there were disagreements on specifics, the political parameters of government were shifted to a new framework of constraints by the establishment of new public institutions in social care, health, education, industry, and housing.

Morgan's judgement is that whatever its reformist aspirations, the Labour government 'was never really a group of social radicals. They adhered to the empire; many of them believed in white supremacy; they, or most of them, upheld the extreme penalty of the rope; they refused to upset the miners by abolishing fox-hunting.'[215] The government appeared more radical than it really was insofar as it had to implement its policies in the teeth of a strong tradition of Conservative opposition to state intervention, and while the reforms were small in themselves, they were magnified by their effects on millions of people. In the final analysis, the legislation of the Attlee government did make a significant difference to the British economy and social policy. However, it did not attempt to reform institutions that were foundational to the social hierarchy, nor did it challenge the traditions of an elite closely identified with state power. 'The fact is that the Labour Party, on the whole, had absorbed uncritically the ideological and institutional defences of the British political system: that it was class- and party-neutral; that it made for "strong" government; that it had been legitimated by a unique and victorious national history.'[216]

The government had instituted a framework of corporate socialism based on the collaboration of unions with the government and big business. While workers enjoyed full employment and welfare for the first time, they were not represented on the boards of the newly nationalised industries. However, Ross McKibbin argues that the members of Attlee's government, even Bevin and Morrison, *thought* they were implementing a socialist programme, 'that it represented both a social transformation and a system of values superior to any alternative. Yet it was a peculiar form of socialism; the socialism of a particular generation, one which drew a clear distinction between the economy and social policy on the one hand, and Britain's status and class system on the other.'[217]

Post-war social change

Post-war Britain remained a disciplined, socially conservative society still dominated by class, observes Kynaston, with the ambitions of the young limited to marriage, family and work. Society had lost none of its prewar insularity, and was steeped in a sense that entitlement to social welfare was a reward for many years of deprivation and exploitation, not to be shared with 'outsiders'.[218]

If there was a continuity of culture through British society, it was the acceptance of class stratification. The idea that joint sacrifices in the war years had created a more egalitarian society was a self-deceiving Labour myth: class and individualism remained at the foundation of social culture. Employers retained their Edwardian approach to management but were constrained by state institutions and union bureaucracies, while the culture of the work environment remained predominantly male. Despite the much-vaunted opportunities for factory work given to women in wartime, they were confined to low-level and routine jobs and most returned to family life at war's end. Workers identified with their class but looked to the unions and the state to ameliorate insecurity of employment while remaining passive enforcers of the consensus. Collectivism in this context was expressed as a moral imperative for embracing community, equality of sacrifice, taking care of children and the elderly. There was a deeply embedded belief that, as the TUC put it in 1948, 'the home is one of the most important spheres for a woman worker,' since entering industry would mean neglecting their 'domestic duties' and the care of young children.[219] Although Labour recognised the importance of women in the welfare state, it approached them as traditional housewives and mothers, not as political subjects. Only 21 of 393 Labour MPs elected in 1945 were women.[220]

The distribution of wealth in society did not change. The fact that manual workers' wages went up by a large percentage, apparently reducing the differential in wages, only reflected the appallingly low wages they were paid in the 1930s. 'The striking fact was that by 1949 a manual worker's average earnings stood at 241 per cent of their 1937 level, whereas the equivalent figure for a member of the higher professions was 188 per cent. Even so, that professional man was still earning as much as a skilled manual worker, a semi-skilled manual worker and an unskilled manual worker put together.' Hours were being reduced and workers now enjoyed paid holidays and greater safety at work. A considerable amount of old-fashioned paternalism still pervaded industrial relations, and although full employment made a difference, the attitudes of employers and management were invariably hostile to organised labour.[221]

Post-war slum clearance and rehousing tended to break up close-knit working-class communities in the inner cities, and the mass industrial working class of the 1930s was eroding as complex technologies developed during the war, such as electronics, differentiated technically trained from unskilled workers. The demographic diffusion of people from the war-damaged cities into new housing estates located in suburban or rural areas fragmented traditional political allegiances and class solidarity. Egalitarianism had reflected the enhanced political power of the working class after 1940; now social change found a more individualist expression. 'Throughout these post-war years, the class divide in Britain remained as pronounced as ever. ... It was, in terms of dress, speech, and entertainment, a more egalitarian society. Yet the middle class remained impervious and impregnable. Indeed, the middle class clearly expanded in size after 1945, reinforced rather than eroded by the welfare state and social engineering.'[222]

Conservative opinion became increasingly embittered, and middle-class hostility to Labour became 'a demoralising influence upon the Labour Government even though the continued support of working people was never seriously in question', remembers Saville.[223] The Labour leaders' belief that society had been changed in an egalitarian direction undermined their appreciation of the class nature of the state and the political resources of the propertied elite, while the middle class regained its sense of grievance at the reduction of its social privilege. 'The Conservative party, accustomed to controlling Parliament, was inevitably thrown off course with the overwhelming Labour victory of July 1945, but not for long ... in its press and on platforms, [it] developed an unrelenting criticism of Labour politics, with populist organisations such as the Housewives' League enunciating in increasingly shrill terms the feelings and sentiments of middle-class England.'[224]

Labourism was unable to come to terms with the way increased prosperity had affected the shift of allegiances within society – the party's leaders repeated the mantra that the Tories would reinstate unemployment, even after Churchill had pragmatically moved his party to the centre and, when returned to office in 1951, avoided industrial confrontation. Since the left had assumed that there would be a fully socialised economy after the war, it had not formulated any kind of plan for dealing with private industry in the mixed economy that had resulted, and had not developed any political alternative to the corporatism of the government's approach to socialism.

The socialist ideal still firmly held by party activists remained utopian in the sense that a better society was assumed to result from parliamentary legislation, given sufficient political will. Immediate nationalisation of the whole economy was deemed impractical, but the extension of public ownership to larger industries became important to the rank and file as signs of a change in power relations rather than of economic effectiveness. However, the specific domestic and international balance of power that underlay the 1945-47 nationalisations had changed in a way that removed this possibility. The country's economic problems had become more severe; flight from sterling after convertibility was imposed made the government dependent on Marshall Aid and the goodwill of the US; and public enthusiasm for nationalisation had waned.

This chapter characterised the undoubted legislative achievements of the Attlee government, which brought about important social and economic changes, that were nevertheless restricted by the limits imposed by the restoration of private capital. The unprecedented scale of social reform encouraged workers to accept wage restraint during the immediate post-war years, while expecting better treatment from employers. Within Labour Party discourse, the leadership enjoyed wide support for its achievement of full employment and the creation of a social safety net, understood by the membership to be taking society in the direction of a socialist state.

The left retained its belief in the orthodox socialist ideal, but it fixated on state-centric nationalisation as the way socialism should be brought about – specifically, through public ownership of the 'commanding heights' of the economy rather than all of industry. More leisure and greater security of income consolidated working-class support for the Attlee government, although civil society and culture remained the stronghold of middle-class individualism.

The next chapter will discuss how the Labour left's political disagreements with the government crystallised around foreign policy and became the foundation of the Bevanite revolt when they fused with the rank and file's hostility to wage restraint after devaluation of the pound and the Korean war drove up the cost of living. In the end, however, Bevan's defence of the principles of orthodox socialism without a theoretical reckoning with the effects of post-war affluence and the way society had changed led him into a political impasse, and he was eventually to capitulate to the right wing, led by Hugh Gaitskell, in the internal party struggle over policy.

Chapter Four
Bevan and the Crisis of Orthodox Socialism

'Bevan did not create Bevanism; as a refusal on the part of a substantial minority of Labour's rank and file to endorse the leadership's drift of policy and as an affirmation of the need for different policies, it had existed in the Labour Party and in the trade unions long before Bevan gave it his name and his gifts; and it endured and grew in strength after he ceased to give expression to it.'[225] Ralph Miliband, 1961

The conflict over Labour's foreign policy

After 1948, the ideological divisions within the Labour Party grew as the economic problems associated with restoring capital circulation created conflicts between the leadership, who had favoured Morrison's proposal for consolidation, and the activists who wanted to continue with the socialist advance. The government's domestic reforms had won it the instinctive solidarity of the working class, however, and overt political disputes within the party centred on foreign policy.

In this chapter, I show how the Attlee government's continuation of Big Power politics abroad came under serious challenge only when its involvement in the Korean War began to threaten living standards and social reform. This was the start of the Bevanite opposition within the party, which connected the struggle of the trade union rank and file against its own autocratic leadership with the campaign within Labour to enact the socialist elements in the party's programme. Despite its support in the constituencies, the Bevanite movement was unable to overturn the domination of the Labour Party by Gaitskell and the right wing, since they were backed by the union leaders' outsize influence at party conferences through their block vote. The mass protests for nuclear disarmament that began at the end of the 1950s bypassed this stalemate by organising outside the party, inspiring a New Left that sought a way out of the political impasse. In tune with the decline of deference in society expressed in the youth rebellion of the 1960s, New Left writers began a seminal critique of the corporate form of nationalisation implemented by the 1945 government, exploring the concept of workers' control.

Political dissent over foreign policy stemmed from the divergence of the government's practice from the orthodox socialist approach elaborated by Attlee himself before the war. Then he had maintained that the international system should be reformed on the basis of a cooperative community of nations, and had rejected the Tory government's single-minded defence of British interests, imperial outposts and commercial networks.[226] However, now that it was in power, the Labour government's approach to international affairs was in marked contrast to these internationalist positions.

Labourist ideology had never challenged the assumption that social reform at home rested on the continuation of empire abroad. As a trade union leader, Ernest Bevin had prioritised the rights of British workers over the left's support for colonial independence in the 1930s. As Foreign Secretary, he now accepted unquestioningly the Foreign Office's assumption that policy should continue to be shaped by national interests, and he only reluctantly acknowledged the independence of India. John Saville recalled that '[t]he starting point for Britain was naturally the colonial Empire, its continuing control a necessary part of Britain's status within the leading countries in world politics'.[227] To compensate for its economic weakness, the government ruthlessly plundered British colonial possessions through manipulating the terms of bulk food purchases and the sterling area arrangements. Raw materials such as rubber, tin and copper from Malaya and Rhodesia could earn vital dollars while foodstuffs from Australia and New Zealand could be paid for in sterling. Africa was assumed to possess hitherto undiscovered geological resources that would compensate for the loss of India. 'Bevin argued that, if the resources of Britain's African colonies could be fully exploited, she might be able to rival the USA as a superpower.'[228] The result was that colonial economic development was subordinated to British economic interests – encouraging cash crops for export, as in East and Central Africa, had the effect of creating local food shortages and increasing the influence of white settlers. Riots in the Gold Coast (now Ghana) in early 1948 were the first post-war challenge to colonial rule. The British had eventually to concede self-government, but only after an imprisoned Kwame Nkrumah won election in 1951.[229]

There was widespread unease within the labour movement over the government's acceptance of the imperial mandate, its suppression of the Greek resistance movement, and its refusal to act against Franco despite his wartime support for Hitler. At the 1946 party conference, the government was attacked for its 'apparent continuance of a traditionally Conservative Party policy of power politics abroad', and it was exhorted to return 'to the Labour Party foreign policy of support of Socialist and anti-imperialist forces throughout the world'.[230] Seventy-two Labour MPs voted against peacetime conscription in the spring of 1947, forming the 'Keep Left' group in parliament, but despite their criticisms of the inadequacies of post-war planning and the pitfalls of sterling convertibility, the group's protest was subdued by MPs' support for the government's domestic agenda.[231]

Party activists, however, remained frustrated by the government's international role. 'It is difficult to overestimate the extent of the gulf between the international policies pursued by the Government and the expectations of many of its supporters,' writes David Howell.[232] The government's foreign policy was clearly at odds with the labour movement's internationalist traditions. Rank-and-file opposition was suppressed by right-wing control of the party machine; Kenneth Morgan observes: 'It is clear from the party archives that [general secretary Morgan] Phillips brushed aside a good deal of grass-roots disaffection in the unions and in the constituency parties. A torrent of protest against Labour's foreign and defence policies, the wage freeze, and the handling of [dissident MPs] Platts-Mills and Zilliacus was simply smothered by the urbane and resourceful general secretary in Transport House.'[233]

There was a significant level of protest from constituency parties, including the disavowal by Kingston Borough Labour Party of 'the new definition of socialism outlined by Mr. Herbert Morrison ... to apply the name "socialism" to a policy which includes the assisting and stimulating of private enterprise is a negation in terms.' CLPs wanted 'more socialism' at home and a more independent foreign policy. By 1949, Coventry East CLP believed that Bevin had become so detached from Labour's traditional policy that he 'should be advised by a council of five from the elected representatives of the people'.[234]

Most Labour MPs shared Bevin's nationalism, however. His anti-communism was compatible with the outlook of labour leaders who viewed the Soviet suppression of social-democratic parties in Eastern Europe through the lens of communist activities in their own organisations. Parliamentary critics of Bevin's foreign policy tended to be new entrants, university-educated and with journalistic rather than trade union connections, who conceived Britain as the nucleus of a Third Force independent of the USA and USSR, exerting a moral influence on world affairs. A reformed 'Keep Left' group in 1951, while accepting NATO and opposed to the Soviet role in Eastern Europe, attempted to relate the Third

Force proposal to colonial nationalism. This created a new basis for left support of revolutionary internationalism, leaving behind the disillusion that now dominated Labour attitudes to the Soviet Union.[235]

The victory of the Chinese revolution in 1949 had alarmed the Foreign Office with the spectre of communist-led insurgencies in India, Malaya and Indo-China (now Vietnam and Laos), and it aimed to shore up military support in the region through British support for the US in the Korean War. By 1951 Hugh Gaitskell, now Chancellor of the Exchequer, planned to double the defence budget from that of the previous year. This was partly due to US pressure, but mainly to the perception that the US needed encouragement to maintain a military presence in Europe to counter a feared Russian thrust westward.[236] Continuing what the government considered the military obligations of Empire, it spent a higher proportion of national income on military commitments than any other country in Europe apart from the Soviet Union, and the bulk of industry research and development was in the defence industries.[237] The military build-up had the economic consequence that while other European countries established a technical lead in machinery and rebuilt their infrastructure, the UK was building tanks and planes. This willingness to spend on armaments was 'the reflex action of ministers to whom upholding Britain's status as a Great Power was a national imperative'.[238]

The left's disagreements over foreign policy merged with a shift in its attitude to the government's management of the economy. Up until this point it had supported a wage freeze, since it continued to hope for a planned economy in which wages and profits would be controlled. Bevan's paper *Tribune* opposed the railwaymen's dispute in 1949, backing the official line that redundancies were necessary to increase productivity before higher wages could be awarded.[239] The union rank and file, however, remained opposed to the TUC's cooperation on wage restraint, undercut by their leaders who continued to support the government with the justification of repeated calls for measures to control prices, extend cost of living subsidies, and limit profits. At the same time, union leaders were aggressive in promoting industrial discipline: Arthur Deakin of the T&GWU in particular was violently hostile to 'unofficial' movements against the union's leadership, especially among his members on the docks.[240] But after strikes of busmen and dockers in 1950, who were resisting the continuation of wartime restrictions on collective bargaining despite Deakin's witch-hunt against union militants, *Tribune* aligned itself with the growing wages movement fuelled by the increases in the cost of living caused by the devaluation of the pound and the start of the Korean War.[241]

The TUC's support for wage restrictions became unsustainable: at its executive conference in 1950, the general council's resolution that requested member unions to freeze existing wage claims was passed by a very thin majority. Conference delegates expressed resentment at the abandonment of physical economic controls and the government's reliance on budgetary management of demand. 'Keynes's economics,' said one delegate, 'are not working-class economics.'[242] The mood of the conference was expressed by one delegate in particular: 'I want to say that none of the women cleaners in the Civil Service will agree to have their wages frozen. Last year, we tried to get a rate of 2 shillings an hour for our work, and all we got offered was Sir Stafford Cripps' farthing and we told him what he could do with it ... We feel that this idea of freezing wages should be applied to some of the higher-ups, but if you ask us to live on our present wage, then the answer is NO, and if that is being awkward, then I will say that we did not vote in the Labour Party in 1945 in order for our position to be made worse.' Despite Deakin's condemnation of 'this policy of smash and grab' at the TUC's General Congress in September, the resolution from the platform supporting wage restraint was defeated.[243]

The Labour left had accepted the drift to war in Korea, reluctant to identify itself with the Soviet bloc, but belatedly opposed British involvement when its effects on living standards and welfare services became apparent. The consequences of alignment with US foreign policy in Korea – inflation, charges on social services, conscription, and anti-communist hysteria – were 'the real father of the Bevanite current,' according to Mark Jenkins.[244] Gaitskell's substantial increase in defence spending, announced in March 1951, was coupled with curbs on NHS resources and the imposition of charges on teeth and spectacles. Bevan called it 'deplorable' to abandon the principle of a free NHS for the comparatively small amount that would be saved, opposing the defence programme on both foreign policy and economic grounds – he was convinced that the resources to implement a programme on this scale could not be realised, and was vindicated in this view by the subsequent Churchill government.

Attlee had moved Bevan to the Ministry of Labour in early 1951, but Bevan found himself in a difficult position when the attorney-general prosecuted seven London dockers in February under the wartime anti-strike Order 1305. Facing a crowd of angry dockers in Bermondsey demanding the repeal of the law, Bevan answered one heckler: 'I will never be a member of a government which makes charges on the National Health Service for a patient.' This precipitated his resignation from the cabinet; defending the ideals of orthodox socialism against the government's rightward turn, he wrote to Attlee that the budget 'fails to apportion fairly the burdens of expenditure as between different classes. ... It is wrong because it envisages rising prices as a means of reducing civilian consumption, with all the consequences of industrial disturbance involved. It is wrong because it is the beginning of the destruction of those social services in which Labour has taken a special pride and which were giving Britain the moral leadership of the world.'[245]

The Bevanite revolt

With Bevan's resignation, the accumulated discontents of the Labour Party's membership found a spokesman and lightning-rod. According to Michael Foot, 'once Bevan resigned, all other left-wing activities were swamped by it'.[246] In Campbell's judgement, it 'opened a Pandora's box of grievances ... to create a deep division in the party which never healed'.[247] But this presentation inverts the relation: there was a deep division in the party after five years of government which crystallised around Bevan after his resignation. Bevanism was an expression of an ideological conflict within the labour movement over the Attlee government's acceptance of existing economic arrangements, its bipartisan foreign policy, and Morrison's centrist political platform. Despite the leadership's conservatism, individual party membership was increasing at this time, and its considerable strengthening between 1945 and 1952 'led to a qualitative transformation after 1951 when the rift at the level of government and the Labour apparatus facilitated the public airing throughout the Party of issues and discussions which had, up till then, been agitating small groups of left parliamentarians'.[248]

Bevan and his colleagues joined the existing 'Keep Left' group in parliament and were immediately dubbed Bevanites. They included Barbara Castle, Michael Foot, Richard Crossman and Ian Mikardo, meeting weekly and encouraging debates among the Labour rank and file, and adopting the 'Brains Trusts' already popular in the constituencies. 'Labour party members attended in their droves. Individual party membership soared to its highest ever level: over 1 million in 1952 and 1953'.[249] The Bevanites' pamphlet 'One Way Only', published in early 1951, addressed the connection between home and foreign affairs by citing the direct experience of factory workers: 'We have seen how the materials we need for our work disappear off the floor of the workshop because of something that's happening on the other side of Asia, and we have seen how the prices of goods in the shops are forced up by raw materials scrambles thousands of miles from our shores.' Its argument was that a reactionary foreign policy was making domestic social reform impossible and worsening the lot of the colonial peoples of Southeast Asia.[250]

The breakdown of wage restraint saw the right-wing union and party leaderships join forces against the Bevanite revolt. Even though the union leaders were making similar demands as the Bevanites for increased government economic control, they saw Bevan as challenging their right to speak for the rank and file and encouraging the opposition to wage restraint that had defeated the TUC General Council in 1950. Deakin told the 1952 party conference of 'difficulties and criticisms from their members' over their support for the party in government rather than focusing on industrial negotiations. The union leaders' hostility to the party left was closely connected to these difficulties: G.D.H. Cole wrote in 1953 that '[t]hey are afraid of Bevanism, not without reason, as calculated to strengthen opposition to "wage restraint" and to collaboration in measures designed to increase productivity'. But they also knew they had to be cautious in case they were rejected by their own membership.[251]

Although the media claimed a major Labour split, the Bevanites emphasised that they were not putting forward an alternative domestic policy, since their proposals were party policies decided democratically at conference that the leadership had abandoned. They referred explicitly to the 1950 election manifesto, *Let Us Win Through Together*, describing its economic plans to be 'as valid now as they were when they were written'. The manifesto promised full employment and higher production, food subsidies to keep down the cost of living, the nationalisation of sugar and cement monopolies, and 'control over capital investment, distribution of industry, industrial building and foreign exchange'. It reiterated the aspiration of ethical socialism 'to create a community that relies for its driving power as the release of all the finer constructive impulses of man'.[252] However, neither the Brains Trusts nor the Bevanites encouraged the re-thinking of socialist ideas in relation to the experience of Labour in power, and they did not devise any concrete plans that addressed how the manifesto's policies could be achieved in the context of a mixed economy, except to continue to call for the nationalisation of the 'commanding heights' of the economy.

Mark Jenkins argues that '[i]f in the main, Bevanite pamphlets exhibit a lack of concrete proposals for domestic reform it is due solely to their commitment to the party programme, which they believed could not be implemented without a major shift in the emphasis of Labour's foreign policy'. Nicklaus Thomas-Symonds rebuts this with the observation that the 'Atlantic alliance had produced the money' in the form of Marshall Aid that allowed the Attlee government to implement its reform programme.[253] But his argument is overly facile: clearly, what Jenkins is referring to and what the Bevanites had in mind was not the earlier Atlantic alliance but the cold war alignment with the US. He is on surer ground when he adds that Gaitskell and Bevan were not really that far apart on domestic policy.

The Tories won the election that Attlee had inauspiciously called in 1951, and Labour was returned to parliamentary opposition. While in the Cabinet, Bevan had been a reluctant supporter of the Atlantic alliance as a financial and military necessity, but the Korean War was a turning point. Bevan now considered that US foreign policy was driven by ideological hostility to communism, and he began to look for alternatives – although Crossman's view was that Bevan was 'almost exclusively concerned to be leader of the party, rather than to formulate left-wing policy'.[254] This was the context for the leadership rivalry between Bevan and Gaitskell, who with Morrison represented the right of the party and who enthusiastically supported the government's Atlanticist policy. Bevan's hostility to Gaitskell was heightened by his antipathy to people whose Labour affiliation was not based on their own experience of working-class struggle. His opposition to German rearmament was popular with the party membership, and Emanuel Shinwell, who had been defence minister, lost his place in the constituency section of the NEC, while Bevan's supporters increased their votes. At the same time, however, the leaders of the general unions, Arthur Deakin of the T&GWU, Will Lawther of the NUM, and Tom Williamson of the GMWU, who had been criticised in Bevan's journal *Tribune* for ignoring their members' views in conference voting, took a decision at Scarborough to stop Bevan ever becoming party leader, switching their support to the parliamentary right wing.[255]

The union leaders were conservative men, impressed by the material progress that had been made since the 1930s, who saw the Bevanites as a threat to the unity of the labour movement. 'Much of the energy and many of the initiatives behind the drive against the Bevanites emanated from such officials. Many union leaders insisted upon unflinching respect for majority decisions: this both lay at the heart of their understanding of Party democracy and (in their view) was the bond that held it together. Factionalism, Tom Williamson insisted, "can have no place in our democratic organisation".' Shaw describes this reasoning as 'social-democratic centralism,' a discipline grounded in trade union traditions that permeated the internal life of the Labour Party. 'Loyalism was in turn reinforced by widespread sentiments of deference towards authority; in this Labour was a microcosm of the wider political culture.'[256]

The parliamentary 'Bevanite controversy' began in March 1952 when the Churchill government set out its defence plan. Attlee decided the opposition should approve it in principle, while questioning the government's ability to carry it out – but 57 Labour MPs defied a three-line whip and voted against it. While the PLP right wanted as a consequence to remove the whip from Bevan, support for the Bevanites in the constituencies escalated. Bevan topped the poll for the constituency section of the NEC at that year's Morecambe conference, and delegates expressed open hostility to Deakin and Lawther, defying the leadership by replacing Morrison and Dalton on the NEC.

Gaitskell fought back with a speech that accused the conference resolutions and speeches as 'communist-inspired', calling *Tribune* 'an attempt at mob rule by a group of frustrated journalists'.[257] He was joined by Deakin, who attacked *Tribune* and the Bevanites as a 'party within the party'. Attlee moved the disbanding of unofficial groups and evoked the spectre of the 1930s experience with the ILP to achieve an overwhelming vote for his proposal, effectively banning the Bevanite group. Labour's parliamentary committee then recommended that all groups within the party be disbanded, and the Bevanites formally did so at the end of 1952. The parliamentary group now began to operate clandestinely, but lost its connection to the organisation of work among the rank and file. While the Bevanite MPs languished after being proscribed, 'the mass work and propaganda side of the group flourished as never before'. This took the form of increased Brains Trust activity in 1953 followed by a drive into the unions in the course of 1954. 'There was a compelling desire to discuss, to air the problems of the movement after the defeat of the first ever majority Labour government. ... The Brains Trusts showed that what was needed was discussion, and that to facilitate this, very little in the way of sophisticated organisation was required.'[258]

After Gaitskell had denounced *Tribune,* the NEC decided to investigate the Brains Trusts, for which there was still an insatiable demand in the constituencies. The union representatives were determined to ban them, not for what was said but for 'the fact that they are organised'.[259] While within party discourse a struggle raged over German rearmament, dockers in Hull rebelled against the T&GWU leaders' refusal to recognize their strike over dangerous work conditions by joining the NASD (blue) union. In the northern ports of Hull and Liverpool, dockers migrated to the blue union, and its call for a strike against compulsory overtime drew a big response from T&GWU members in London. This was much more than an inter-union membership dispute, it was an important struggle by the rank and file to free themselves from Deakin's bureaucratic leadership. *Tribune* came out in support of the NASD strike, and Deakin unsuccessfully demanded action against the paper, but its support for the right of trade unionists to join the union of their own choice led to record sales between October and November 1954. The union leadership covertly fought back by reviving the trade union group within the PLP, aiming to protect the parliamentary leadership against the left.[260]

The resistance of the party right wing

The high point of Bevanite influence in the party was in 1954, after the US had pushed for both West German 'independence'[261] and its inclusion in NATO. *Tribune* argued that this would only antagonise the Soviet Union and remove the possibility of its agreement to German reunification as a neutral state. At the party conference that year the *Tribune* position was only narrowly defeated by the block votes that were controlled by the unions' bureaucratic leadership, and in which the rank and file had little say. It also lost in the parliamentary party by a mere two votes. The conflict had a wider significance insofar as it foregrounded the ideological gulf between those who accepted the cold war anti-communism of the US and those on the left who, like Bevan, demanded a policy that would recognise the validity of the anti-colonial struggle despite its characterisation by the US as pro-communist.[262] When Arthur Greenwood died, Bevan announced his candidacy for party treasurer, although he knew that the block vote of the union leaders meant he faced certain defeat. His decision was based on his conviction that the union membership would eventually overcome its domination by the right wing, and his campaign precipitated a radical questioning of undemocratic processes that had been commonplace in the unions.[263]

Bevan was nearly expelled after he confronted Attlee in parliament over Labour support for Tory foreign policy, which included building a British H-bomb. The Bevanites had abstained on the agreement on a European Defence Community Agreement, and the docks dispute continued to antagonise Deakin. Bevan was accused of persistently attacking party and union leaders, refusing to accept majority decisions, and forming an organised group with its own press.[264] Gaitskell told Richard Crossman that 'Bevanism is and only is a conspiracy to seize the leadership for Aneurin Bevan', and in the same conversation, compared Bevan to Hitler. Gaitskell's bile is evidence that their ideological differences expressed a real tension in the relation between the party leadership and the base.[265] The response throughout the wider labour movement was decisive – Transport House began receiving protests from CLPs and union leaders like those of the NUR and NUM, forecasting a huge row at the party conference. Although the PLP voted to withdraw the whip, Attlee intervened and persuaded Bevan to agree a statement of apology rather than be expelled.

When Attlee finally retired at the end of 1955, Gaitskell was elected leader by an overwhelming majority of the parliamentary party, since Bevan had not succeeded in increasing his support from MPs much beyond the 1952 rebels. In his 1955 campaign for party treasurer – won again by Gaitskell – he attacked the union block votes, saying that in reality 'it is the leaders of the general unions who are in effective control of the Labour party'.[266] The Bevanites' perspective was that a strong left-wing presence in the party leadership would commit Labour to a more radical programme. Their strategy signally failed when Bevan's drive for the leadership ended in December 1955. The left had made little headway on policy documents – 'the fifties were a decade when revisionist sentiments made significant headway at the top of the party, with the place of public ownership reduced, and a growing desire to court rather than influence existing electoral preferences'.[267]

The history of the party leadership's attempts to rein in Bevan and submit him to bureaucratic discipline is an inverse reflection of the strength of the Bevanite movement in the rank and file. It reveals the hostility of the party machine at that time to left-wing sentiment and the organisational lengths it was willing to go to crush it. Shaw comments: 'Though social democratic centralists genuinely believed that vigorous central direction was in the interest of the Party as a whole, there is little doubt that throughout this period the NEC used its powers to promote the factional cause of the dominant right, both locally and nationally.' Significantly, the right retreated in 1955 when elections were looming and, with redistricting, MPs needed membership support in the constituencies to get re-elected.[268]

Bevan's support within the parliamentary party itself was limited because most Labour MPs were concerned to maintain party unity. The economy had recovered, leading to a consumer boom, with the Tories maintaining full employment and the welfare state. Many parliamentarians understood this to have satisfied what they thought of as socialism and they became an essentially conservative force, uninterested in further reform. 'The memory of 1931 was painful; the achievements of 1945-51 were a cement joining many of them to the leadership; the belief that dissent damaged electoral prospects was shared widely. ... Such emotions were carefully fostered by political and industrial leaders.'[269]

Although left sentiment and increasing militancy began to be reflected in the unions with the election of Frank Cousins as leader of the T&GWU in 1956, Bevan could see no way to overturn Gaitskell's leadership. He accepted the post of Shadow Colonial Secretary, while asserting his right of free speech within the party. After Nasser nationalised the Suez Canal, Bevan eloquently opposed Eden's use of military force at a mass rally in Trafalgar Square. His opponents for the position of party treasurer were split between three right-wing candidates, and this fragmentation of the vote allowed Bevan to be elected. Rather than a victory for the left, in practice it marked Bevan's acceptability to the party leadership, and he was promoted to Shadow Foreign Secretary.

In his exhaustive study of Bevanism, Mark Jenkins concludes that the movement's political weakness lay in its failure to grasp the repressive role of the Soviet bureaucracy in world politics. What eventually separated Bevan from the Bevanite movement was his desire for détente with the Kremlin after the revolutions of 1956 in East Germany and Hungary, when he moved closer to the policy of negotiation with the new liberal Stalinist regimes, a core plank of the multilateralist viewpoint of the party leadership. Bevan perceived the world as 'divided into two blocs with a neutral bloc trying to emerge between them'. He believed the reformed Stalinist leaderships could be negotiated with to establish a neutral bloc in Central Europe – and in order to restrain the military threat of the superpowers, Britain would need possession of nuclear weapons in order to negotiate with both sides.[270] Bevan's notorious speech at the 1957 Brighton Labour Party conference threw his support behind retention of the H-bomb, and was understood by his erstwhile supporters as a renunciation of his previous beliefs, although it was consistent with his drift towards a pragmatic accommodation to power. He challenged his critics that while they could only pass resolutions on the subject, in practice a British Foreign Secretary would have to negotiate with some means of influencing the US and USSR. Would they send him 'naked into the conference chamber?' he asked.

When Bevan reconciled himself to Gaitskell's leadership, he appeared to have lost 'what seemed essential in Bevanism – its style of revolt', as Geoffrey Foote remarks.[271] The coherence of the left was shattered, and disillusion set in. Gaitskell used the 1959 electoral defeat to argue that increasing affluence and the party's identification with public ownership was behind a declining Labour vote and proposed to remove 'Clause Four' from the party's constitution. But the symbolism of the clause meant that leaders of large unions with many old-style loyalists opposed Gaitskell's proposal. In 1960 the party conference passed a motion in favour of unilateral disarmament, against the position of the NEC. Gaitskell called on MPs to ignore the vote, announcing to delegates that he would 'fight and fight again to save the party I love', beginning a campaign which ended in the overturn of the resolution the following year.

The limits of Bevanism

At party conferences, Gaitskell counted on the block votes controlled by the right-wing union leaders to support his leadership position, but in the constituencies, Bevan had 'energised the constant fund of traditional idealism ... [as well as] elements who responded vehemently to what they considered as disloyal criticism. Within the unions, Bevanism evoked the strongest positive response in those organisations with significant Communist factions ... although in policy terms the Bevanite leadership position was far closer to the Labour moderates than to the Communist Party.' However, on the domestic front, '[t]here was no examination of the assumptions behind the Government's economic strategy, the failure to change the pre-existing managerial hierarchies in the newly nationalised industries, or the readiness with which existing economic practices and incentives had been accepted'.[272]

Bevan, as we have seen, had accepted the principle of a mixed economy as long as the party retained the intention of nationalising its 'commanding heights'. He retreated further at the 1957 party conference, agreeing that Labour should restrict its nationalisation plans to the industries privatised by the Tories, steel and road haulage. While dubious about Tony Crosland's proposal for the government to own shares in the largest industrial companies instead of nationalising them, Bevan had no alternative suggestions about how public ownership could be increased. The Bevanites' uncritical acceptance of the party's domestic programme had become a political weakness: 'Belief in public ownership was an abstract principle without practical proposals for its implementation.'[273]

The party's leadership struggle had been confined within the ideological limits of Labourism and had little impact on public opinion generally. The left, including Bevan, continued to maintain that a Tory government would inevitably mean the restoration of unemployment – but Churchill's concern to avoid industrial confrontation facilitated a close relationship between the government and the TUC, concessions on wages, and the maintenance of full employment throughout the 1950s. "The great Bevanite arguments took place not against a backdrop of industrial discontent, but in a period when many trade unionists accommodated themselves more than adequately to the Churchill-Butler variant of the post-war consensus.'[274]

Since Bevan's perspective was limited to parliament, he was unable to consistently leverage his extra-parliamentary support against the right. Hilary Wainwright's researches in the party archives found 'overwhelming support for Bevan in the constituency parties, and how this power base was rendered marginal by the bloc vote of all the major unions ... although changes were taking place in the unions, subterraneanly, on the shop floor, the Bevanites had little political inclination to build any direct association with shop-floor activists ... Bevan's reverence for the House of Commons, stemming from his belief in its power as the "sword at the heart of private property", meant that he and his followers saw little political significance in the growth of shop-floor power.'[275] Bevan and his colleagues had developed their political ideas at a time when socialism had been understood narrowly in terms of the economic reform of a capitalism in crisis. The Attlee government's legislation displaced any debate about the class nature of the British state, which the left, like the rest of the party, continued to consider a neutral instrument for social reform.[276]

The Labour Party establishment dealt with dissent with a heavy hand. The banning of the Bevanite group and the attempted expulsion of Bevan himself revealed a deep authoritarian streak in the right-wing leadership, disregarding the concerns and democratic voice of the rank and file.[277] However, many in the membership retained their support for Bevan's basic positions, asserting that Labour would have retained office if it had enhanced its nationalisation programme after 1948. In the late 1950s, 'many ordinary Labour members considered socialism to be largely a matter of implementing Clause IV of Labour's constitution. For those in agreement with the leadership, however, electoral success depended on dispensing with the commitment. Both sides had separated themselves from an emphasis on ethical transformation, so much to the fore in the 1940s.'[278]

Mark Jenkins has countered the depiction of Bevanism as a purely parliamentary phenomenon by demonstrating that within the labour movement it was 'a powerful mood or current of revolt against the direction taken by the Labour cabinet between 1949-51, and against the direction of the Attlee-Deakin leadership in both foreign and domestic policy after the election defeat of 1951'.[279] The Bevanites' conception of socialism was an economy rationally controlled by the state, thus ensuring the most effective use of manpower and natural resources. But the Attlee government's achievement of full employment without centralised state control of industry – albeit at the cost of political subordination to the US Treasury – left Bevan little alternative to making the compromises necessary to implement basic social reform. On the philosophical level, the Bevanites remained trapped in the analytical categories of orthodox socialism, which viewed society as a struggle between an undifferentiated manual working class and identifiable monopoly capitalists, but with the difference that social reform was thought to be dependent on the party leadership's commitment to socialist policies.

The fatal flaw of Bevan's conception was the idea that the popular will could only be expressed through parliament as the central power that would implement social change, denying agency to extra-parliamentary activities. His political dualism took the form of equating the symbol of power – parliament – with real class power, and the symbol of socialist priorities – nationalisation – with socialism, and led him to mistake the shifts in the Eastern European bureaucracy for the social upheavals underlying them.

In Place of Fear

In 1952 Bevan took advantage of his reprieve from office to write a book about his political philosophy, *In Place of Fear,* which was published in a blaze of publicity and quickly sold 37,000 copies. For the book, he combined chapters written before he became a minister in 1945 with others hastily produced after his resignation. Although it was a publishing success, many felt 'puzzled, even defeated' by the fact that it was primarily an exposition of orthodox socialist arguments against capitalism, at a time when the left was searching for a fresh political perspective on a society that now had full employment and welfare provision.[280] Bevan's definition of democratic socialism was the acceptance of the obligation to choose between possible alternative kinds of political action, rather than follow a dogmatic formula for changing society. However, he blended this pragmatic approach with a justification of extended public ownership as a way to subordinate the profit motive to the general needs of society, in the circumstance that 'large aggregations of capital have coagulated into monopolies ... in which profit is a clear tax on the community'.[281]

Bevan resolved the clash of socialist principles with the compromises of government by separating them into coexisting domains. For example, his book gives an ethical socialist justification for free healthcare: 'The collective principle ... insists that no society can legitimately call itself civilised if a sick person is denied medical aid because of lack of means.' But he gives a pragmatic reason for funding the health service from taxation rather than insurance, because this uses a pre-existing system 'already in the possession of most modern states'.[282] While he remarks that he finds it 'painful' when a Labour spokesperson justifies socialist legislation on exclusively practical grounds, he fails to show how workable policies could be derived from socialist principles. In other words, a policy should be justified in socialist terms even though it may be a pragmatic solution to a problem. Despite the fact that, as he admits, his compromise agreement with the medical profession had many flaws, he declared that 'a free health service is pure socialism and as such it is opposed to the hedonism of capitalist society ... [it] is a triumphant example of the superiority of collective action and public initiative applied to a segment of society where commercial principles are seen at their worst.'[283]

In the 1920s Bevan had been a strong syndicalist, but after the defeat of the General Strike he became an advocate of parliamentary democracy as a weapon in the class struggle. Socialists had to display audacity in applying 'the full armament of democratic values to the problems of the times,' he wrote.[284] He defines the issues of capitalist democracy as 'either poverty will use democracy to win the struggle against property, or property, in fear of poverty, will destroy democracy'. This aphorism was not based on a consideration of a wide sweep of history, however, but on the symbolism of specific events – the role of unemployment in the collapse of the constitution and rise of Hitler in Germany, as opposed to the election of a Labour government in Britain that would 'expose wealth-privilege to the attack of the people.'[285]

Since he considered parliament to be the ultimate seat of power, Bevan did not cite the trade unions or public protest as a factor in defeating potential resistance by 'wealth-privilege.' Instead, he gives credit to Britain's unwritten constitution which gives parliament a 'revolutionary quality' that 'exposes all rights and privileges, properties and powers, to the popular will.'[286] Since communal interests could only be expressed through parliament, gaining positions in the Labour Party executive was key to expressing the general will, rather than engaging with the collective will expressed by the labour movement's rank and file. He rejected Keynesian methods of economic regulation since they did not change the social power of capitalist ownership but saw the problems of nationalised industries as only an issue of improving ministerial oversight and allocating sufficient civil servants.

Bevan concedes that a mixed economy was the only politically practicable policy at that time, rejecting the purism of left critics 'who in practice would socialise nothing, while in theory they would threaten the whole of private property'. In the future, private property should yield to socialist priorities, but in the short term, 'parliamentary power is to be used progressively until the main streams of economic activity are brought under public direction'.[287] He remained committed to a centralised, top-down form of state ownership, understanding industrial democracy in terms of cooperation between workers and management rather than workers' control of management. Nationalised industries were the cornerstone of economic planning, but the advance to socialism, he says, is predicated on 'the extent the workers in the nationalised sector are made aware of a changed relationship between themselves and the management. The persistence of a sense of dualism [conflict] in a publicly owned industry is evidence of an immature industrial democracy.'[288]

He did not oppose national defence, but he did oppose a paranoid fear of Russia that exaggerated its military strength and led to the building of a vast military capacity at a level that threatened social reform.[289] His belief in the possibility of the liberalisation of the Soviet Union after it had absorbed the Eastern European states was consistent with his renunciation of unilateral disarmament in 1957; for him, Britain had a responsibility to exert moral leadership in the world, and to have any kind of diplomatic influence it had to retain its nuclear weapons.

The aftermath of Bevanism

The Churchill government's avoidance of industrial conflict and acceptance of the welfare state and managed economy after 1951 disoriented the left. Its resolutions to party conferences became more the reaffirmation of a moral stance rather than a practical alternative to party policy. Bevan's capitulation to the Labour leadership had emphasised the restrictions of a perspective dedicated to achieving leadership positions in the party, leaving the Bevanites at a political and theoretical dead end. Ideologically the left was hamstrung by the political centrality of the Cold War, and by their optimistic assumption that the post-war reforms provided a platform for socialist advance: 'post-war experiences, [on the Bevanite interpretation] suggested that the state could serve not just the interests of capitalists, but, alternatively, those of the working class provided that Labour had a clear set of priorities, and a keen determination.'[290]

The first important theoretical challenge to the orthodox socialism of the Bevanites came from the right. For a number of Labour intellectuals like Richard Crossman, John Strachey, and Anthony Crosland, state intervention in the economy had fundamentally altered British capitalism. Since full employment and rising living standards had been achieved, they considered there had already been an altered distribution of economic power between capitalists and the state. Crosland, who self-consciously styled himself a 'revisionist', argues in his 1956 book *The Future of Socialism* that to all extents and purposes the capitalism of the 1930s, where individual proprietors could close down whole industries with no concern about its social impact, no longer existed. Capitalism had not collapsed, as the left had expected it to, but instead had metamorphosed into something different. The separation of private ownership and managerial control had made business more responsive to political pressures, and the state could use fiscal policy if necessary to encourage socially responsible business decisions.[291]

Experience showed that ownership of the means of production was no longer the key to the nature of society – workers in the Soviet Union were no better off than in Britain or in the US – so nationalisation could not be considered a precondition for socialism. More importantly 'what is unjust in our present arrangements is the distribution of private wealth', and nationalisation had done little to redistribute it. It was the class antagonism created by resentment against this social inequality that lay behind the 'militant, class-conscious leftism' in the Labour Party; the Bevanites' resolutions at party conferences calling for more nationalisation and state planning were therefore 'Quixotic tilts' at a nonexistent enemy. Instead, a state investment trust should be provided with public funds to take over inefficient firms and under-utilised assets.[292]

Socialism should realistically be defined in terms of social welfare and social equality, thought Crosland, which was a matter of increasing the part of national income directed at the social services and therefore dependent only on the will of the government. In order to realise true socialist ideals, the first priority of Labour should be education reform, which was 'of far greater significance to socialism' than nationalisation, since changes in the educational system could undermine the managerial class's assumption of social superiority. A Labour government should democratise entry into the independent public schools; propagate comprehensive schools; and allot greater resources to raising standards in secondary moderns. Moreover, instead of deploring affluence, 'socialists must acknowledge the link between rising consumption and equality in "felt" living standards,' so that the working class could enjoy the material comforts hitherto only available to the privileged few.[293]

For Crosland, socialism was a matter of deciding how to apportion the abundance that would arise from an ever-expanding economy, and reducing inherited class status. His book was essentially a description of the practical aspirations of the Labour right in the 1950s, accepting self-interest rather than the traditional socialist values of fellowship and cooperation as the determinants of social policy; the denial of these traditional values was, however, 'only an explicit acknowledgement of the practice of the Attlee Government,' an intellectual justification of the post-1945 consensus that dispensed with the orthodox vision of a nationalised economy.[294]

As Crosland's book was being published, reports of Khrushchev's 'secret speech' detailing Stalin's crimes began to circulate, precipitating a crisis among intellectuals in the Communist Party. The disillusion created by the Soviet invasion of Hungary in the same year combined with the opposition of students to the British invasion of Suez to create a broad 'New Left' outside the Labour Party that rejected both Bevanism and Stalinism as ultimately sterile, reviving a radical culture that had stalled with the political stalemate within the party. Towards the end of the 1950s mass demonstrations had begun over the issue of nuclear weapons. Pressure for unilateral nuclear disarmament grew inside and outside the party; after Bevan's speech to the 1957 conference, 'the unilateralist movement developed outside the party's official channels ... an upsurge of radical feeling unparalleled since the Popular Front agitations of the thirties,' with the first anti-nuclear march from Aldermaston held in 1958.[295] The newly-founded Campaign for Nuclear Disarmament (CND) channeled a genuine social movement involving large numbers of disenfranchised women and youth: the emerging youth culture of the late 1950s adopted the campaign as an expression of identity, while many women were politicised by it and later became active in the feminist movement of the 1970s.[296]

Inspired by the rise of the New Left, the Marxist writer Ralph Miliband addressed the limitations of Bevanism in his influential book *Parliamentary Socialism*. He argued that the dogmatic loyalty of the Labour Party to parliamentary rule had inhibited it from radical reform. 'The leaders of the Labour party have always rejected any kind of political action (such as industrial action for political purposes) which fell, or which appeared to them to fall, outside the framework and conventions of the parliamentary system,' he wrote. The Bevanite left, like its predecessors in the ILP and Socialist League, had accepted the same limitations, which was why it had never been able to successfully challenge the party leadership. 'Throughout, parliamentary Bevanism was a mediation between the leadership and the rank and file opposition. But the parliamentary Bevanites, while assuming the leadership of that opposition, also served to blur and to blunt both its strength and its extent. Themselves limited by their parliamentary and executive obligations, they fell back on the politics of manoeuvre, and were regularly outmanoeuvred in the process.'[297]

He considered the resignation of intellectuals from the Communist Party after 1956 to have greater political importance. While some had dropped out of politics, and others joined with Trotskyists to found the Socialist Labour League (SLL), Miliband was attracted to the intellectual collaboration of John Saville and Edward Thompson. The two historians had founded the *New Reasoner* after their original dissident 'Reasoner' publication had been suppressed by the Communist Party bureaucracy, seeking to revive the less dogmatic socialist tradition of Tom Mann and William Morris. In 1959, Saville explained the rationale for the new publication as a response to the failure of the left to theorise the welfare state and full employment: 'The

Left in domestic matters has produced nothing of substance to offset the most important book of the decade – Crosland's *The Future of Socialism* – a brilliant restatement of Fabian ideas in contemporary terms. We have made no sustained critique of the economics of capitalism in the 1950s, and our vision of a socialist society has changed hardly at all since the days of Keir Hardie.'[298]

Miliband enthusiastically accepted Saville and Thompson's invitation to join the editorial board of the *New Reasoner*, and hoped to convince them to join with the Labour left in an attempt to steer the party in a socialist direction, but they turned instead to the group around the Oxford-based publication *Universities and Left Review*. This had been established by a number of students, including Stuart Hall and Raphael Samuel, who had an aversion to both the right-wing revisionists and leftist orthodoxy that evaded issues connected with the post-war reshaping of workers' consciousness through the spread of consumerist mass culture. The Oxford group's 'culturalist' approach to the social process implied that all aspects of economics and politics had equal weight, so that 'workers' self-management could not be regarded as less critical than the nationalisation of a steel company'. Between 1957-59 both groups channeled frustration with the labour movement's bureaucratic suppression of rank-and-file opinion into an enthusiastic support for the Campaign for Nuclear Disarmament (CND), which represented a more democratic grassroots alternative.[299]

In 1960 the two separate publications were merged in the *New Left Review*, calling for the development of a theory of culture as part of a break from the straightjacket of orthodox interpretations of Marxism that had assumed socialism would automatically result from public ownership, and reaffirming the importance of culture over economics and participation over bureaucracy. Miliband opposed the merger at the time on the grounds that the two groups represented very different approaches to the labour movement, and was broadly vindicated when Thompson broke with the publication in 1963. Miliband then proposed the founding of a new journal that became the *Socialist Register*, under his and Saville's editorship. Thompson went on to recover the history of the English radical democratic tradition in his landmark work, *The Making of the English Working Class*. The key argument of his book was that the consciousness of an identity of interests between working men and women was not solely the product of being herded into the cotton mills of the early nineteenth century, but their experience of increased exploitation was mediated through a popular discourse based on memories of Jacobinism, village rights, notions of equality, and craft traditions. The working class 'made' itself in the course of a battle against the imposition of the capitalist order in England: 'It is the political context as much as the steam-engine which had most influence upon the shaping consciousness and institutions of the working class,' he asserted.[300]

His socialist humanist philosophy was developed out of his struggle with the Communist Party's authoritarian control of party discussions, opposing the economic determinism of Stalinism by reaffirming the central role of human agency. William Morris's understanding of the evolution of man's moral nature was an essential complement to a Marxist historical analysis, he thought: 'Economic relationships are at the same time moral relationships ... there is a moral logic as well as an economic logic, which derives from these [production] relationships.' He reasserted the socialist purpose as 'a society of equals, a cooperative community' as against the revisionist idea of 'equality of opportunity' within an acquisitive society. Public ownership did not automatically create a socialist society: nationalisation had to be accompanied by a transformation of social attitudes – including the abolition of the profit motive and the democratisation of the labour process.[301]

Thompson began to re-evaluate the experience of the Attlee government from an historical perspective, beginning by rejecting Labour's gradualism and the cataclysmic Leninist model of revolution: he argued that both ignored the popular pressures that had shaped institutions and forced adjustment to them by capitalist interests. He denied that there is 'some *automatic* relationship between social ownership and socialist institutions or moral disposition: that the superstructure of a "good society" *must* grow in a certain way once the basis has been established'. The utopian protest, 'the vision of new human possibilities constrained within old forms' is an essential part of the socialist dynamic.[302]

Fundamentalist thinkers concluded that no real advance had taken place under Attlee, since the government's reforms had been contained within the system. But, Thompson argues, these concepts of pure revolution should be discarded. 'We must, at every point, see *both* – the surge forward *and* the containment, the public sector *and* its subordination to the private, the strength of trade unions *and* their parasitism upon capitalist growth, the welfare services *and* their poor-relation status. The countervailing powers are there, and the equilibrium ... is precarious.' Thompson's optimism came about 'because the advances of 1942-48 *were* real, because the socialist *potential* has been enlarged, and socialist forms, however imperfect, have grown up "within" capitalism'.[303]

Thompson also took issue with the 'workerism' prevalent in the Communist Party and Bevanite left, arguing that the separation between industrial workers and the rest of society should be abandoned. 'Alongside industrial workers, we should see the teachers who want better schools, scientists who wish to advance research, welfare workers who want hospitals, actors who want a National Theatre, technicians impatient to improve industrial organisation.' His perspective enlarged the basis for socialism in a way that encompassed the social changes brought about by the expansion of the welfare state, and by extending it beyond the industrial working class he supported a positive appreciation of grassroots protest activities like CND.[304]

The political fortunes of the New Left were in fact closely bound up with the rise of the anti-nuclear movement. It had aimed to combine CND's cultural and political protests and the youth rebellion with the socialist traditions of the labour movement, but when the unilateralist movement began to decline in the early 1960s the New Left's political influence also dwindled. Early drafts of Labour's 1961 platform, *Signposts for the Sixties*, reflected New Left concerns such as the role of the media and democratic control of industry, but these issues were replaced with an emphasis on modernisation and technological advance, the theme of the party's new electoral campaign.[305] The New Left's political decline corresponded to the protest movement's reorientation towards the election of a Labour government, and the *New Left Review* itself became increasingly academic.

In this chapter, I recounted the rise of the Bevanite opposition to the Labour Party leadership over the retreat from the socialist elements in its programme. Insofar as the Bevanites conveyed the frustration of labour activists, it represented a real opposition to the right-wing bureaucracy in the unions and the party. But it became locked into the struggle for party leadership without a strategy to overcome the stranglehold of the union block vote. Moreover, the Bevanites could not resolve the contradiction between the ideal of a socialist economic policy and the party's commitment to a mixed economy. Since the welfare state and full employment remained popular, and strike struggles were swiftly defused by government and employer intervention, the conflict over nationalisation and foreign policy remained confined to the party's internal discourse. At the same time, the expansion of the welfare state was creating a new layer of professional and administrative staff in education, health and social services which tended to oppose bureaucracy and the unions' influence in the Labour Party; this, together with affluence and greater access to education, contributed to the undermining of the collectivist social relations that had rested on political passivity and deference to authority.[306]

An emerging youth culture challenged the old hierarchical values of society, expressing a popular discontent and a romantic rebellion, while CND rejected traditional authority in favour of direct action. The New Left, connected to both these movements, had presented an important ideological challenge to both the Bevanite left and the revisionist right, especially with its stress on the need for people's direct involvement in the political decisions that affected their lives. It was a significant break from the centralising ideas of orthodox socialism. In the next chapter I shall discuss how the New Left's ideas about direct democracy were assimilated by a revitalised Labour left in the context of an unprecedented surge in union militancy, leading to a re-thinking of the post-1945 concept of the relation between socialism and nationalisation.

Chapter Five

Harold Wilson in Office and the Rise of a Labour New Left

'The greatest gain in the three years' work that has been done in Upper Clyde is the transformation of the labour force from people utterly dejected by the failures of private management; the restructuring of the unions; and the assumption of responsibility. Now the Government have awakened a force in Scotland, and I believe in industry generally, that will not easily be put back.'[307] Tony Benn, 1971

The first Wilson government: 1964-70

There were four Labour governments in the turbulent 1960s-70s, under Harold Wilson and James Callaghan, which used Labour's links with the trade union bureaucracy in an attempt to discipline the mass strike movement of the period. This had a material effect in undermining support for the Labour new left's struggle for an alternative to the economic strategy forced on the government by the international banks. However, despite the left's defeat, a new conception of socialism developed that was linked to Tony Benn's campaign for popular democracy.

The economic background of the social and cultural shifts in the 1960s was a sustained reduction in the rate of profit as a consequence of the overaccumulation of capital built up during the extended post-war boom. Combined with full employment and rising raw materials costs, the result was price inflation and intensified international competition. From the early 1960s, British manufacturers found they were at a relative disadvantage because of low industrial productivity. Although fundamentally this stemmed from lack of investment in technology and infrastructure, employers blamed high wages and called for government controls on unofficial strikes that were becoming increasingly effective in industries like car manufacturing, bypassing the reluctance of union leaders to engage in industrial struggle.[308]

In this chapter I discuss how the unprecedented expansion of industrial militancy in the 1960s and 1970s encouraged the development of a new left within the Labour Party that mounted a formidable challenge to the right-centrist leadership, finding a spokesperson in Tony Benn. He was sensitive to the political forces that eventually resulted in Thatcherism and he developed a conception of socialism oriented to making practical changes in the immediate present that would strengthen the working class and democratically empower the public. In conjunction with a strategically experienced group of shop stewards, he encouraged an experiment in bottom-up socialist planning that devised a company-wide plan to manufacture socially useful products that would replace arms industry production and retain jobs, a conceptual development that had no parallel among even the most politically conscious industrial militants. It resolved the labour movement's traditional separation of immediate tasks from ultimate goals.

The short-lived euphoria over Labour's election victory in 1964, after 13 years of Tory rule, was based on the expectation that it would continue the work of the Attlee government and resume the advance towards socialism. Harold Wilson had become party leader the previous year, using his earlier association with Bevan to gain the support of the left. However, taking office in the middle of a balance of payments crisis, and with a small parliamentary majority, Wilson's plans for reform on the basis of technology-driven economic expansion were shelved in favour of a prices and incomes policy that would curb wage inflation with the collaboration of the TUC.

With Wilson, '[t]he rhetoric of science, expertise, planning, purpose and public service was in the ascendant. This was Fabian revivalism ... It was a language of social revolution that thereby engaged the sympathies of the left; but it was the language of modernisation, dynamism and progress and that gave it a more general appeal both within and outside the Party.'[309] As with the Attlee government's use of the vocabulary of planning while in practice avoiding the necessary coercion, Wilson's planning rhetoric functioned as a cover for an accommodation with the existing structures of economic power. The Bevanite left was unable to project any alternative to Wilson's technocratic view of socialism because it shared the same strategic assumption of the need to make the party electable, placing its faith in the ability of a Labour government to direct a politically neutral state. At the same time, the party's core working-class constituency became disillusioned with the government, expressed in apathy and electoral abstention, because of discontent with its attempts at wage control and the contraction of the traditional industries that formed Labour's base of support.[310]

The government was faced with a choice between deflation and devaluation to deal with the growing balance of payments problem. Wilson opted for deflation and avoided devaluation by relying on IMF loans, which opened up the government to pressure for sweeping cuts in public expenditure. Its reform plan had assumed a faster rate of economic growth, but it chose instead to defend the exchange rate and continue with military spending and capital exports, with the result of worsening the outflows of sterling. A new election in 1966 finally gave Labour a workable majority. Wilson initially resisted Treasury demands for a more deflationary budget, but a run on sterling led to further spending cuts and the statutory imposition of wage restraint. Devaluation was avoided in order to retain US support for the pound, but 'the fact remains that the decision not to devalue in July 1966 represented the triumph of short-term over long-term considerations. It represented the victory of the Treasury over the DEA [Department of Economic Affairs]. ... It made plain too that traditional Treasury and Bank of England goals were still in the ascendant and that, at root, Labour still craved respectability in the eyes of the City.'[311]

From 1966 the government initiated direct state intervention in the economy through the Industrial Reorganisation Corporation. Great hopes were placed in the new Ministry of Technology, but, as its Minister, Tony Benn's experience of bankrolling corporate mergers in order to achieve economies of scale convinced him of the futility of this form of state support, given the intractable structural problems underlying the industrial decline it was meant to solve. The government was finally forced to devalue the pound in November 1967, but it still needed an IMF credit of $1.4 billion, which was made conditional on more cuts in welfare spending. The Labour Party's membership dropped significantly: those who remained were more likely to challenge the party establishment than previously and the constituency parties were now well to the left of the leadership. Although Wilson was able to neutralise hostile opinion in the party by refusing to aid in US bombing directly or to send troops, mass opposition to the Vietnam war had built up, primarily based on a liberal anti-war sentiment, but supplemented by a left perspective that the Vietnamese struggle was an episode in the colonial revolution.[312]

The class loyalties that formed the glue of the social order were eroding as militant trade unionists challenged government attempts at wage regulation. In the mid-sixties, an academic study found that affluent workers were more attuned to local shopfloor groups than national unions. This was a new kind of populism, 'hostile to hierarchy and large-scale organisation, essentially individualist, but capable of making the local group a powerful instrument of industrial action'. Workers' militant responses to speed-up and erosion of their wages were mediated by a change in attitudes towards society and inequality, the decline of deference and an assertion of workers' rights.[313]

The government's strategy for its prices and incomes policy rested on the TUC acting as an agent of social control over the militant rank and file, but the political balance in the unions was changing. Left union leaders like Frank Cousins and Hugh Scanlon had replaced the right-wing leaders who previously would have unconditionally supported the government. The TUC general council was hostile to the idea of policing member unions, and in 1968 Wilson commissioned former Bevanite Barbara Castle to draft a law that would restrict wage increases. The document that resulted, *In Place of Strife*, proposed to extend recognition for official collective bargaining agreements while persuading union leaders to act against unofficial strikes.[314] Castle 'had always been a strong economic interventionist, advocating rational planning as the road to socialism. In contrast, she saw little in union addiction to differentials and sectional rivalries that was compatible with her vision.'[315] The opposition of the rank and file to the plan meant the TUC had to back down from its acceptance of government intervention, and after the party NEC and trade union MPs opposed the legislation, legal sanctions were replaced by a 'solemn and binding agreement' with the government in order to avoid a damaging split in the labour movement.

Benn's ministerial experience had made him uncomfortable with the contradiction between the technocratic strategy he had followed as part of Wilson's government and his democratic populist orientation. He began to publicly express his concern about this at the end of the 1960s, advocating decentralisation and devolution of government; the main issue for him was how to build mass support for involvement in radical social change. Benn thought industrial militancy had been triggered not only by the heightened expectations of post-war affluence, but also by the public's higher level of education that had improved its ability to think critically, and the availability of enhanced media information about current affairs.[316]

His disillusion with Wilson's leadership grew after the government's deflationary policies forced further cuts in public spending. The turbulent student protests of the period, responding to the civil rights movement in the US, the May 1968 general strike in France, political liberalisation in Czechoslovakia, and the Tet offensive in Vietnam, were not reflected in the Labour Party and tended to be antagonistic to it. At the same time, the strike movement was surging out of the control of union officials. In an effort to overcome the gulf he perceived between the party and those who had voted for it, Benn called for workers to be directly involved in the decisions that affected their lives: 'People want a much greater say,' he pointed out. 'Much of the industrial unrest – especially in unofficial strikes – stems from worker resentment and their sense of exclusion from the decision-making process,' he continued. 'We are moving rapidly towards a situation where the pressure for the redistribution of political power will have to be faced as a major political issue.'[317]

The reality of the post-war consensus was that the commitment to full employment, growth and welfare was superimposed upon a traditional structure of authority and understanding of British international interests, an accommodation that rested on the hierarchies associated with a large and deferential industrial working class. The belief in Britain's world power status had justified high levels of military spending and the maintenance of the strength of the City of London. The Wilson government adopted with little debate the priority of defending the international status of sterling and the financial hegemony of the City.[318] Its perpetuation of the traditional structure of authority is especially shown by its role in sending troops into Northern Ireland. Although the issue of discrimination against Catholics over jobs and housing was well-known to Wilson, who counted many Irish Catholics in his Huyton constituency, he downplayed calls for reform until the violent police suppression of civil rights marches in 1968 made them inescapable.

Wilson observed the convention that the Westminster parliament could not discuss Northern Irish affairs, which were considered to be the exclusive responsibility of the devolved parliament in Stormont. This allowed British governments to distance themselves from the discrimination and gerrymandering perpetrated by the dominant Unionists. Wilson put pressure on the Unionist prime minister, Terence O'Neill, to introduce reforms, but their grudging implementation was too little, too late, and rioting in Belfast in 1969 changed the focus of protest from political and economic issues to that of the sectarian nature of the Ulster police. Roy Hattersley, then acting Minister of Defence, sent in troops, who were welcomed at first by the beleaguered Nationalist community until they began to impose curfews and house searches. As the government was drawn into deeper involvement, it began to perceive the problem in colonial terms and the emphasis of policy was shifted from reform to security. Hattersley blamed the continuing violence on 'sinister elements' stirring up the Catholic population, a narrative adopted by subsequent governments to justify the use of political repression, and the subtext shifted to the failings of the Irish rather than the historically violent imposition of partition that established the Unionist-controlled statelet.[319]

Howell concludes that Wilson's government marked the endpoint of the trajectory of the form of the socialist ideal that had become accepted after 1945. The government's record 'had a devastating impact on the party. ... Most clearly it was evident that the social democratic inspiration was dead. It had been nurtured after 1931, it had had its heroic hour after 1945, and it had failed to give guidance since then. ... Now the vision had withered, the potential for major reforms seemed virtually dead and the coalition showed signs of disintegration.'[320] Despite this pessimistic evaluation, however, the decline of 1945-style social democracy had opened the way for a rethinking of strategy by the left.

The party's membership had collapsed during the first Wilson governments. But outside the Labour Party there was a 'virtual explosion' of political activity at national and local level that was sceptical about the nature of the state and traditional parties of the left, and had a tendency to romanticise the possibilities of radical direct action. Student politics, the women's movements, and anti-racist campaigns were seen by young activists as a way to bypass the stifling bureaucracy of Labour and the traditional organisations of the working class.[321] Extra-parliamentary leftists such as Trotskyist groups gained ideological currency because of the divergence of the government from the post-1945 socialist ideal. However, these groups were unable to overcome the philosophical dualism they shared with the Bevanites: they did not extend their conception of socialism beyond that of a fully nationalised economy, and workers' control was advanced as a slogan that did not challenge the exclusively trade-unionist orientation of the shop stewards' movement.[322]

Public opinion shifted in line with union militancy and the generational expectation of a socialist advance from the achievements of 1945, but was alienated by the government's incomes policy. Although by early 1970 the government had succeeded in gaining control of the balance of payments, it was at the cost of extreme deflation. Unemployment was rising along with prices. Labour Party membership was in decline, and the government's lacklustre performance allowed the Tories to win the 1970 election.

The Heath government 1970-74

Edward Heath came to power determined to end Labour's policy of bailing out unprofitable companies, or 'lame ducks' as he called them, and proceeded to dismantle state industrial agencies. But when Rolls Royce came close to bankruptcy over its commitment to manufacture the advanced RB211 engine, the government was forced to nationalise it as the only way to save the nation's premier engineering firm. The same issue arose over Upper Clyde Shipbuilders, a product of a previous government reorganisation. Heath planned to close two of its four yards, making nearly 6,000 redundant, until the workforce occupied the yards in July 1971. The government's U-turn encouraged the Labour left to push for an unapologetic economic interventionist strategy.

The breakup of the international Bretton Woods system that pegged currencies to the dollar resulted in a loosening of money controls that facilitated speculation in commodities and drove up the cost of raw materials. The oil crisis of 1973 eventuated in a worldwide economic slump and a steep decline in the rate of profit in manufacturing, which depressed capital accumulation and led to a high level of unemployment throughout Europe. The pressure to drive down wages so as to restore profitability created the conditions for an explosion of industrial and social turmoil under Heath's administration.[323]

Determined to contain industrial militancy, the government passed an Industrial Relations Act that set up a court to arbitrate strikes. But it could not legislate away spontaneous unofficial strikes through which wages had been driven up. Unofficial strikes had escalated from 4.7 million strike days in 1968 to 11 million in 1970 and 23.9 million in 1972.[324] The unions objected to the provision for individuals to opt out of membership, regarding the measure as elevating individual rights over the group, an affront to trade union tradition. The TUC leaders insisted that unions must 'respect the rule of law' and much of the official union resistance was passive non-cooperation. But the Act succeeded in uniting the larger unions with the Labour Party and encouraging unofficial resistance.

In the context of this upsurge in militancy, Tribune group MPs made a call for more public ownership in the party's next manifesto, taking up the question of the accountability of Labour representatives and the election of the leader at conference rather than by the PLP. The party's most prominent former Bevanite, Michael Foot, had previously demanded a 'strong shift leftwards', but now strongly opposed the Tribune MPs' demand for an inquest into the Wilson government's record. He intervened to prevent the possibility of 'a furious attack on the leadership' from the left. After Wilson appointed him Shadow Leader of the House in 1972, he worked to maintain a common accord between the parliamentary and trade union leaders; his defence of the parliamentary prerogatives of rightwing MPs who voted with Heath on the bill to join the Common Market against their furious constituency members, and his 'overarching concern with party unity', positioned him to clash with Benn's critique of internal democracy in the party and accompanying re-evaluation of extra-parliamentary movements.[325]

In early 1972, a miners' strike escalated when the strikers picketed power stations to prevent the removal of coal stocks, and with public opinion on the side of the miners, the government capitulated. A railway strike, followed by industrial action over the imprisonment of five dockers under the new laws, led to further setbacks for the government. Then OPEC raised oil prices by 75 per cent, and, faced with an overtime ban by power engineers and miners, the country was put on a three-day week. When the miners launched another strike in early 1974, Heath called an election over the issue of 'who rules Britain?' but the falloff of Tory votes gave Labour a slim majority of three seats.

The early resistance to Heath's government 'became political, but primarily in the anarchic sense of "bugger your laws"'. The defiance of the Pentonville Five dockers in 1972, the UCS work-in in 1971, and 102 similar occupations between then and 1974, was not an expression of political radicalism but of a defensive struggle for trade union rights, and even the most militant sections of the working class did not reject the social and economic system in which those rights were embedded.[326] In early 1974, just before the election, Benn argued that the Heath government's clashes with the unions had put class struggle back at the centre of British politics: 'Unless and until there is a major social reform to make our society fairer and more equal, workers will not co-operate in wage control where they have bargaining power and if they have the strength to resist ... They want a sharing of power and an enfranchisement of the community ... and not the corporate ideas which are being put forward by this government,' he told the House of Commons.[327]

Although Benn resisted calls to build an organised faction within the parliamentary party, ' "Bennism" *did* have a strong base in the party – and a growing one. ... The leadership role he played lay in his clear articulation of the new left's understanding that "our long campaign to democratise power in Britain has, first, to begin in our own movement".'[328] Although CLPs submitted over 500 resolutions on constitutional reform to the 1973 conference, the NEC was able to defer discussion until after the 1974 election and the issue was shelved. However, as the campaign for changes to the party constitution heated up in the mid-1970s, more young people with experience of community action and influenced by Benn began to rethink working within the Labour Party. They tended to be active in local organisations like tenants' associations, unlike old Labour which depended on patronage within the council bureaucracy, and they resisted the paternalism of the established Labour administrations. Many socialist women and minorities were encouraged to join the party by an increase in democratic access at local government level that appeared to offer more opportunity for them to influence the party's policies. However, these new members also brought with them experiences of participatory democracy that clashed with the traditional hierarchies and inflexibility of procedures in local constituency parties.[329]

From the New Left to the Bennite Left

The New Left of the 1960s had little direct impact on political discourse, despite widespread dissatisfaction with Labour's policies when in power. Ralph Miliband had come to the conclusion that, because of its ideological domination by the reformist leadership, the Labour Party could not be transformed into an instrument for advancing socialist policies. However, some of the social critique included in the 1967 *May Day Manifesto*, edited by leading New Leftists Raymond Williams, Stuart Hall, and E.P. Thompson, was later reflected in the work of the party's economic research department.[330]

A more direct channel for the incorporation of New Left ideas into the Labour Party was through the Institute for Workers Control (IWC), which was set up in the late 1960s by Ken Coates, Tony Topham, and Michael Barratt Brown. Coates became its principal spokesperson, arguing that the experience of the Morrisonian model of nationalisation since 1945 had shown that the orthodox socialist strategy had to be revised. The institute organised a series of well-attended conferences which attracted the support of rising left union leaders Ernie Roberts and Hugh Scanlon of the AEU, and Jack Jones of the T&GWU, articulating opposition to proposals of workers' 'participation' in management, which threatened the loss of union independence over potential redundancies. The IWC considered that workers' control should be seen as an extension of collective bargaining rather than an alternative to traditional trade union methods of resistance to management.[331]

Full employment had facilitated the consolidation of rank-and-file organisation around the shop stewards' movement, but in the late 1960s workers were confronted with the problem of industrial reorganisations involving mergers and takeovers. With the encouragement of the IWC, work-ins and sit-ins were tried as an alternative to plant closures, including at GEC in Liverpool in 1969 which Tony Benn visited as Minister for Technology. Coates sought to re-orient the New Left to the shop stewards' movement, scorning the *New Left Review's* 'talk of "hegemonic" aspirations which ignored the practical need of workers to defend their own interests'. His appeal was buttressed by the wave of strikes and demonstrations against the Heath government.[332]

While Labour was in opposition, Benn began a reassessment of the party's corporatism, having experienced first-hand the influence of multinational corporations, international finance, and US policy on British economy and politics. His analysis of the breakdown of consensus politics and its connection to the changes technology was making in society enabled him to articulate the concerns of an embryonic new left within the party, which was seeking to answer the problems of the decline of the British economy and the failures of the Labour government.[333] He considered the 1970 defeat to be due to the party's concentration on top-down government rather than the role people could themselves play in solving their own problems. He proposed that '[i]t must be the prime objective of socialists to work for the redistribution of political power', and he included in that goal industrial democracy to be achieved by legislation and union negotiation.[334]

Benn was inspired by the resistance of Upper Clyde Shipbuilders workers to the threatened closure of the yards, and in turn supported their campaign and occupation. He told parliament: 'Over the years I have seen the labour force on Clyde about-turn from a defeated, demoralised and divided group engaged in demarcation disputes and unofficial strikes into a determined and responsible body of men welded into unity, into defending the public assets which have been made available to them by this House. ... The men have rediscovered by what they have done their self-respect which they never had under private management in the past.'[335]

Benn's immediate support for the occupation initially angered Wilson, who soon backed down. But the head of the TUC, Vic Feather, 'was furious, absolutely wild with anger that I was talking to shop stewards when he was trying to get the whole thing to stop,' Benn wrote later.[336] He already had extensive contacts with the stewards after being responsible for shipbuilding in the previous Labour government, and headed a march of up to 70,000 workers through Glasgow. He told a mass meeting: 'We are seeing the birth-pangs of industrial democracy,' but he also made clear that the shop stewards 'were not trying to create a little pocket of revolution in the capitalist world but were trying to engage in a serious industrial and political campaign'.[337] Crucially he took up the New Left critique of the statism of Labour's nationalisation tradition, influenced by his IWC connection. This marked a fusion of Benn's political development with the militancy of the most advanced elements of the shop stewards' movement, and he became a determined advocate for industrial democracy.

Benn embraced the radical proposals for an interventionist economic strategy originating from Labour's policy and research department, which became incorporated in *Labour's Programme 1973*. It proposed to reindustrialise Britain through import controls, planning agreements between the state and leading companies to govern investment, and a National Enterprise Board (NEB) that would act as a state holding company and a means of public investment in profitable industries, famously calling for 'a fundamental and irreversible shift of the balance of power and wealth in favour of working people and their families'. Although in fact moderate in scope, it encountered strong opposition from British business; the details of the proposals were not as important to it as the reflex of the ruling elite to defend 'managerial prerogatives'. Short-term profitability and suppression of unions took precedence over a long-term plan that attempted to address the structural weaknesses of the British economy – even though the plan was based on European state models.

The strategy incorporated into the programme was based on the work of socialist economists in the party's research department, in particular Francis Cripps and Stuart Holland. Keynesian social democracy had failed, they thought, because it had not taken into account the concentration of capital in multinational corporations which were able to subvert government control of the economy. It was clearly the fact of unregulated capital flows between multinationals and their foreign subsidiaries – in the guise of transfer pricing – that had undermined the value of the pound. Holland advocated redirecting the outward flow of capital back into the British economy to protect the sovereignty of the nation state against the multinationals. Public ownership had been concentrated in infrastructure and declining industries; instead of this, Holland advocated nationalisation of the leading 25 companies in the expanding and profitable sectors of the economy, which now constituted the 'commanding heights'. Through purchasing shares in these companies the NEB should influence decision-making in line with a planned programme of expansion.[338]

Planning agreements could be given teeth through pressure on private companies by the economic clout of the extended public sector. Moreover, unions could be coopted into the planning process to implement a 'social contract' that would redistribute wealth, increase spending on welfare, and shift decision-making in favour of workers. Only as part of a social contract could a non-inflationary rate of wage increases be sustained. Import controls were likewise intended to reduce the outward flow of capital from the UK and channel investment into manufacturing through import substitution for the UK market.

This did not break from Keynesianism as much as create conditions for Keynesian strategies to be effective, through state intervention to impose price restraints as part of a counter-inflationary policy. Import controls were linked to exchange controls in the plan, aimed at curbing the power of currency speculators. Confronting the power of the City, the Treasury and the Bank of England over financial markets, the plan connected the analysis of Britain's industrial decline, on which the industrial strategy rested, to the difficulties faced by nation states in controlling the rapidly expanding financial markets.[339]

The viability of a socialist strategy based on workers' control was enhanced by the growth of employment in the public sector, the increased self-confidence of workers after two decades of full employment, and the strength of shop-floor organisation. The sit-ins of the early 1970s had raised the question of the wider social costs of plant closures and the need to broaden the basis of economic decision-making.[340] Institutional economist Geoff Hodgson focused on the extension of democracy as the central agent of social transformation. 'Economic democracy was also a necessary corrective to the ignorance of decision-makers in general and economic planners in particular, and was, therefore, a fundamental means of improving the flow of information.' Where decision-making was confined to a professional elite, 'mistakes were more likely to be made and more difficult to rectify'.[341]

Resolutions adopted by the party conference and what the parliamentary leadership would support diverged sharply. The left aimed for a mass campaign to mobilise public approval for the industrial policy, while the leadership wanted to first water it down and then to ignore it. The internal battle was thus twofold – one over the National Executive Committee's (NEC's) economic plans, and another over the implementation of decisions democratically arrived at by conference. The NEC's plan fudged these points, and so the left on the Industrial Policy Subcommittee concretised the proposal by including Holland's proposal to nationalise 25 leading companies. The Shadow Cabinet rejected this programme and, while Benn gave it a strong defence, left-wing union leaders – including Jack Jones who had earlier supported the plan – avoided conflict with the party leaders over the issue. Wilson immediately disowned the proposals, working to get them eliminated from the manifesto.[342]

The left on the NEC, led by Benn and Mikardo, aimed to use the resolutions on socialist policy passed by the conference to strengthen their hand against the parliamentary leadership in preparation of the party's manifesto. Their emphasis on industrial democracy reflected the new left critique of the statist nature of Labour's nationalisation tradition. One reason for the success of the left in pushing radical economic strategy at the party conferences was the leadership's inability to develop its own economic policy. However, while able to shift the discourse of the party to the left, 'it had achieved very little in terms of democratising the party or changing its structure so that socialist mobilisation would replace "parliamentary paternalism"'.[343]

The 1974-79 governments

After Heath was brought down by the miners' strike, a minority Labour government was elected which returned Benn to the Ministry of Industry, and for a short time he and Eric Heffer were able to campaign for the implementation of the party's radical industrial policy, using state resources to offer support for workers' initiatives in the struggle against redundancies and factory closures. This encouragement from within the government led to groups of trade unionists coming forward with plans for reorganisation of production, such as the well-known Lucas Plan. The chronicler of the plan, Hilary Wainwright, comments: 'Without political support it is unlikely that the [Lucas] shop stewards would have felt confident of selling something as bold as the alternative Plan to their membership. The membership needed to believe there was a chance of success, only then would they support radical proposals like the alternative Plan.' While Benn and Heffer remained in the Department of Industry, many groups of workers came forward with proposals for sustaining production, usually in response to threats of factory closures.[344]

Labour's industrial strategy was launched in the middle of a huge workplace mobilisation, mainly in defence of jobs. Much of this militancy derived from an 'instrumental collectivism' that was not inherently radical. 'But neither did it defer to established patterns of managerial authority; and a significant layer of the leadership of this instrumental working class ... *was* politicised,' say Panitch and Leys.[345] Trade union activists had high expectations of the Labour government in its first few months, from a general understanding that it would bring large corporations under social control. They assumed the government would carry out the policies on which it was elected, and so there was no necessity for organised pressure for the new industrial policy. However, shop stewards in different parts of the country independently decided to discuss the implications of the policy. Because of the dearth of information coming from union central offices, shop stewards from Vickers and Swan Hunters shipbuilders on Tyneside came together to discuss for themselves planning agreements, workers' control, combine committees, the NEB and nationalisation.

What had caught the Tyne shop stewards' imagination was the prospect of 'workers' control with management participation'. It was because of their impression that their allies in government gave them a source of political power over their managements that the stewards believed there was an opportunity to control the investment decisions of the companies, as a means of guaranteeing job security for the future. 'The assumption was that workers could prepare their own proposals and then win the backing of the Department of Industry,' a report commissioned by a group of trades councils explains.[346]

One of the most important of the plans presented to the Department was the one developed by the Lucas Aerospace shop stewards' combine committee.[347] The committee had led important strikes against factory closures and redundancies, that had achieved a remarkable cohesion among the rank and file but were still fundamentally defensive in nature. Militancy alone had no answer to the reorganisation of entire industries that the employers were beginning to embark on, but the background of industrial militancy had driven the election of a Labour government on a manifesto that included nationalisation of the aerospace industry. The stewards were well aware of the reservations of their members about this policy. However, central to their strategy of saving jobs was to urge the government to bring the Lucas combine into public ownership.

In 1974 the stewards sent a delegation to urge Benn to include Lucas in the government's nationalisation proposals, but he was not in a position to do so; instead, he suggested, the committee should be involved in drawing up a corporate strategy that would find 'ways of producing our way through a slump'. When they returned to their factories, the stewards initiated a debate among their membership about the limits of old-style nationalisation and created a detailed plan for manufacturing socially useful products as an alternative to factory closures and redundancies.

More significantly, they developed a new concept of nationalisation that re-thought the nature of the work process itself, pioneering schemes in which the tactile knowledge of shop-floor workers would be combined with the scientific knowledge of technicians. Production methods and products were to be socially responsible and environmentally sustainable. The products themselves, suggested by rank-and-file workers, were designed to utilise the existing technology in the Lucas factories and existing skill-sets, so as to preserve resources and jobs. They included medical equipment, alternative energy technologies such as solar cells, hybrid petrol/electric vehicle drive trains, braking systems, submersible vehicles, and remote-controlled systems for underwater oil rig repairs. Altogether, they made up far-sighted plans that would, if implemented, have put Lucas technology far in advance of contemporary manufacturing corporations.³⁴⁸

Industrial democracy had been a theme for Labour's left intellectuals and appeared in the party's programme, but it was still abstract. The Lucas stewards made it concrete, pioneering a 'bottom-up' form of planning for which there was no precedent. 'By campaigning for an alternative production and employee training plan the Combine were attempting to influence the Company's corporate investment programme. ... Their emphasis was on direct shop-floor involvement and the extension of collective bargaining, as opposed to the introduction of "worker directors" or other forms of minority participation in management.'³⁴⁹

This was in marked contrast to Bevan's view that the advance to socialism was dependent on the extent to which workers in nationalised industries 'are made aware of a changed relationship between themselves and management', implying collaboration between management and workers but keeping existing social divisions. The Lucas stewards' idea was to integrate management and workers on a basis of equality, and following their logic, Wainwright rephrased Bevan to read: 'the extent to which public ownership is an advance towards full socialism depends on the extent to which workers *create* a changed relationship between themselves and management in the course of achieving public ownership.'³⁵⁰

As an indication of just how remarkable this conceptual advance was, and how dependent on the specific combination of sympathetic government minister and strategic sophistication of the combine committee, the industrial militancy of the 1970s produced no comparable development even among the most politically-conscious trade unionists. Alan Thornett, a leading militant at Morris Motors' Cowley plant, joined the Trotskyist SLL in 1966 because it appeared to provide an explanation of the bureaucratic role of CP union officials in the industry. But his association with Trotskyism did not guide him to break from his 'productivist' outlook. He confesses: 'We saw no problem in ever-expanding production, and took little interest in the product we were producing ... Our concern was for wages and working conditions in the plant. If these were right, we did not question what was produced. Even the alternative plan produced by the Lucas Aerospace shop stewards in the mid-1970s, to turn military production into socially useful products, had little impact on us as an example of what could be done in the car industry to achieve environmentally sustainable production.'³⁵¹

While Benn sought to channel union militancy into a political struggle for greater power in industry and the state, the rest of the cabinet – including the former Bevanites – were furiously opposed to his politics, joining with the Treasury and hostile civil servants in a hysterical attack on the industrial strategy. At the same time, the more political shop stewards remained a minority in the trade unions, while the union leadership did little to advocate for the strategy. The 1974 election had done nothing to resolve what Benn termed a 'crisis of consent'; it was the Labour government's inability to tackle this crisis that strengthened Thatcher's hand, even though the party's published manifesto was more radical than any since 1945.[352] When Benn finally presented his Industry Bill in March 1975 he called it a plan for 'far-reaching democratic socialist reforms affecting the relations between the community, management and workers and ... designed to deal direct with the problems of manufacturing industry that lie at the root of Britain's present industrial and economic weakness.'[353] His objective was to extend industrial democracy to make firms accountable and 'bring about the shift in the balance of power towards working people' needed to overcome industrial problems. However, Wilson and the cabinet immediately diluted the proposals still further. 'If the Left, with minor setbacks had hitherto proved triumphant as regards the formulation of policy, the Right still dominated the Cabinet and thence held the levers of political power ... this power was used in particular to shape the content of the White Paper brought forward by the Department of Industry ... Thus the compulsory dimension of planning agreements was absent from the White Paper as it finally emerged.'[354]

Through a combination of extra-parliamentary pressure from employers and the opposition of the PLP leadership, the industrial policies were turned into little more than 'a source of finance for manufacturing industry' and 'a means of rationalising and reorganising British industry' in response to the pressures of international competition. Wilson's manoeuvres were carried out without any objection from the union leadership, so there was little labour movement resistance to the gutting of the radical proposals. The joint trades council report surmised that 'trade union members often thought the original policies were being implemented. After all the names were the same: "NEB", "planning agreements", "industry Bill"; Tony Benn was still in government ... There were very few public signs of the changes that had gone on behind the scenes.' The report concludes that even if the manifesto's policies had been carried out, 'the experiences brought before this inquiry reveal power structures which cannot be overcome primarily by a parliamentary majority'.[355]

Disillusionment with the Wilson governments and rising inflation and unemployment had increased militancy in the unions and more combative leaders were elected. Jack Jones of the T&GWU, together with the TUC, insisted on a Keynesian reflationary policy that planned financial flows and mandated the investment strategies of large industrial firms. Foot was particularly concerned not to allow a breach between the party and the left union leaders, becoming what Benn called the leadership's 'belt and buckle' with the industrial wing. 'Healey and Callaghan were the senior members of the Cabinet, but Michael's presence was essential because he ensured the support of the unions and the always restive left of the party,' writes Foot's biographer.[356]

Foot's crucial role was to persuade the union leadership to accept the government's 'social contract', providing a left cover for chancellor Denis Healey's insistence on wage restraint. He persuaded the union leaders they would be treated as 'partners' in economic decision-making if they were to maintain voluntary wage restraint. This was a weak partnership insofar as it gave overriding primacy to keeping the Labour government in power despite the severe economic crisis. 'As the Minister most trusted by the unions, Michael played a vital role [in negotiations with the TUC]. He was thus brought into close and regular contact with Denis Healey ... Now, they were allies in their determination to maintain the Labour government and make a success of the concordat with the unions.'[357] In April 1975, faced with another sterling crisis, Healey cut expenditure and increased taxation, 'in effect abandoning Keynesianism by putting the conquest of inflation before the maintenance of a "high and stable" level of employment'. The renunciation of Keynesianism inadvertently legitimized Thatcher's monetarist critique: 'the gap in Labour's economic thinking which had been covered by Keynesianism since the 1940s was embarrassingly re-exposed.'[358]

Benn's experience with Brussels bureaucrats as a minister in 1974 had convinced him that the Common Market was based on free-market orthodoxy and was inimical to democracy in its member states. His concern to sustain the democratic basis of parliamentary rule motivated him to establish another constitutional precedent by pressing for a referendum on the Market, campaigning to leave it. However, the Labour Cabinet had already committed to the terms of Market membership, and, according to Benn, the referendum's pro-Market outcome was used by Wilson 'to reassert the primacy of the parliamentary leadership over the party and the unions'.[359] Wilson was emboldened enough to demote Benn, although union leaders prevented him from being sacked outright; he was shifted abruptly to the Department of Energy in June 1975.

Now a dissenting minister in the government, he supported wholeheartedly the rank-and-file campaign for democracy within the Labour Party, as a strategic goal important in the ultimate aim of democratising the British state. He used his ministerial position as far as possible to campaign on this issue, guided by his acute perception of the danger to the labour movement posed by the Tory Thatcherite wing in the context of the continuing economic crisis. In 1976 the pressures from the Treasury to capitulate to the market and abandon government efforts to boost the economy were bolstered by the claims of monetarism. Benn attempted to counter this ideological influence by again presenting an alternative economic strategy that would avoid proposed cuts in public spending, but in the face of fears of a collapse of sterling Jim Callaghan and the rest of the Labour cabinet determined that the cuts should be made, the priority of full employment should be abandoned, and Benn's proposals for selective restrictions on trade and capital flows repudiated. The government's Declaration of Intent to the IMF in 1976 indicated just how far the party leadership were prepared to go in accepting their compulsion of monetary control and fiscal 'restraint'.

After Wilson resigned in 1976, Benn contested the party leadership in order to openly advocate for change in economic policy, open government and a greater role for MPs, as opposed to the party leaders, turning to the experience of the 1945 government and the writings of Clement Attlee to find arguments for the extension of public ownership. The election was eventually won by Callaghan; meanwhile Benn continued to campaign for constitutional reform within the Labour Party and the accountability of the parliamentary leadership to the party membership. 'The new left's project had been sustained in the Cabinet only by Benn, whose influence on policy was effectively neutralised by Wilson with the support of the rest of the Cabinet, the civil service, and media and business opinion. Crucial to this outcome was the fact that the union leadership had failed to give serious support to the industrial strategy.'[360]

Benn and the transformation of the socialist ideal

The left-wing opposition that developed around Benn reflected a grassroots movement in the Labour Party influenced by the demands for more democracy within the unions. Benn's thesis was that public support for left policies had to be won by directly raising political issues, supporting community groups and broadening the base of party membership.[361] He was encouraged by and spoke for the radical political impulses emanating from the militant shop stewards' movement that opposed the wage freeze complicity of the union leadership. In the course of this he undertook a major revision of the socialist ideal, incorporating much of the cultural liberalization of the 1960s, and posing the issue of popular rather than parliamentary sovereignty.

In her book, *Labour: A Tale of Two Parties*, Hilary Wainwright detected the formation of a political trend that sought to go beyond the framework of Labourism to create a new relation between trade unionists and the government. This tendency took the experience of the 1945 government and developed from it a critical concept of nationalisation and of work.[362] Benn gave this movement an ideological justification by conceiving the early history of the Labour Party as implicitly supporting workers' control, drawing attention to the fourth paragraph of the party's famous Clause IV which committed to 'the best obtainable system of popular administration and control of each industry or service.' From this phrase, he claimed, 'we can draw our authority for the present pressure for industrial democracy ...'[363]

Benn's unique contribution to the socialist ideal was his determined advocacy of the idea that people should directly participate in government, rather than having the popular will interpreted for them by a class of professional representatives. More than that, he constantly formulated policies in such a way as to allow those affected by them to creatively modify their practical application. Perhaps his greatest legacy was his support for the legitimacy of extra-parliamentary activism, which was continued by the Corbyn movement. Benn's receptivity to the ideas of rank-and-file activists had enabled him to give them a powerful voice in the Cabinet, the NEC and party conference, contributing to the development of a socialist economic policy. His support of the Lucas Aerospace shop stewards helped them turn the idea of workers' control from a slogan into a practical proposition.

Hilary Wainwright describes how Benn's approach to government extended political authority beyond parliament. He considered ministers should be accountable to the Labour Party and the labour movement, and by the same token the movement should work enthusiastically for the policies jointly discussed and agreed. During his brief period as Minister for Industry he began to develop these ideas in practice: preparing government Green Papers for 'meetings with trade-union officials, local authorities, local employer associations, shop stewards and gatherings of working management whose support is essential if our policies are to succeed'; encouraging shop stewards organisations to draw up production plans that would save jobs and meet local needs to be backed by the government in negotiations with management. What alarmed British industrialists was that 'Benn, a Cabinet minister, was seeing shop-floor representatives independently; he was going round the country encouraging workers in their demands, building confidence, raising expectations, giving out information. In a sense it was as much Benn's democracy – of a radical kind – as his socialism, in the conventional sense of state intervention, which caused the panic and loss of confidence.'[364]

The intensely creative period of the left in the 1970s was dependent on the synergy of Benn's eloquent presentation of the initiatives of Labour activists with the strength of the shop stewards' movement. The new left's greatest achievement, however, was 'its vision of a radical broadening of the public arena, tapping the talent and energy of ordinary people and bringing them into new positions of power and responsibility in the state. No doubt this vision was imperfectly shared, but there is also no doubt that when Benn articulated it he struck a powerful chord.'[365]

This is also the context for understanding his fascination with the seventeenth-century English revolution. Beginning in 1971, Benn attempted to develop his understanding of contemporary political battles by mapping the party's right and left wing onto the factions in the Civil War. He noted in his diary that Heath and the City financiers represented the King and Court, the parliamentary party the Presbyterians, and Trotskyist groups the Agitators in the New Model Army. 'The Levellers are broadly the labour movement as a whole,' he thought.[366] Directly inspired by the Upper Clydeside work-in, he sought to legitimize the direct action of the rank and file by situating their struggle in the history of the fight for democracy in Britain. Many commentators have misread the significance of this radical history for Benn's thinking: it was not the source of his ideas, but rather he re-imagined it as containing the potential for labour democracy and workers' control of industry. He wrote: 'The Levellers ... represented the aspirations of working people who suffered under the persecution of kings, landowners and the priestly class and they spoke for those who experienced the hardships of poverty and deprivation. ... Their advocacy of democracy and equality has been taken up by generations of liberal and socialist thinkers and activists, pressing for reforms, many of which are still contested in this country to this day. The Levellers can now be seen ... as speaking for a popular liberation movement which can be traced right back to the teachings of the Bible.'[367]

Benn understood the biblical message to be one of promoting egalitarianism and social justice, a radical protestant interpretation that privileged dissent over received authority, and which also linked back to the seventeenth-century English revolution. He wrote: 'The best of the Christian tradition of social action has always been revolutionary, democratic and humane, in challenging wealth, power, privilege and injustice, whether under kings, conquerors or commissars.' His interpretation of morality was distinct from those in the labour movement, like R.H. Tawney, who made a moral critique of capitalist social relations a justification for social reform by an enlightened legislature. Morality for Benn was not a means of criticizing society so as to illustrate some utopian future, but an ethical imperative to act on socialist principles in the here and now, negating the dualism long endemic in the labour movement. The New Testament call to 'love thy neighbour' Benn considered to be an egalitarian imperative to reject injustice, quoting the Levellers' assertion that 'in Christ there is neither bond nor free'. The socialist interpretation of the Good Samaritan, he thought, is to be 'less concerned with the personal salvation of the traveller who was stripped and beaten than with his immediate need for medical treatment, accommodation and food in this world, here and now'.[368]

The early 1970s was a fertile period for rethinking the Morrisonian corporatist model of nationalisation and questioning the social relations of production with the idea of workers' control – occupations, cooperatives, the Lucas Plan, were all features of this era. Previous nationalisations had not changed management, said Benn: 'We will change it by going back to a very basic principle of socialism ... those who invest their lives in industry are at least as strongly entitled to control it as those who invest their money.'[369] As the economic crisis began to bite, factory closures and redundancies across industry had resulted in occupations and sit-ins in defence of the right to work. Benn regarded them as experiments in workers' democracy that challenged existing forms of ownership and control. They were important because 'they revealed a readiness to extend the vision of labour beyond pay. Men at Meriden or the *Scottish Daily News* or Kirkby were transformed not by anything that was done by government, but by their readiness to take responsibility.' Rather than posing the abolition of wage-labour, in a conventional Marxist sense, Benn saw the potential within this movement to 'extend the vision of labour beyond pay', to develop meaningful forms of work that produced goods necessary for society, rather than for profit. In other words, instead of a revolutionary government abolishing wage-labour from above, Benn advocated that people should find creative alternatives to it through experiments in workers' democracy – with encouragement and support from the state.[370]

Although the co-ops failed – they could only have had a chance of success in a climate of prosperity – they had demonstrated that industrial democracy could work in practice. Benn concluded: 'A real co-operative option open to workers at the crucial moment during a pay claim, or under threat of redundancy or collapse or a merger, would change their prospects. ... I have no doubt whatsoever that those three co-operatives played a tremendous part in boosting the self-confidence of workers by showing them the possibility of another route. Without such practical examples, nothing can ever be done.'[371] He had a high opinion of the trade unionists from the UCS work-in, the cooperatives and from Lucas Aerospace that he had worked with, crediting them with giving him 'an education in the real meaning of practical socialism which no books or teachers could have matched'. Benn saw that industrial rationalisation had faced management, scientific and technical staff with the same prospect of redundancy as production workers, which meant that all the skills necessary for an alternative strategy and management in industry were available to the labour movement. He wrote that: 'In Britain we have over a long period of struggle actually bred a quality of collective leadership within the trade union movement which is quite capable of assuming a leading role within the framework of democracy which simply wouldn't have been true at the time of the General Strike in 1926.'[372]

Benn's great merit was to advocate practical changes in the immediate present that would strengthen the working class and empower the public to decide how society should be improved. This was a philosophical advance that overcame the dualism of orthodox socialism inherent in separating immediate reforms from an abstract ultimate goal. Consistently democratic, it posited a far more powerful social force than manifestos or legislation alone. He became the primary advocate for making nationalised industries accountable to workers and consumers, attempting to suggest 'practical ways in which many of our existing institutions can be adapted from their present role as props of the status quo.'[373] This meant developing 'workmanlike plans' (in Attlee's phrase) to resolve problems of industry and the economy, and in this way to concretise socialist approaches to dealing with the crisis, involving unions in the process of industrial reorganisation.

The right dispenses with full employment

After Wilson's resignation in March 1976, the ascendancy of the parliamentary right wing did not give it political success. It had not grasped, unlike the new left and Thatcher, that the post-war mode of social democratic regulation had become unsustainable. Resistance to the retreat from Keynesianism entailed by the 1976 IMF loan was undermined by the acceptance of the Cabinet of the belief, promoted by the Bank of England and the Treasury, that public spending was out of control.[374]

The renunciation of Keynesianism and surrender to monetarism by the government was 'a defining moment in the politics of globalisation'. Healey's Letter of Intent to the IMF explicitly repudiated the left's proposal for exchange controls, which would have set back the globalisation trend considerably. The point was to establish 'financial discipline' and abandon the universalist ideal of the welfare state, as Callaghan did at the 1976 party conference. But the defeat of radical proposals aimed at curbing the pressures from financial capital made Thatcher's claim 'there is no alternative' only more plausible. The leadership's acceptance of monetarist economics also precipitated a more determined effort by the Labour new left to fight the right's domination of the party.[375]

The new left's plan for capital controls in its Alternative Economic Strategy (AES) stemmed from its recognition of the forces leading to globalisation. In the early 1970s its focus was on the growth of multinational corporations; by the end of the 1970s it emphasised the growth of international finance. Benn made the growing scope and power of financial markets the basis of his assertion that the 1976 IMF crisis showed they could force any left-wing government 'to pretend that it wished to follow policies that have in fact been imposed by the pressure of world bankers'.[376]

Thatcher's calls for 'law and order' were immeasurably helped by the Labour leadership's condemnation of the public-sector workers' strikes in 1978-9. And Callaghan's public attacks on the NEC's plans for public ownership of the banks, together with Thatcher's offensive against the public sector, combined to create an ideological climate that reversed public attitudes to nationalisation and privatisation. Support for nationalisation had increased among voters between 1964 and 1974, but between 1974 and 1979 this plummeted.[377]

The appeal of Thatcherism was that it had rooted itself in the disillusionment of the working class with the form of social democratic statism to which previous Labour governments had been committed, argued cultural theorist Stuart Hall. 'That type of "statism" implied a very distinct view of the state itself – as a centralised bureaucracy, a neutral beneficiary, which ... was largely *experienced* in negative and oppressive ways.' Thatcherism's ideological assault was successful because social democracy 'represented the dominated classes as passive recipients, as clients of a state run by experts and professionals over which people have no real or substantive control'. Labour governments had served 'to *discipline* the classes [they] claimed to represent'.[378] Benn and the new left understood that the struggle for popular democracy in relation to the state had as a necessary precondition confronting the undemocratic character of the party's own institutions. The Campaign for Labour Party Democracy (CLPD) was set up as a direct response to Wilson's vetoing of the commitment to nationalise 25 leading companies in the 1973 programme. It was successful in building alliances within the party to push through constitutional changes, such as mandatory reselection, that would make MPs more responsive to the membership. But it was sucked into an internal power struggle that overlooked the need to explain the issues to the broader labour movement.[379]

The new left was isolated from the union leadership because of the rank and file's reluctance to attack the government. A deep sense of loyalty to Labour, and the fear of the effects of high inflation on real wages and jobs, meant that many union activists had refrained from opposing wage restraint. From 1977-8 onwards, however, union conferences repudiated their leaders' cooperation with the government. This did not necessarily represent a shift to a more political opposition, even though there was a significant layer of union activists who supported the Alternative Economic Strategy, but they depended for their success at conference 'on a complex organizational alliance with those disillusioned with the detailed industrial impact of the policies. ... They simply wanted more flexibility to bargain and rectify anomalies that had created havoc in their pay structures. ... What might be labelled a "social democratic economism" remained the predominant ethos in the bargaining strategies and political practice of British trade unionism.'[380] The idea of an alternative economic strategy was kept alive through resolutions passed at the 1977 and 1978 party conferences, but while union delegates voted for it, their leaders did not campaign for it among the membership.[381]

The internal party battle over constitutional reform focused on the NEC's draft of the election manifesto that called for the abolition of the House of Lords, a wealth tax, compulsory planning agreements and the nationalisation of the construction industry. However, the final manifesto was based on a new draft hurriedly put together by Callaghan, using his prime ministerial authority to excise any mention of the party's democratically agreed policies and essentially to promise the electorate a return to the failed corporate consensus – in contrast to the Tories' radical proposals of tax cuts and limits to union power.[382] The union leaders could not sustain their support for the government's incomes control policies, but maintained their partnership with the government out of fear of a Thatcher electoral victory. They were unable to contain a new outbreak of rank-and-file militancy among the lowest paid workers in the public sector, and the confrontation between the government and its own supporters in the 'Winter of Discontent' fatally weakened it.

The 1979 election was a much greater strategic defeat for Labour than was realised at the time. The Callaghan government's turn to monetarism and slashing of public expenditure had destroyed the material basis of post-war social democracy. The Tory right was able to capitalise on Labour's crisis and incorporate the electorate's burgeoning anti-Labour, anti-state and anti-equality sentiment into its free market doctrine. Thatcher succeeded in building an ideological consensus around national patriotism, competitive individualism and an authoritarian state, assembling a new social bloc with a discourse of 'choice' and 'Victorian values' that was later used to justify attacks on social movements such as women's and gay liberation. Her central aim was to expunge the idea of the welfare state and force an acceptance of the market as the only true economic reality.

In this chapter, I chronicled the evolution of the Labour left's political discourse from technocratic modernism to radical democratic socialism. The combativeness of the working class in this period was bound up with full employment and the decentralised system of industrial wage bargaining that enhanced the influence of shop stewards, which then amplified the militancy of workers on the shop floor. Although related to the rise of radical populism, it stayed primarily at an anti-authoritarian level, and was further limited by the Labourism of the union bureaucracy and the hostility of the parliamentary party. The Labour new left was defeated, not only because it was in a minority in the cabinet and PLP, but because industrial support was lacking.

The socialist ideal had to be re-imagined at an ideological level, and its new form did not emerge spontaneously from the experience of militant trade unionism. Tony Benn critically re-evaluated the practice of the first Wilson government and was both inspired by the workers' tactic of occupations as a form of resistance to factory closures and in turn inspired them. But his support did not mean bringing theory into the working class from outside, in a Leninist sense. It represented a fusion of the Labour new left's struggle for an alternative economic strategy with workers' struggle against factory shutdowns and redundancies. His emphasis on practical, concrete socialist solutions to the immediate problems facing the working class distinguished his approach from the dualism of the Bevanite left and from Trotskyist groups' calls for nationalisation disconnected from the actual course of working-class struggle.

The high point of this phase was Benn's ministerial encouragement of the Lucas shop stewards' combine committee. His initial assistance was crucial in helping the Lucas Plan get off the ground, since he represented the elected government which 'has a legitimacy in the eyes of the majority of people, over and above any particular economic institutions or interest. ... Without this support, the Combine delegates would have found it very difficult to gain support for the plan from their fellow stewards and trade-union members.'[383] The important relation between state support (as embodying the general will) and the creative problem-solving approach of the Lucas stewards to factory closures led to a qualitative change in consciousness: it produced a new concept of nationalisation and a concrete, bottom-up model of socialist planning. Industrial militancy on its own could not make this conceptual leap without that social dynamic; although the rightwing in the government dissipated and defused the Lucas plan, the ideas it generated were immediately available when the political environment changed.

The lack of interest of the union leadership in the left's alternative economic strategy, and its active hostility to the Lucas stewards' achievements, kept this development isolated and the crisis of social democratic politics allowed Thatcher to take power. She was able to change the ideological outlook of the ruling elite by turning to populist capitalism and empowering the upwardly mobile. But the context in which this took place was one where the globalisation of production and trade, together with rapid movements of international capital, had already broken down the nationally circumscribed economic arrangements which had been the basis of Labour's Keynesianism. In the next chapter, I discuss the impact of Thatcherism on the Labour Party and the politics of New Labour. Although its accommodation to the privatisation of much of the public sector by Thatcherite governments enabled electoral successes, the 2008 financial collapse demolished New Labour's 'third way' and the Blairite leadership lost its authority; it was unable to answer Tory attacks that blamed Labour for economic mismanagement and overspending on welfare.

Chapter Six
New Labour's 'Modernisation' Project

'I think that socialism had been almost underground in the Labour Party for the last 20 years, you couldn't mention socialism as a Labour member.'[384]
Pat, retired teacher, 2016

The socialist ideal in retreat

After 1979, Labour had to contend with the victory of a Thatcher government that built on the post-war shift away from unionised heavy industries to small, high-tech companies based on microelectronics with a workforce divided between highly skilled engineers and low-paid and unorganised assembly workers. The explosive growth of the international finance system facilitated the relocation of production to the global South. The apparent inevitability of this transformation was the ground for a changed relation between government and society during the Thatcher period, as the government sought to change the political culture by removing the responsibility of the state for individual welfare. Some consider that the rise of New Labour was a capitulation to this social reconfiguration, while its supporters argue that it expressed a genuine adaptation of social democracy to the new global economy. However, while New Labour's practice differed from that of the Tories, it remained within the framework of free-market neoliberalism.

The newly-elected Thatcher government, buoyed up politically by the manufactured image of union culpability for the winter of discontent, immediately began to put in place legislation to restrict trade union activities. Applying monetarist dogma to the economy, its first deflationary budget was aimed as a deliberate blow against working-class collective action, intensifying the industrial recession and pushing unemployment over three million. In response to this diminution of trade union strength, the TUC leadership retreated and 'repeatedly threw its influence ... against militancy and against challenging the government through industrial action'.[385]

The Tories' drastic economic measures were only the prelude to a sustained attack on post-war social-democratic reforms. A ferocious budgetary squeeze that increased taxation and cut public spending reduced manufacturing output by 15 per cent in 12 months, and the deflationary pressure was continued in the 1981 budget even though the economy was clearly in recession. The government's early abolition of exchange controls allowed a massive outflow of capital from the UK: British financial institutions increased their holdings of foreign assets by £75 billion in the following nine years.[386] But it also ensured the influence of financial markets on changes in interest rates through the risk of unmanageable flows of capital, and forced through the internationalisation of the London stock exchange and a rapid expansion of credit that financed a consumer and housing boom. It was both an extension of the power of global capital into the British economy and the start of the financialisation of the UK, tying London financial markets into international circuits of capital accumulation and reordering economic activities and social relations through the 'marketisation' of finance.

The Tories' programme of selling off council houses, privatisation, and cutting taxes was 'designed to dislocate [Labour's] core constituency' by making the more prosperous sections of the working class individualistic homeowners. They had grasped the dynamic of social change and 'engaged in systematic social engineering' to realise their strategy.[387] Thatcher's famous phrase 'there is no alternative' meant in practice a fundamental change in the role of the state: it would no longer intervene in the economy to safeguard jobs but would remove perceived barriers to corporate efficiency and innovation through deregulation and privatisation, substituting market solutions for the social safety net. The Tory narrative concentrated on changing the perception of welfare, blaming trade union power, dependency culture, Labour administrations, and the unemployed themselves rather than acknowledge any governmental responsibility for individual and collective well-being.

The Thatcher government both took advantage of and accelerated the physical erosion of the industrial working class that formed Labour's base. Its electoral victories in 1983 and 1987 encouraged a bolder implementation of its attack on the collectivist consensus, which was achieved through a process of overcoming various political and institutional restraints. The defeat of the miners' strike in 1985 marked an important shift in the balance of class power and allowed Thatcher to extend the scope of her economic restructuring. The central government increased its control over the finances of local authorities, introducing new systems of regulation that caused local agencies 'to focus obsessively on their performance ratios without much concern for the real content of their remit'. Public services were divided into separate agencies subjected to consumer choice, which led to 'replacing an administration obeying the principles of public law by a management ruled by the common law of competition'.[388] The individualisation of the relation between the state and the social subject had a profound effect on the political space in which Labour operated, while the Labour Party itself was transformed through a series of electoral defeats in which the conflict between left and right was overtaken by the new terrain marked out by Thatcherism.

In this chapter I track the way that Kinnock's 'modernisation' project, concentrating policy-making in the leader's office, both reflected the new political landscape and paved the way for the rise of New Labour. The leadership of Tony Blair and Gordon Brown repudiated the egalitarian trend of Labour policy and accepted the Thatcherite reconfiguration of the state. In government, New Labour sought to bring state institutions in line with business practices. While increasing spending on social welfare, they introduced market relations into welfare provision and encouraged the flow of speculative capital into the City, doing nothing to correct the imbalance of financial accumulation. The 2008 banking crash ended their pretensions to a 'third way' social democracy, but they left the Labour Party with a legacy of centrist MPs who share Blair's perspective that social problems are cultural in nature and have no connection to power and financial privilege.

After defeat in the 1979 election, the initial response of the party membership was to move sharply to the left. Amid recriminations against the failure of the Callaghan leadership, delegates to the 1980 conference supported radical resolutions calling for an extension of public ownership with industrial democracy, a substantial cut in arms expenditure and a 35-hour week. Benn won a huge ovation when he called for 'self-management as an alternative to market forces', and elaborated the role of workers' cooperatives and alternative industrial plans produced by workers themselves rather than by a centralised state.[389]

The left won all seven constituency places on the NEC, the high point of the left's influence at that time, and individual party membership continued to grow as many joined from extra-parliamentary movements and pressure groups. At the 1981 conference the campaign for internal party democracy was taken further, endorsing the mandatory reselection of MPs and replacing their exclusive role in electing the party leader with a new electoral college that included constituency parties and the unions. Soon after, Callaghan resigned to ensure his successor would be chosen under the old rules; Michael Foot was elected by the party's MPs, while Denis Healey was elected unopposed as deputy.

The fact that Foot stood for the leadership was a response to the rapid leftward shift in the party. MPs recognised that only a leader associated with the parliamentary left could get enough support in the constituencies and unions to contain and neutralise the momentum of change. Although he was the parliamentary favourite, the aggressively right-wing Healey openly disagreed with the policies decided at party conference, and did not have the confidence of the rank and file. Moreover, party activists were preparing to challenge his credentials as leader. There was 'a real danger of an irrevocable split in the party. In the event, it was the choice of Michael as leader – accepted however grudgingly, both by Healey's followers and by Benn's – that averted the catastrophe.'[390]

Foot's exclusively parliamentary orientation and obsession with keeping a Labour government in power at all costs epitomised the weaknesses of Bevanism after it had lost the strength it had derived from popular support in the labour movement. His primary concern was to maintain the party's parliamentary institutions and safeguard the link with the union leadership, but he also believed the democratising project of the new left would 'destroy parliament' if carried to its logical conclusion.[391] Foot met with union leaders soon after the 1981 conference to assure them that the constitutional changes for leadership election would not upset the power balance within the party. Despite this manoeuvre, the rumoured defection of right-wing MPs (who would later form the SDP) created a perceived threat to the shadow cabinet. By attacking those who he understood to be upsetting the party's fragile parliamentary coalition, like the Trotskyist 'Militant' tendency and left activists Peter Tatchell and Ken Livingstone, Foot provided ammunition for Thatcher's ideological onslaught on Labour-controlled local authorities, helping her make 'socialist' a term of abuse.

Defying Foot's appeal for unity, Benn stood against Healey for the deputy leadership, losing by only a narrow margin after Neil Kinnock attacked him in *Tribune* on the grounds that Benn was sowing division in the party. The effect of this intervention was to provide 'soft' left MPs with political cover to abstain and allow the election of Healey by a very small majority; Kinnock had effectively split the left by using his reputation as a Tribunite to play on the party's consummate desire for unity. His sabotage of Benn's campaign ingratiated him with the union bureaucracy and the shadow cabinet.

The left had forced the right onto the defensive on the policy front, but Healey's slim victory was the signal for a behind-the-scenes effort to claim back control of the party apparatus, using the press to attack Benn and his supporters. 'The right aimed not to suppress, but to discredit and isolate the

(Bennite) left by tarring it with the brush of extremism: hence the imagery of 'bully boys', the analogies with Eastern Europe and the accusations of intimidation and brutality ... Many senior right-wing Labour politicians possessed good contacts in the media and were only too ready to utilise them to mobilise opinion against the left.'[392] According to Michael Meacher, 'There was never less than half a page of vitriol in the press per day and the source was the right wing of the Labour party. They were feeding stuff into the press even though it did cataclysmic damage to the Labour party.'[393]

Behind the near-pathological intensity of the right wing's hostility were the challenges to the autonomy of the parliamentary party posed by the constitutional changes in the election of the party leader and mandatory reselection. By legitimising extra-parliamentary authority, the reforms had undermined the independent role Labour MPs expected to play in maintaining the stability of the state and defending the 'national interest'. To avoid criticising the unions, which still provided the bulk of the party's finances, Labour politicians blamed the left for the threat to their position; the most incorrigible of them later split from the party to form the Social Democratic Party (SDP). However, the departure of Jack Jones from the T&GWU in 1981 had opened an avenue for the right-wing union leaders to use their block vote to displace the left on the NEC's policy committees. As a result, the election campaign committee excluded Benn and Dennis Skinner and was dominated by union leaders and shadow cabinet ministers, who failed to contact or mobilise grassroots groups who could have provided ideological support.[394]

The manifesto on which the election was fought had been the product of an extensive democratic consultation within the Labour Party, resulting in a document that reflected the party's balance of forces at the time. It contained many elements of the left's alternative economic strategy, aiming to counter the Thatcher-initiated recession with an £11 billion 'emergency programme of action', incorporating massive investment in industry. Import duties and exchange controls would be re-imposed to 'counter currency speculation and to make available – to industry and government in Britain – the large capital resources that are now flowing overseas'. A national investment bank would put resources from North Sea oil revenues into industrial priorities, and a new national oil company would begin to bring the North Sea oil industry into public ownership. Privatised industries would be re-nationalised, and 'significant public stakes would be taken in electronics, pharmaceuticals, health equipment and building materials; and also in other important sectors, as required in the national interest'.[395]

These were specific proposals for a framework to restrain the uncontrolled movement of capital and channel it into industrial regeneration. It was not a plan for a command and control economy, as is sometimes suggested, but assumed a mixed economy in which the private sector would be subject to a complex system of state regulation. However, fierce opposition to the manifesto from the shadow cabinet and right-wing MPs presented a divided party to the electorate and allowed Thatcher to dominate the election campaign with her jingoistic celebration of the war in the South Atlantic. Foot's leadership expressed the lack of coherence and unity of purpose in the party; 'the political timidity and staggering lack of imagination in the presentation of Labour policies was a reflection of the huge gulf between those who had created the policies, the party's rank and file, and those responsible for presenting them, the shadow cabinet'.[396]

The 1983 election defeat

Labour made a disastrous showing in the election, in part because the defection of the SDP had split the anti-Tory vote. The right wing blamed the left of the party and the manifesto for the defeat, taking no responsibility for their lukewarm handling of the campaign; instead, the voters were presumed to have decisively rejected left policies. Foot immediately resigned as party leader, and a number of union leaders began to promote Kinnock as his successor. At the party conference that year Kinnock won a substantial majority in the electoral college because he was still perceived as a supporter of Labour's left-wing programme and especially of nuclear disarmament, which won him constituency support. His room for political manoeuvre at this time was limited by the continuing influence of the left in the party and on the NEC. Balancing between the constituency left and the parliamentary right, Kinnock began to centralise policy decision-making in his own office. He launched a new group of policy committees that combined NEC representatives with members of the shadow cabinet, with the ultimate objective of diluting the influence of party activists on policy through the party conference. Key positions on the committees were assigned to leadership supporters.

After its re-election, the Thatcher government began to implement the results of four years of preparations to take on the miners' union. In 1984 it initiated various provocations to push the miners into strike action with the intention of destroying a pillar of the labour movement and removing the most important obstacle to the dismantling of the nationalised coal industry. The TUC was split over opposition to the Tories' anti-union laws, which were always intended to be used against the miners. When the Coal Board management announced the closure of a major pit in Yorkshire, without the customary consultation with the union, it precipitated immediate strike action against the wishes of union officials.[397] The rank and file of the Labour Party responded spontaneously to the miners' strike by giving it material and moral support, but the leadership did all it could to distance itself from the struggle. Kinnock intervened at the party conference to vehemently condemn all picket-line violence, avoiding any expression of solidarity. 'As the strike progressed and the miners became weaker, Kinnock and the parliamentary right became stronger. The NUM's ultimate defeat led to a loss of confidence at all levels of the labour movement. ... The defeat of the miners was a disaster for the labour movement but a victory for Neil Kinnock.'[398]

The strike had political implications far wider than Kinnock's leadership of the party. Thatcher's determination to defeat the miners didn't stem only from her visceral hatred of their union but also from her ideological commitment to dismantling the post-war consensus. Her policy was aimed at removing an important obstacle to international capital's penetration of the UK economy, in the form of the miners' cultural attachment to their industry despite the corporatist structure of the management. They considered the blood, sweat, and lives expended down the pits to have given them a form of ownership, and that nationalisation had made the mines a community resource that the government was wilfully breaking up with unnecessary closures. 'We are protecting the people's coal,' wrote miners' leader Mick McGahey in April 1984.[399]

By mid-1985 Kinnock recognised that the left had fragmented after the miners' defeat, and took a more combative stance at the party conference, launching an impassioned critique of Scargill's handling of the strike, and more significantly on the Trotskyist 'Militant' leadership of Liverpool council. As a result of his ideological onslaught, a pro-leadership majority was restored in key party institutions.[400] Expulsions of Militant and non-Militant members proceeded apace as the NEC turned to a tougher managerial regime. They were aided by a shift in constituency opinion as the Liverpool public sector unions turned against Militant's use of a patronage network to award council jobs to its supporters. By the 1986 conference Kinnock had reasserted control, through the expulsions of leading Liverpool Militant members, and many of Benn's supporters abandoned him as the left began to fragment, lining up behind Kinnock in a 'realignment' of inner-party forces. This political shift gave Kinnock the chance to build a coalition on the NEC that would not question his leadership. The demoralisation of the rank and file after successive electoral defeats was key in enabling Kinnock to achieve these organisational changes, cementing his personal authority within the party's decision-making bodies. 'At the base of the party, it was clear that realignment enjoyed real but limited support. A frustrated membership desperately wanted a way out of the impasse of electoral and industrial failure and internecine strife.'[401]

The Kinnock leadership did not immediately replace the 1983 manifesto's policies, but instead gradually watered them down. Policy changes involved 'a shift in attitudes and presentation' and not principles, according to Kinnock, but gravitated to a 'pragmatic and largely consensual reform signaling the abandonment of any sustained challenge to the power and privileges of business'.[402] Kinnock's advisers Charles Clarke and Peter Mandelson developed 'a new emphasis on packaging and presentation ... and there was a new emphasis on glamour and glitz. From this there followed a downgrading of the party conference.' But 'organisational transformation was no less significant than programmatic, not least because sweeping changes in ideology and policy could not have been accomplished in its absence'.[403]

The campaign for the 1987 election epitomised the political bankruptcy of the new leadership. Its manifesto, *Britain Will Win with Labour*, answered Thatcher's government with tired slogans that harked back to Keynesian economic management, such as 'community and caring', 'investment in people and in production'.[404] Its target was the 'traditional labour voter', which as Stuart Hall pointed out, was code for 'back to the respectable, moderate, trade-unionist, male-dominated working class'. Kinnock's familial image 'carried not a single echo or trace of feminist struggles over two decades ... [and] signalled the distancing of Labour from all those "fringe issues".'[405] Kinnock also tried to suppress the demand for Black sections in the Labour Party, which he claimed was divisive. The growth of Afro-Caribbean and Asian communities in major cities, which consistently voted Labour but were politically marginalised, was the basis for a campaign for racial justice within Labour. Unofficial Black sections were set up to ensure the selection of ethnic minority politicians in winnable parliamentary seats, despite the opposition of the party leadership, and in 1987 succeeded in electing three Black MPs in London and one in Leicester.[406]

Despite the manifesto's glitzy presentation, Labour was again defeated, and even though the campaign strategy was wholly in the hands of the right, Kinnock and his supporters continued to blame this failure on the left. He was able to survive the electoral setback because the presidential style of the election insulated him from its consequences; the soft left was reliant on his patronage and the Bennite left was weakened by defections and defeats.

The 1987 defeat

The election loss in 1987 had a greater impact on the party's membership than in 1983, because the labour movement appeared to be helpless against an unstoppable Tory onslaught. 'Defeatism and despair … allowed the leadership to impose a top-down, authoritarian rule the like of which the Party had not seen in decades.' Political debate in party bodies was stifled and anyone who dared question the leader's wisdom was attacked for 'disloyalty'.[407] A new communications directorate was set up, headed by Peter Mandelson, with autonomy from the party's leading bodies and reporting directly to the leader. It began to influence policy-making using market research techniques, treating voters as consumers of policies. Mandelson considered the party's problem to be that it was perceived as too left-wing, and that the media had to be won over by presenting positive stories. Since the media was uniformly hostile to the party's policies, Mandelson instead promoted Kinnock as a vigorous leader who would trounce the left.

Kinnock initiated a major Policy Review, a three-year plan to produce a new statement of party positions in the light of the electoral defeats. The plan was endorsed by the conference, despite opposition from the Bennite left; after defeating a challenge from Benn for the leadership, Kinnock was able to secure a majority on a new 'Statement of Aims' in 1988 that embraced the value of markets, abandoned unilateral nuclear disarmament, and removed any reference to planning and nationalisation. Interventionist economic policies were scrapped in favor of cooperation with business. This 'modernisation' of the party's policies was based on the perception that the success of Thatcherism was connected to the rise of an affluent sector of the working class, which meant abandoning the values of collective action and replacing them with consumer-based individualism. Kinnock established a new think tank, the Institute for Public Policy Research (IPPR), creating 'a new Labourite party-expert configuration – office-seeking "modernisers" flanked by strategic aides and progressive policy specialists, informed by the new ethics of a changed [free-market] economics profession'.[408] He joined with the right-winger Roy Hattersley to endorse the supremacy of the market, and by 1989 dispensed with his supporters on the soft left who had continued to advocate Keynesian solutions to economic problems, like Michael Meacher and Bryan Gould, replacing them with rising stars Tony Blair and Gordon Brown. They brought with them an aggressive assertion of a new political identity defined in opposition to the failures of 'Old Labour', and reflected a shift in the intellectual climate that generated social theories strongly critical of benefit claimants' alleged dependency on state welfare.

The parliamentary party was encouraged to become disconnected from the views of its constituency organisations when the mandatory reselection of Labour MPs was abolished in 1990. Since parliamentary candidates were now carefully vetted for support for the leadership, careerists dominated the selections and the PLP shifted increasingly rightwards. Kinnock was opposed to protests against the Tory poll tax, despite its unpopularity with the public, but a near-riot in London forced the government to abandon its plans, and shortly afterwards Thatcher was ousted from the party leadership. However, Labour got no electoral benefit from the Tory debacle. The ejection of Thatcher from the Conservative leadership changed the political landscape, but it also demonstrated that much of Labour's apparent support in by-elections was little more than an anti-government protest. The party could no longer campaign on the basis of demonising Thatcher; however, the party leadership discouraged discussion of alternative strategies, and at the 1991 conference contentious debates were kept to a minimum. It resembled a US-style political rally, with Kinnock anointed as the prime minister in waiting. Priority in debates was given to parliamentary candidates who heaped praise on the leader.[409]

The absence of major policy differences with the Tories characterised the election campaign, which was controlled tightly from party headquarters. The party itself was failing: its membership had dropped precipitously and there were few available for the basic work of campaigning among the electorate. Media publicity and mass mailings were no substitute for active volunteers on the ground. The Labour right's conversion to financial orthodoxy led it to accept the Tory government's disastrous entry into the pre-euro Exchange Rate Mechanism (ERM) at a too-high exchange rate – politically accepting unemployment of 2.5 million or higher – which made Labour's economic strategy indistinguishable from the Tories'. Labour could then claim no credit when the government was forced to pull out of the ERM after spending billions to shore up the pound and allowing it to be devalued.

Assessing the effectiveness of Labour's 1992 campaign, Shaw points out the way the tabloid press mocked Labour's indecisiveness and amplified and elaborated the Tory message. The Tories altered the perception of high unemployment by blaming either the unemployed themselves, technological change which demanded leaner industries, or world market forces. 'Because the questions of causal (and moral) responsibility were answered with such clarity, because the explanation often tapped existing sentiments in the popular culture ... their object of "depoliticising" unemployment was achieved.' While the Tories were able to communicate a clear vision, Kinnock's concern to return Labour to a safe centrism prevented it from generating a distinct identity, leaving 'a vacuum which the Conservatives and the tabloids were able to fill by foisting on it a host of damaging attributes'.[410]

Blair's rolling coup

Labour's unexpected defeat in the 1992 election led to Kinnock's resignation in favour of John Smith, but the modernisers and their media allies continued to attack the union connection. The demoralisation of the membership removed much of the opposition to the party's rightward turn, and opened the door for the modernisers' promotion of the merits of market competition. Minkin comments that although the modernisers 'were essentially centrists with a yearning for electoral success, they developed an unusually Bolshevik attitude to their historic role and an attraction to the virtue of fundamental party change'.[411] Under Smith, the centralisation process slowed down and a more traditional leadership style was adopted, but after his sudden death in 1994 Tony Blair was elected with a surge of membership support, and Kinnock's managerial regime was revived.

Despite Blair's victory, Minkin points out that he 'had in practice only a narrow base of committed supporters of his full political project'.[412] Blair himself had little affinity with the traditions of the labour movement, and he surrounded himself with like-minded people from the professional and managerial class. Colin Leys noted that 'he operates in a milieu based on a different ethos, an ethos of professional politics based on higher education, management skills, and the culture of the communications industry'.[413] Blair effected what Minkin calls a 'rolling coup' that redefined the role of party officials from 'civil servants' representing the members to partisan 'political organisers' loyal to the leader.

The electoral failures under Kinnock were seen as resulting from an incomplete separation from 'Old Labour', the 1992 defeat in particular convincing the modernisers that Labour had to distance itself from the party of the 1983 manifesto and memories of the winter of discontent. The new strategy was to court 'middle England' voters who they imagined to be 'aspirational, consumer-oriented, and individualistically minded' and opposed to more taxation and 'wasteful' public authority spending – and was strongly influenced by the successful orientation to the centre by Clinton's New Democrats in the US.[414] Blair pressed for the replacement of Clause Four (and its symbolic connection with the unions) as a step to convince the public of the party's modernisation and to assert his own authority. He rebranded the party as 'New Labour' soon after becoming leader to emphasise its break from traditional Labour policies and its new acceptance of neoliberal economics. For Blair, a partnership between government and business was needed to achieve economic growth as a foundation for social policy, declaring in 1995 that 'Old Labour thought the role of government was to interfere with the market. New Labour believes the task of government is to make the market more dynamic, to provide people and business with the means of success.'[415]

During the 1980s, socialist women had joined the Labour Party because they perceived that it was democratising and offered an opportunity for them to remain a distinct political force. However, Kinnock and the modernisers suppressed the demand for separate women's sections (as well as black members' sections) because of their fear that such autonomous groups would derail the leadership's centralising thrust.[416] Instead, women were incorporated into the party elite, and a women's rights post was created in the shadow cabinet. As the leadership sought to distance itself from 'Old Labour', greater significance was placed on bringing women into leadership roles, and party conferences advocated all-women shortlists in vacant seats to increase the proportion of women MPs. 'Feminists inside and outside the party ... tended to celebrate the decline of ... the "tough patriarchs" with their entrenched "sandwiches and beer routine".'[417] However, the participatory and non-hierarchical approach to organising that characterised radical feminism was lost. Although a record 101 women Labour MPs were elected in 1997, they were far from being feminist actors influencing policy. Centralised elite control by the New Labour leadership meant that 'these women were likely to remain loyal and quiescent' and their political impact was generally considered to be negligible. In particular, the government's decision in late 1997 to reduce the benefit payable to single parents, announced by leading feminist Harriet Harman as secretary for social security, disillusioned many extra-parliamentary and Labour feminists. New Labour had appropriated feminist criticism of welfare state paternalism, but was perceived as opportunist in relation to women voters, being reluctant to overhaul equal pay and sexual discrimination legislation.[418]

It was not only Blair who wanted the party to more closely mirror what he assumed to be a more electorally popular free-market outlook; the cohort of modernisers, and especially his close collaborator Gordon Brown, were active participants in constructing this ideological shift. Brown concluded that the threat of higher taxes had destroyed the party's electability. From Clinton's campaign, he had absorbed a deference to global markets when formulating economic and social policy. In a 1994 Fabian pamphlet, 'Fair is Efficient,' Brown argues that the key to restructuring employment is 'a new opportunity-based economics', that requires the state to institute skills training for the unemployed so as to enhance their value to the economy. Welfare programmes were re-focused on the requirement for individual effort, rather than a government commitment to redistribution.[419] As shadow Chancellor, he set up a team consisting of Ed Balls – a market-oriented economist, who had studied under Clinton guru Larry Summers at Harvard – and Charlie Whelan, a spin doctor. Their approach to the perceived problem of Labour's economic competence was to 'reassure the media and the markets that Labour was "prudent" in the sense that, in line with conventional economic thinking, it was committed to free markets, globalisation, and central bank independence'.[420]

Labour's 1997 campaign closely emulated the neoliberal policies of Clinton's US administration, with a specific manifesto for business and calling for restrictions on universal welfare. Although not in the manifesto, Brown gave the Bank of England independence soon after taking office, insisting that New Labour could reconcile its prudent fiscal management with Labour's social goals.[421] Blair committed the future government to 'enhancing the dynamic of the market, not undermining it', and made it clear that government borrowing and spending were not going to be increased above the fiscal projections of John Major's Tory government.[422]

This was carried through into Labour's electoral programme. Labour had abandoned re-nationalisation of privatised utilities such as electricity, gas and water, and British Rail in 1992, and in 1997 the party's manifesto declared the government would 'leave intact the main changes of the 1980s in industrial relations and enterprise. We see healthy profits as an essential motor of a dynamic market economy.'[423] The whole idea of public ownership was held to be hopelessly old-fashioned. Richard Heffernan writes that this shift in approach reflected the influence of Thatcherism as 'the agency of a fundamental and far-reaching policy departure [privatisation] that called into question the very premises upon which nationalisation was predicated'.[424] However, this diagnosis does not take into account how Thatcherism had also achieved a deeper and more fundamental change in the processes of governance by introducing corporate management practices into public administration. The evaluation of the performance of public institutions on the basis of competitive efficiency began to alter the nature of interactions between them and individual clients. In turn, social subjects internalised market criteria for their actions: decisions became based on individual advantage through consumer 'choice' rather than on a conception of the social good.

Pierre Dardot and Christian Laval draw a distinction between the restructuring of the state 'from without, by massive privatisation of public enterprises ... but also from within, by the institution of an evaluating, regulating state that mobilizes new instruments of power and, along with them, structures new relations between government and social subjects.' Neoliberal governments, they argue, actively exploit the freedom allowed individuals so that of their own accord they end up conforming to the behavioural norms of competition, which means accepting that every social relation can be reduced to a depersonalised transaction in terms of costs and benefits. 'Neoliberal subjects' are produced who are not exposed to overt compulsion, but are required to engage completely in their professional activity. They are expected to work for companies as if they were working as entrepreneurs for themselves, abolishing any sense of alienation from the enterprise. These subjects must continually adapt to the incessant change demanded by competitive markets, thus internalising market rationality. As Thatcher put it: 'Economics are the method. The object is to change the soul.'[425] There was a limit, however, to the extent Thatcher could cultivate this entrepreneurial attitude among her core supporters in the middle class over the course of her government. She had to be content with instituting strict rules of central monitoring, financial accountability, and productivity onto social and educational institutions, which New Labour was to take much further.

New Labour in power: a neoliberal economic platform

Eighteen years of Thatcherite governments had devastated the industrial heartlands in the North and accentuated the migration of resources and population to the South-east. But, after winning the 1997 election, New Labour made no effort to reverse the consolidation of financial power in the City of London, considered by the new government as inevitable and even necessary for economic prosperity. The key to New Labour's class role is that it took over from a Thatcherite government at a moment when it was unable to continue governing: there was mass opposition to the poll tax, riots in inner-cities across the country, coinciding with an upheaval within the Tory party itself.

The destabilising effects of hardcore monetarism had motivated the World Bank to retrench on free-market fundamentalism. It produced a report in 1997 explicitly advocating a larger role for the state in maintaining social stability while allowing markets to flourish. Deregulation was not in itself sufficient to ensure global integration, the report concluded; states were encouraged to reform government institutions to make them more accountable to civil society and increase their ability to regulate social problems. The Bank encouraged more privatisation of public services and the introduction of competitive bidding into government spending on health, education and transport.[426] New Labour's policies closely paralleled this shift in the form of governance.

New Labour had already committed to continue Tory spending levels when it came into office, primarily to ratify its credibility with the international bond markets. Brown, as Chancellor of the Exchequer, believed that the government's role should be 'not only to support but positively enhance markets'. Fiscal discretion was combined with what he called 'light-touch' regulation of the banks, in effect encouraging the creation of debt as the foundation of economic expansion. The financial markets could be harnessed to the cause of social reform, he thought, by recycling profits from the financial sector into social spending. But the result was that significant costs of public welfare were transferred from the state to the private individual. Priority was given to reducing government debt, cutting public spending from 40 per cent of GDP in 1991 to 38.1 per cent in 2001.[427] Brown's economic management was premised on attracting speculative capital to the City of London, arguing that globalisation forced the government to follow economically 'rational' policies. Despite his claim that the government was constrained by the need to appease global investors, New Labour was pro-market from conviction. It believed that business 'creates wealth and jobs and sustains our quality of life', as the minister for trade and industry, Patricia Hewitt, remarked.[428]

Although social programmes like Sure Start and welfare-to-work initiatives, together with real increases in benefits and extra spending on education and healthcare, had achieved a material improvement for the poorest families, the net effect of New Labour's policies was to leave income inequality at the same high level as under Thatcher. What was reduced was the disparity between the poorest and those on median incomes – not the inequality between the poor and the very rich: in 2002 the top 1 per cent held 23 per cent of personal wealth, an increase from 18 per cent in 1990. The narrowing of absolute inequality was not a priority for the government because it was accepted as necessary for a market economy within a globalised economic system. What was a priority was combating 'social exclusion', promoting 'employability' through skills training, together with restructuring welfare to match the needs of the job market – providing advice on job searches, enlarging the gap between benefits and pay, instituting a minimum wage and tax credits for families. It also set conditions for benefits that workers had to accept, the duty to take available jobs and training. But it ignored the loss of quality industrial jobs that had resulted in a de-skilling of the workforce and an erosion of working-class confidence.[429]

Political decisions were justified by the mantra of external global imperatives in a rhetorical sleight of hand that avoided responsibility for unpopular social and economic reforms. However, in the two domestic areas where New Labour got the most opposition from within the party – healthcare and education – policy choices reflected the preferences of key ministers rather than any perceived external constraints.[430] Price stability would be maintained through a deregulated labour market which would hold down wage levels, making the cooperation of the TUC unnecessary. Employee rights were restored to some extent through EU legislation. But the government limited its coverage to full-time employees – at a time when the numbers of part-time and temporary contract workers had ballooned in the aftermath of Thatcherite government policies. Resistance to EU provisions for protection of these workers and the continuing political marginalisation of the unions meant that many low-paid jobs were taken by immigrants. 'The UK was one of only three countries in Europe where employers could legally hire temporary workers on lower pay and poorer conditions than other [fulltime] staff.'[431]

The drive to make benefits conditional on skills training was part of an attempt to increase social cohesion through the discipline of paid work, especially targeted at the younger, single, unemployed. Brown's chief economic adviser, Ed Balls, had observed that US labour market deregulation had increased wage inequality and social dislocation, especially among unskilled younger men. 'It is, therefore, significant that while the [Labour] New Deals covered a wide range of economically inactive claimants, the strongest emphasis (and extension of conditionality) was applied to a social group which could most readily be identified as a threat to the security of the insecure middle class voters to whom New Labour pitched its strongest appeal.'[432]

Rather than the absolute hostility of Thatcherite governments to unions, New Labour recognised their role in workplace representation. The government mandated a minimum wage, strengthened employee rights, and adopted the EU Charter. But the retention of legal restrictions on strike activity, insistence on a lightly regulated labour market and the introduction of private management practices into the public sector reflected a managerial antipathy to organised labour. Manufacturing contracted sharply; under Thatcher's successor, John Major, it had been 20 per cent of the economy, but dropped to 12 per cent under New Labour. Low-wage, flexible working conditions were actively encouraged by Blair in order to attract corporate investment. However, public spending was still constrained to Tory levels; spending on social services was increased after the government's first two years in office, but it was combined with a centralising drive for controls on service provision.

In the late 1990s, Clinton, Blair and other European left leaders had agreed on the need to reform public intervention, aligning themselves more closely with corporate management techniques. The strategy continued the 1980s Tory policy of applying the principle of efficiency in the public sector through auditing agencies. Private Finance Initiative (PFI) was resuscitated from the Thatcherite legacy – essentially it was an accounting device to keep capital expenditure off the public spending figures, which leached funds from public entities over the long term and guaranteed cash flow to private corporations. Under New Labour these contracts mushroomed in all areas of public provision, including the NHS and education. Since they appeared to offer solutions to pressing needs for investment, they fostered a new public management rationality that 'operates much more effectively than any radical discourse by undermining ethical and political resistance in the public and community sectors'.[433] As with the banking sector, profits were privatised and risks socialised – government would always have the obligation to step in to bail out failing large projects. Brown was 'passionate' in his support for PFI: he considered that the public sector was inefficient and ineffective in managing large projects because, according to the Treasury, it had 'no incentive to make a profit or recoup the cost of capital'.[434]

New Labour's second term: conditional redistribution

New Labour was re-elected in 2001, but the continuation of Tory-determined public spending levels in the government's first two years had created a crisis within the health services such that Blair was forced to announce a major boost to its budget. In 2002 the NHS received a substantial increase in funding, but just as with benefits, the cash infusion came with conditions. The government had become concerned about cost efficiency, and shifted to a command and control mechanism that reflected its scepticism about the ability of the service to continue long-term improvements without drastic reform. While resources were pumped into the sector, 'renewal' also implied introducing private investment, meeting market criteria of efficiency and value, managerial command structures, and undermining working practices and collective bargaining.[435]

The introduction of markets into social provision – in the name of encouraging consumer choice – was accompanied by a welter of targets to be met at the service level. At the same time, accountability was removed from the public realm: the quality of service was now governed by opaque contracts agreed by corporate entities whose highly paid CEOs took no responsibility for people's actual welfare. The cost of maintaining the NHS internal market rose to 10 per cent of its budget, soaking up any increased funding. While PFI allowed the building of new facilities, it was the rationalities of investment that guided their construction rather than a medical assessment of the population's needs.[436] *The Guardian* reported that the ultimate consequence was that, by 2017, 700-odd PFI schemes had an estimated capital value of less than £59.1 billion, 'yet taxpayers will end up paying out more than £308bn for them, well over five times that sum. PFI is a gift to the City which has resulted in, as the PFI expert Allyson Pollock acidly put it, "one hospital for the price of two"'.[437]

A clear break from the traditional Labour approach to health services was to institute choice, competition and private sector involvement within the NHS. New Labour's initiative 'represented an explicit effort to re-engineer the culture of the public sector and to lessen the role of professional norms in favour of market or instrumental rationality'.[438] The agency had always trusted professional expertise in the provision of treatment, but now an agenda of consumer choice and preference was to override the medical establishment. The faith in central control evaporated and a new initiative of decentralisation was launched. 'Foundation Trusts' were set up, with independent control of their assets; private provision of healthcare was encouraged in order to put competitive pressure on NHS hospitals to become more efficient. Decentralisation, which was claimed to empower the individual, was in fact connected to the restriction and simplification of what the individual could choose, and to increased concentration of power at the top. Centralised administrative bodies closely monitored the actions of those at the front line of service provision, through the introduction of targets and complicated systems of performance measurement.[439]

New Labour's education policy encountered active resistance within the party when the government broke with Labour's traditional support for comprehensive schools and retained many Tory innovations. The Tories had weakened the role of local authorities, given extra funding to self-governing schools, reintroduced selection and initiated performance tables based on exam results. Blair kept these measures and accelerated the fragmentation of the school system through the introduction of 'faith schools', and 'city academies'. These were set up in deprived areas, publicly funded but allowing external sponsors to have disproportionate influence over curriculum, admissions and head teacher appointments. In its second term, the government introduced more stringent performance management with a host of centrally-set standards; encouraged competition between schools for league table standings; gave successful schools more autonomy and put struggling schools in 'special measures'; and encouraged new types of private providers. Teachers were especially antagonised by the retention of the authoritarian OFSTED inspection regime, whose powers further debilitated local education authorities, and a 'blame game' management culture based on private sector practices.[440]

Devolution of powers to Scotland and Wales, which seemed to run counter to New Labour's drive for centralised state management, was in reality an acknowledgement of regional imbalances arising from the increased financialisation of the economy. In Northern Ireland, devolution rested on the power-sharing Belfast agreement of 1998, which made the British government legally neutral between the Nationalist community's demand for a united Ireland and the insistence of Unionists on remaining part of the UK. In Scotland, 'the decline of Scottish indigenous industry and the relative attachment of the Scottish middle class to the potential of the state as an instrument for progressive social change' accentuated its divergence from New Labour's electoral target of Middle England, itself a product of the Thatcherite restructuring of the economy that favoured the south-eastern based financial industry.[441]

New Labour's conviction that the media's ferocious attacks on Kinnock had damaged the party's electability led Blair to make a bid to cultivate relations with the tabloid press. At Mandelson's urging, Blair flew to Australia to meet the billionaire owner of the Sun, Rupert Murdoch, who then became a frequent visitor to Downing Street. The media strategy went together with Blair's presidential style of party management and government, relying on a group of advisors and spin doctors rather than his parliamentary Cabinet, which 'produced a drastic curtailment of debate on substantive issues by anyone who could be publicly held accountable'.[442] Opposition to the government's policies within the party was stifled by its managerial structure and close vetting of parliamentary candidates to weed out dissent: decision-making was now confined to the leader's small coterie, excluding even members of the Cabinet. Public opposition was fragmented by the decline of union strength and the absence of a political alternative. Party management was under the firm control of functionaries centred on the party's headquarters in London, made easier by the shedding of disgruntled members, but heavy-handed control of CLP elections in 1998 and the requirement that CLPs submit conference motions to the National Policy Forum provoked opposition even from loyalists. At the same time union opposition to private sector involvement in public services was ignored.[443]

Blair's crusading morality rationalised state and ideological support for US imperial aims in Kosovo, Afghanistan and Iraq on the grounds of 'humanitarian intervention'. His office was instrumental in developing the narrative of 'weapons of mass destruction' in Iraq which was taken up by the US administration as justification for its invasion in 2003. Coupled with the war on terror was the attack on migrants. Invasive policing and surveillance was targeted in the main at British Muslims – between 2002 and 2009 the administration passed four acts on terrorism, five on immigration and asylum, six on policing and crime – severely curtailing civil liberties. By 2006, more than 3,000 new criminal offences had been created, their number markedly accelerating towards the end of Blair's premiership.[444]

The aftermath of the 9/11 attacks in the US led to a further concentration of power, with Blair relying on a handful of close advisers. Having committed to support the US in Iraq, Blair had hoped to replicate Thatcher's success as a war leader. But public and party opposition to war was intense; curbing this voice meant controlling the discussion in every party forum. Machine loyalty to the leader began to frustrate both the party grassroots and union leaders. At the 2002 party conference, the leadership resolution supporting force was carried on a show of hands rather than a card vote, after a debate heavily rigged in favour of Blair's position.[445] The Stop the War coalition was formed in 2001 outside the party, drawing together left organisations with the Muslim community and the energy of the anti-globalisation movement to protest the US invasion. A two million-strong demonstration in February 2003 signalled public alienation from New Labour; one of the platform speakers was Jeremy Corbyn, and activists from the coalition were later to join his election campaign. Blair's support for Bush was the last straw for many of the remaining politically-active members, who had expected the government to follow what they considered to be an ethical foreign policy. The Leader of the House of Commons, Robin Cook, who had been Foreign Secretary for five years under Blair, resigned from the Cabinet in protest.

When MP George Galloway was expelled from the Labour Party for his outspoken opposition to the Iraq war, the Trotskyist Socialist Workers' Party saw this as an opportunity to build a left electoral alternative to Labour. They sought to create a coalition from the diverse forces of the anti-war movement – disillusioned Labour supporters, trade unionists, radical Muslim activists and pacifists – and launched the 'Respect' party in 2004. It achieved an electoral base in East London and Birmingham where large Muslim populations who normally voted Labour had been disenchanted by Blair's support for the war. However, Respect's reliance on ethnic patronage in these areas for votes meant that divisions in the Muslim communities were imported into the party, and the alliance broke up in 2007.[446]

The attrition of Labour's membership over disappointment with the government's policies culminated in a drop of 25,000 members in the first six months of 2004, leaving a total of 190,000 compared to over 400,000 in 1997 when Blair became prime minister.[447] The decline in individual membership strengthened the unions' position in relation to the party leadership in the run-up to the 2005 election, and they began to coordinate their activities with respect to the party. Despite election victory, by the following year party loyalists began to dissent from the leadership: the 2006 conference overwhelmingly carried a motion from the Unison union urging the government to 'rethink the headlong rush to a competitive system' in the health service and calling for a moratorium on key planks of its NHS marketisation strategy. An NEC motion critical of the government was narrowly defeated by 16 votes to 15.[448] Resistance to the continued centralisation of policy came from both the party mainstream and the traditional right. Blair was 'unable to extend the rolling coup in a way which removed limitations on his leadership and management' and he was eventually forced out of the premiership by Brown in 2007.[449]

The economic crash

The hyper-financialisation of the economy had made it vulnerable to international finance's intrinsic volatility. Defaults on subprime mortgages in the US created a liquidity crunch in the money markets that European banks had come to rely on. In August of 2007 the largest bank in France, BNS Paribas, suspended payments on three of its investment funds, and the following month the fifth largest lender in the UK, Northern Rock, needed emergency support from the Bank of England as depositors queued outside its doors. Brown's strategy of encouraging financial asset bubbles as the basis of economic expansion disastrously collapsed when the liquidity crisis spread to the Royal Bank of Scotland in 2008 and forced him to provide a massive capital infusion to the banking sector. 'What Gordon Brown had portrayed as a new British economic miracle was actually an economic mirage. ... Brown had mistaken an unsustainable consumer-fuelled, property-driven and ultimately debt-based boom for a new British model of macroeconomic stability and fiscal prudence.'[450]

Because of its dependence on consumer debt, the British economy was so exposed to the credit crunch that Brown was forced to underwrite the entire financial sector with public funds – according to the National Audit Office with £850 billion by December 2009 – condemning the public sector to a decade of retrenchment. The rationale for the bailout was to insure depositors and restore the supply of credit to the consumer economy. Government debt increased to 82 per cent of GDP, while at the same time unemployment increased by half a million people. The huge increase in public debt was predominantly the result of the reduction in the tax take because of the sharp decline in taxable economic activity. Although Brown attempted a neo-Keynesian investment programme to restore the economy, it was done only to shore up the existing growth model, it being understood by international markets that Keynesianism would eventually be abandoned when balance was restored to public accounts.[451] By saving the banks, Brown also saved the debts that people owed to the banks, leading to a spike in foreclosures and a wave of business bankruptcies. Although these crisis measures averted a collapse of the banking system, the high level of the budget deficit became the focus of relentless Tory political attacks.

What is significant is that New Labour had no effective reply to the Tory claim that Labour overspending caused the crisis. Brown had based the government's social spending projections on the unsustainable tax revenue from the overheated financial sector, but refused to accept that his abdication of regulation on bank asset requirements or encouragement of inflation in the property market was in any way connected to the need for a massive bank bailout; he could not sustain a coherent intellectual alternative to free-market neoliberalism because he and New Labour had faithfully followed Thatcherite prescriptions for the economy. He had ignored the fragility of a growth model based on credit, and the discrediting of the left had removed the authority of intellectual resources within the party that could have undertaken a serious analysis of the collapse of the financialised economy.

New Labour's ideology: The Third Way

According to Blair, New Labour had discarded ideology: 'what matters is what works'. This claim is belied by New Labour's hostility to any allusion to socialism and its repudiation of the egalitarian values of organised labour, even those expressed from a right-wing Keynesian standpoint. Since Labour's earlier attempts to tackle the problems of globalisation and British industrial decline with a left policy in the 1970s were rejected *a priori*, Blair approved the Thatcherite restructuring of the economy as inevitable and 'necessary acts of modernisation'.[452] The corollary of this position was the neoliberal idea that the free movement of capital constrained government policy; capital flows, or markets, were conceived in like vein as external structures that directed individual decisions towards the common good.

For New Labour, there could be no return to the Keynesian welfare order, while at the same time the worst social effects of Thatcherism were unacceptable. A synthesis had to be produced which would win elections, would not challenge the fundamental pattern of social inequality that had crystallised under fourteen years of Thatcherite governments, but would allow the alleviation of the worst forms of disadvantage. The leadership had to retain the party's traditional support by reaffirming social democratic themes of equality, social welfare and full employment, while at the same time advancing a market-friendly approach to the economy.[453] The resulting synthesis, Blair's 'Third Way', elaborated a neoliberal argument in its entirety, placing markets in a realm outside human intentions and interests, and making them a rationale for disciplining the working class to accept a low-wage, polarised financial economy.

The goal of the Third Way was to construct a framework that allowed market forces to work properly as a condition for economic success and employment. Individuals were expected to adapt to the new reality of globalised capital, rather than being protected by the state against its exploitative pressures. Similar language to Blair's was used by European parties like Germany's SPD and Sweden's SAP, as well as Clinton's New Democrats in the US, which Stephanie Mudge describes as characterised by 'market-friendliness, antidogmatic pragmatism, and a brand of welfarism that elevated work, adaptability, and personal responsibility over security and state provision'. She argues that this language, which she calls 'neoliberalised leftism', was distinguished from straightforward neoliberalism by a particular blend of market emphases with pragmatism and work-centric welfare.[454] While it is important to distinguish this rhetoric from that of the new right, it is also necessary to stress that it remains within the bounds of the neoliberal project as a leftist variant of neoliberalism, and represents a fundamental break from the collectivist traditions of social democracy.

Academic assessments of New Labour are divided between those who interpret it as continuing neoliberal policies, and those who argue that increased state intervention and spending on social services distinguished it in principle from Thatcherism. Both Heffernan and Hay, for example, consider that Labour accepted the neoliberal consensus created by a succession of Thatcherite governments.[455] This view is firmly rejected by sociologist Anthony Giddens, an early influence on Blair, who refuses to accept 'the simplistic idea that New Labour was just a continuation of Thatcherism. Labour's policies involved extensive government intervention in economic life.'[456] Mark Bevir, likewise, claims that New Labour falls clearly within the broad social democratic spectrum; its Third Way is a 'refashioning of one strand of social democracy' responding to the political issues raised by the New Right. Connell argues more strongly that New Labour's 'commitment to state intervention means it cannot, in our view, be classified as simply neoliberal'. In government, it has 'shown a commitment to redistribution not only of opportunity but of income in favour of the poor (especially the working poor). This redistribution has not been unconditional – it has been designed to reinforce certain "desirable" behaviours, principally paid work – but it has certainly taken place.'[457]

The perception that increased government spending on welfare kept New Labour within the bounds of social democratic values disregards the evidence that a limited redistribution of wealth is perfectly compatible with a neoliberal approach to managing financial markets. As David Harvey has shown, neoliberalism was a political project to restore and consolidate class power, not a set of economic prescriptions, and therefore could be flexible in relation to the specific role of the state. The one constant principle for neoliberal governments was to protect the solvency of financial institutions regardless of its impact on the population in general. Harvey locates the third way individualisation of welfare, education and healthcare in neoliberal concepts of individual freedom: success or failure 'are interpreted in terms of entrepreneurial virtues or personal failings (such as not investing significantly enough in one's own human capital through education) rather than being attributed to any systemic property (such as the class exclusions usually attributed to capitalism).'[458]

New Labour in reality was an adaptation of government to the post-Thatcherite world, where the creation of an economic underclass had increased the insecurities of the middle-class voters that Labour hoped to attract. It was distinguished from Thatcherism – which was indifferent to the devastation of working-class communities – insofar as it aimed to alleviate the worst poverty and sought to integrate the unemployed into society by mandating training to accept the work-discipline of menial and low-paid jobs. The social democratic concept of social citizenship, which meant entitlement to state support, was replaced by one of 'social inclusion' through market reciprocity. All citizens should have the chance to better themselves through paid work, but also must take on the responsibility to take care of their own needs. The new government strategy was to promote 'employability' through skills training, together with restructuring welfare to match the needs of the job market. The community nurtures individual choice, but at the same time enforces the responsibility of the individual to get a job and contribute back to the community. 'Rights and responsibilities go together,' said Blair; in practice this meant denying benefits to those who did not take advantage of the opportunities for finding work that the state presented to them.

While New Labour's concept of citizen as demanding consumer fits the description of the 'neoliberal subject', at the same time neoliberal governments were creating a counter-subject through the individualisation of social responsibility. Sociologists detected a cultural trend toward what they describe as personalized or 'individuated' politics, or as Dardot and Laval put it, 'a radical individualisation that leads to all forms of social crisis being perceived as individual crises and all inequalities being made the responsibility of individuals'.[459] Where states are indifferent or unresponsive to citizens' concerns, individuals are impelled to challenge government policy independent of established political structures. Coming together on specific issues, such as climate change or austerity cuts, protesters discovered new affinities with like-minded people and created for themselves a means for the voices of all individuals to be heard through non-hierarchical participatory democracy. The 1999 mass protests in Seattle against the World Trade Organisation, the protests in Genoa against the G8 summit, and later the movement against the Iraq war, expressed a growing rejection of governments' complicity in extending corporate globalisation. They also launched a new generation of activists committed to developing new techniques of radical democratic decision-making for use in mass civil disobedience movements.[460]

Although there was resistance to specific New Labour policies from within the unions and the party membership, the parliamentary party regarded Blairism as a necessary adaptation to unchangeable economic necessities that enabled them to win elections. While Blair was the most loquacious advocate for neoliberalism in government, he faced no opposition from within the Cabinet or the parliamentary party except for the small group around Tony Benn. Blair's ideological reinterpretation of social democratic values like welfare, equality, and fair employment continues to exert a powerful influence on many within the PLP.

Eric Shaw makes the point that 'the redistributive dimension within British social democracy was always coupled with a second one, the ethical socialist'. Although Blair stressed the responsibilities of welfare recipients to society, this did not apply to the rich, who were entitled to accumulate huge sums without making any corresponding contribution to the social good. Labour had never condemned profit-making as such, but the accumulation of individual wealth had to have some kind of moral justification. When Blair dismissed concern at the growth of inequality as 'the politics of envy' and that 'we need more successful entrepreneurs' in his introduction to the

1997 manifesto, he signalled a clear break with the ethical socialist tradition of fellowship, cooperation and service.[461]

In this chapter, I trace the process by which the Labour leadership was captured by a neoliberal 'modernising' cohort. It was a reaction to a series of electoral defeats, but began with an ideological assault on the Bennite left. Policy-making was concentrated in the leader's office while debate within the wider party was stifled, and Kinnock and Blair's 'modernisation' project reversed the democratic gains made by the membership in the 1980s. Labour's leaders were not constrained by the globalised economy, despite their rhetoric, but consciously chose the policies they wanted to follow. They took many elements of their 1997 programme from Clinton's 1992 New Democrat platform, rejecting socialist alternatives *a priori* and becoming enthusiastic cheerleaders for the market. In government, the trope of modernisation was used to justify the imperative of adapting to the global economy, in particular the removal of constraints on the City of London. Minimally redistributive policies replaced the ethical socialist orientation in Labour's tradition, and members voted with their feet by leaving in droves. Discussion of socialism was actively suppressed within the party until the 2015 leadership election.

In the next chapter, I discuss the way that Labour's membership asserted itself against the parliamentary party, attracting the anti-austerity protest movement into Labour Party politics, and restoring socialist discourse with Corbyn's campaign for the leadership. His election energised the rank and file and it felt empowered to decide policy, rather than being handed it from the party central office. The hostility of many centrist MPs to this development derives from their certainty that the party should continue to advocate socially liberal policies that do not directly challenge the structure of political and economic power, preserving their role of confining dissent within the orbit of elite parliamentary privilege. Like Blair, they are closer to the world of corporate lobbyists and media pundits than to their own electorate. They consider themselves guardians of Labour as a 'responsible' party that accepts that the economy should be dominated by international markets sustaining financial speculation and real estate inflation, while state budgets would be balanced by public service cuts. In other words, they have thoroughly internalised New Labour's 'third way' version of the neoliberal consensus.

Chapter Seven

Jeremy Corbyn and the Resurgence of the Socialist Ideal

'There's no such thing as Corbynism. There is socialism, there is social justice, there are radical manifestos.'[462] Jeremy Corbyn, 13 December 2019

The party's rejection of New Labour

The decisive vote for Jeremy Corbyn in the 2015 Labour leadership election confounded political commentators, who struggled to explain it. They focused on either his personal character or the political machinations that got him on the ballot. But they refused to acknowledge what was in plain sight: the attraction of his ethical socialist philosophy after decades of neoliberal discourse. It rallied a grassroots coalition of party members, returning ex-members, and activists from anti-austerity social movements, giving Corbyn an overwhelming mandate. His policy statements and interventions show that his moral authority was won from a consistent participation in challenges to the British state's imperialist role and the rule of the socially privileged. The strength of the movement supporting Corbyn grew from resistance to the effects of austerity cuts on civil society and young people's perception that there was no economic future for them.

The 2010 general election had been a disaster for New Labour. Economic uncertainty dominated the electoral campaign, with all major political parties agreeing that public service spending would need to be cut in light of the deficit. Labour Chancellor Alistair Darling admitted that the party was planning cuts that were 'deeper and tougher' than even those made under Thatcher.[463] Although politicians tried to link economic problems to immigration, academic studies found that voters' attitudes on the issue were more closely linked to questions of identity than migration. Gordon Brown spoke of the need for 'British jobs for British workers', while the Tories committed themselves to reducing immigration to 'tens of thousands' rather than hundreds of thousands per year.[464] Labour's vote fell from 13,518,167 in 1997 to 8,609,527 in 2010, losing a total of 94 seats. Even though the Tories gained more MPs than in any general election since 1931, they still did not win an overall majority.

The end result was a Tory and Liberal Democrat coalition, led by David Cameron and Nick Clegg, which embarked on drastic austerity measures ideologically justified by the framing of the financial crisis as a 'crisis of debt', allegedly caused by New Labour's overspending on the public sector. The politics of deficit reduction through austerity cuts to public services rather than tax increases guaranteed the domination of the Tories in the coalition. Cuts in public sector spending and pay contributed to a downward pressure on wages with the outcome of displacing the burden of the recession onto wage earners. The low interest rate 'quantitative easing' policy of the Bank of England had the effect of pushing up share and house prices, at the same time that the government extended disciplinary 'workfare' arrangements that drove more people into low-paid jobs and 'zero-hours' contracts.[465] Through its encouragement of asset inflation, the coalition and subsequent Tory governments facilitated an upsurge of rents and real estate prices that has visibly swelled the numbers of homeless and forms a mechanism for direct wealth extraction by global capital.[466] At the same time, these governments progressively defunded welfare services, introducing the 2012 Health and Social Care Act that allowed NHS medical services to be outsourced to 'any qualified provider'. In 2015, private companies won 40 per cent of all contracts, diverting billions of pounds away from the public agency. Closures of A&E departments and the downgrading of public health made the NHS increasingly unable to cope with annual spikes of flu infections and left it disastrously unprepared for the Covid-19 pandemic in 2020.[467]

In this chapter I show that Labour's membership rejected the failed leadership of New Labour, opening a space for the resurgence of social democratic thinking through the nomination of Corbyn as party leader. New members who joined the party out of social protest movements were inspired both by Corbyn's opposition to austerity and the participatory democracy that characterised his approach to politics. Labour's 2017 election manifesto challenged the dominant neoliberal narrative and was a key factor in overturning the Tory government's majority. Despite confusion over the party's Brexit policy, the 2019 conference adopted a raft of radical policies that originated from grassroots activists. Defeat in that year's election saw Corbyn step down as leader, but despite the new leadership's rapid rightward shift under Keir Starmer, there is continuing membership support for the party's radical manifesto. In fact, its policies are even more relevant to the way the coronavirus pandemic has fractured society along its systemic fault lines.

Immediately after the 2010 election, Gordon Brown resigned as Labour leader, and the subsequent contest for the leadership was won by Ed Miliband, regarded as 'soft left', defeating the Blairite candidate, his brother David. Although a majority of the party membership had voted for David Miliband (it was the union votes that gave Ed the victory), over the course of the next five years there was a marked change in the members' mood as Ed Miliband ended the leadership's close control of party discourse. At the same time, the unions stepped up their efforts to restore their influence on the party. The rhetoric of Miliband's first conference speech shifted away from New Labour's deference to markets and the City, denounced inequality and the Iraq war, and repudiated the authoritarian approach to civil liberties. At first, he supported mass protests against austerity cuts and increased student fees, but by 2012 began to backtrack and refer to 'difficult choices' that would have to be made. Shadow chancellor Ed Balls fleshed out this acceptance of the Tory narrative by telling the *Guardian*: 'I am afraid we are going to have to keep all these cuts' and committed to keep public sector pay frozen – bringing him into sharp conflict with the unions that represented public sector workers.[468]

The critical moment in the coalition's regressive austerity measures came in 2013. The bedroom tax, the overall benefit cap and council support reductions produced an absolute increase in poverty in the poorest sections of society.[469] However, in the face of these cuts, the Labour leadership committed itself to a welfare spending cap and compliance with rigid fiscal rules, pledging to match Conservative plans to cut the welfare bill. Miliband said: 'The next Labour government will have less money to spend … Social security spending, vital as it is, cannot be exempt from that discipline.'[470] According to *New Yorker* writer John Cassidy, the leadership's agreement with the Tory principle that punitive reductions in spending were essential to reduce the budget deficit, except that Labour would do it slower – 'austerity lite' – reflected a political judgement by Miliband that the electorate would not respond to an anti-austerity policy.[471] But it also meant that the ongoing resistance to austerity would bypass the party, as direct action groups like UK Uncut, Occupy, and the People's Assembly against Austerity emerged. Their collective response was mediated by a moral critique of inequality and drew on the methods of horizontal democratic decision-making learned from the anti-globalisation movement. Within the party itself, new members were attracted to Miliband's more radical policies like the energy price freeze, the mansion tax, a halt to NHS privatisation, and his opposition to bombing Syria in 2013.

The left steadily increased its vote on the NEC between 2012 and 2014 as the rank and file rejected Blairite candidates and 'voted by a clear majority for candidates opposed to austerity and austerity lite', as NEC member Christine Shawcross put it.[472] But the party leadership made a political blunder by supporting the unionist establishment's 'Better Together' campaign in the 2014 referendum on Scottish independence. The independence vote was understood by many Scottish voters as a way to push back on Westminster-dictated austerity, and the leadership's stance alienated much of its working-class constituency. The former Labour strongholds of Glasgow, Dundee, North Lanarkshire and West Dunbartonshire voted for independence while Inverclyde and North Ayrshire voted 'no' by very narrow margins. The Scottish Labour party was seen as having split the independence vote, and the electorate took its revenge in the 2015 general election when the SNP, which had led the independence campaign, took 40 of Labour's seats and left it with only one MP.[473] In England, the Lib Dem vote collapsed after its association with the austerity policies of the coalition, many of its supporters departing for the Green Party,[474] and a full Tory government took power. Once more the Labour leadership failed to challenge either the Tory narrative that the economic crash was due to overspending on social services, or the media barrage blaming the problems of the welfare state on benefit 'scroungers'. Labour's shadow work and pensions minister Rachel Reeves amplified this discourse, telling the *Guardian*: 'We are not the party of people on benefits', claiming that Labour only represented 'working people'.[475]

After the election defeat the Blairites had expected to reclaim the party leadership. But members were sick of the authoritarian party management that had denied them a democratic voice, and they resisted a return to the hegemony of New Labour neoliberalism. The introduction of one-member-one-vote by the Collins Review in 2014 created an opportunity for them to make their voices heard in the leadership election. In fact, it was on the initiative of two mainstream members that an influential Facebook petition was launched appealing for an anti-austerity candidate to be nominated, a sign of the shift in grassroots opinion.[476] The movement of the membership to the left created a space for Corbyn to join the election, opening up a new political discourse facilitated by social media. His candidacy attracted people from the anti-austerity movement into the ambit of Labour politics, joining the party specifically to vote for him. Largely self-motivated groups sprang up in his support, which were later tied into a national structure with the formation of Momentum.

Corbyn's nomination transformed the nature of the leadership campaign – volunteers found that prospective supporters needed little persuading once they learned about his presence on the ballot. A definitive turning point was the PLP's abstention on the Tory budget which cut £12 billion from benefits, threatening to plunge 40,000 children into poverty.[477] Shadow chancellor Chris Leslie described the policy as 'necessary', and refused to oppose, or even criticise, most of the budget's key decisions. Parliamentary leader Harriet Harman also accepted the austerity agenda – like Rachel Reeves, she claimed that opposition would allow the Tories to represent Labour as 'the party of benefits'. Corbyn was the only leadership candidate to vote against the budget, and his close colleague John McDonnell declared he would 'swim through vomit' to vote against the cuts.[478]

Corbyn and his colleagues both reflected the intensifying grassroots opposition to austerity and contributed to politicising the extra-parliamentary protest movement with a moral stand that distinguished them from the rest of the political class. Their principled position also resonated with the party's existing supporters. In his book, *The Candidate*, Alex Nunns drew attention to the transformation of loyal party sentiment after 2010, something that is often overlooked compared to the political shift in the leadership of the unions or the visible flood of new members into the party in 2015. Michael Calderbank of the Brent Central constituency explained this change in the membership by the turn away from New Labour which 're-legitimised more traditional Labour. There was a decisive belief that the Blair years were behind us and we had to move on from the Iraq War, we had to acknowledge mistakes, we had to recover a sense that Labour stood for something different. … None of the answers that were coming through from the party's top were connecting with those basic realities [like the housing crisis], and suddenly Jeremy was there making the case for rent control, making the case for regulating the banks, and it got an echo.'[479]

From early July of 2015, a surge of popular support for Corbyn saw more and more people come to his rallies and volunteers signing up for his campaign. Polling in August found not only that Corbyn had enormous support among newly-joined members, but also led among those who had joined before 2010 when the party was under the leadership of Blair and Brown. At the same time, the unions played an important role by supporting his candidacy: Corbyn won the backing of Unite the union and Unison, as well as the smaller postal workers' union, the communication workers, ASLEF and TSSA. The election result gave him 59.5 per cent of the total votes cast, shocking the PLP: of the 36 MPs who had signed Corbyn's nomination papers, only 14 actually voted for him. While Labour's membership had responded to its experiences of austerity by moving to the left, the PLP remained trapped in a neoliberal Westminster bubble. Labour MPs would take public positions on 'progressive' causes like restrictions on payday loans and gay rights, but would not criticise New Labour's record of extending the principle of welfare individualisation, which the coalition then used to make absolute reductions in benefits.

Corbyn's vision of nationalisation embodied the re-thinking the party had undertaken in the 1970s, that sought an alternative to the corporate bureaucracies created by Attlee's government. Announcing his plan for the railways, Corbyn declared: 'I want the railways back in public ownership. But public control should mean just that: so we should have passengers, rail workers and government too, cooperatively running the railways ... in our interests and not for private profit.'[480] His Bennite stress on democratic participation at all levels offered empowerment to party members who had been shut out of decision-making under the Blair regime. Nunns comments that 'every aspect of Corbyn's candidacy, from his own selfless demeanour to the specific form of rail nationalisation he was proposing, was about inviting people to take part.'[481]

The opening up of a space for socialist discourse encouraged a new generation of activists, who had rejected party politics and had come to political consciousness through the leaderless social protest movements, to join the Labour Party in order to support Corbyn, attracted by his own participation in the protests and his orientation to grassroots democracy. His reputation and style as a politician marked him out as different from New Labour. After becoming leader, he appointed a shadow cabinet that included 16 women and 15 men, a first in British history. As leading feminist author Selma James pointed out, he sought not only to achieve gender balance in parliament, but also pay equity for women who are 'over-represented in the lowest-paying sectors: cleaning, catering and caring – vital sectors of our economy, doing valuable work, but not work that is fairly rewarded or equally respected.'[482] A letter signed by James and over 70 prominent anti-racist intellectuals said that 'no other British politician in recent memory has been so dedicated to working with us in our communities, in order to overturn racism and achieve justice for those of us facing oppression and injustices'.[483]

Corbyn's politics were not just a re-run of his mentor Tony Benn's: they had been updated over the years, incorporating the outlooks of environmental and social justice movements. Moreover, he championed an ethical foreign policy that took on board the interests of the global South, in particular defending the rights of Palestinians, apologising for the British role in the Iraq war, and indicating he would end collusion with military dictatorships like Saudi Arabia.

The social basis of the Corbyn 'movement'

Corbyn's support embodied both a left tradition within Labour and something qualitatively new. Phil Burton-Cartledge argues that a mass of individuals atomised by neoliberal society became activated through their reception of the politics of the leadership campaign. He categorises the new membership as either originating from the network of existing left activists, or as potential Labour supporters who had been alienated from the party by the Blair leadership.[484] However, to describe them as consisting of a 'mass of individuals' misses the qualitative turn from individualised radical protests to the politicisation of specific social layers that entered the Labour Party. Activists from movements such as Climate Camp, UK Uncut, the mass student protests against tuition fee increases, and the anti-war and anti-austerity movements who had specifically rejected parliamentary politics, saw in Corbyn something worth joining the party for. Moreover, a new class – the precariat – had been created by the global economy, working low-wage insecure jobs on zero hours without benefits. It included many young college-educated people with huge debts and no prospects, who joined the Labour Party and Momentum in large numbers.

The anti-austerity activists who joined Corbyn's campaign moulded its innovative approaches to organising and policy. They brought with them the concept of non-hierarchical democracy and the idea of building a better society in the here and now, rather than relying on state reform achieved from above. These ideas merged with Corbyn's emphasis on grassroots democracy to create a new politics that sought to use the central power of the state to support bottom-up participatory organisation of the economy. As Nunns puts it, Corbyn's anti-austerity message, fused with his Bennite ideas, sounded fresh to a new generation. His vision 'felt both contemporary *and* like a return to Labour's core values'.[485]

Younger members of the precariat were organically drawn to the campaign's participatory message. Liam Young, who was 19 when he got involved, writes that the reason it attracted young people was because its new politics was 'centred on young people's value-driven desires to change the world for the better – through collective solidarity, respect and equality'. Despite Corbyn's age, his anti-war activism 'spoke to the wider scope of what he stood for: primarily, what is fair and just'. Young had worked part-time at Sports Direct when doing A-levels so he could pay for books. However, earning only £3.50 an hour and spending most of it on fares and food, 'I was doing exactly what is asked of all of us, but I received no real reward for it. This is the same story for many people my age. It is why so many decided that it was time to get involved at this election [in 2017], because for so long we had been sold a vision that never seemed to come to fruition.'[486]

A lecturer at Goldsmith's College in London described his students' situation in a letter to the *Guardian*: 'it has been plain for some time that there has been a rising tide of political resentment reflected in social media networking, demonstrations and packed meetings. It just had no focus until Corbyn came along. The irony (and the untold press story) is that many young Corbyn supporters are not particularly left-wing ... they face an insecure job future, enormous debts and soaring rents. Yet no one seemed to be paying attention to their predicament and addressing their concerns.'[487]

Left journalist Richard Seymour argued that Corbyn's leadership victory was made possible by his mobilising a 'radicalised minority', a coalition of 'politically polyamorous young people, trade unionists, and left-wing supporters of Old Labour'.[488] But Seymour's use of quasi-sociological categories does little to clarify the dynamic of the movement that built up around Corbyn, attributing agency to the activists and strategists in the campaign rather than exploring the spontaneous activities of party members and the public. For example, Seymour describes in detail the response to Corbyn's unexpected appearance before a crowd of concert-goers at Tranmere Rovers football ground during the 2017 general election campaign. His advisers thought it a risk; but while he was speaking, the crowd began to sing the now-familiar refrain 'Oh Jeremy Corbyn'. Their reaction 'wasn't because of Corbyn's personal magnetism,' Seymour explains; it would not have happened without 'a profound change taking place'. He didn't mean any profound social or political change expressed by the concert-goers, however, but had in mind the ability of social media to circumvent the official political narrative.[489] Social media did play an important part in Corbyn's campaign, but it didn't *create* a 'Corbyn movement'. It facilitated a new discourse around Corbyn's leadership bid that enabled many people who were self-organising in his support to emerge as a movement. However, it was the discourse itself that connected like-minded people together in a movement from below.

Interviews with Labour members and supporters conducted by this author in October 2016 found that those who supported Corbyn were not motivated by any specific policies, instead singling out his ethics and recognising their own beliefs reflected in his approach to socialism. My findings are consistent with interviews carried out by the *Guardian* after

Corbyn's first speech at the party conference in 2015: Claire Wigzell, Leeds: 'He speaks as an ordinary person talking about things that really matter to him. It is not brilliant rhetoric but it is authentic and real.' Patricia Neira, Tynemouth: 'Lovely to hear more about activism, human rights and social justice – socialism at its best, and it's a welcome change from the New Labour "Tory appeasement" way of doing things.'[490]

A return to ethical socialism

As Brent Central's Michael Calderbank indicated, existing Labour members' responses to austerity and inequality were mediated by their conception of what Labour should stand for. Their support for Corbyn stemmed not only from his commitment to bottom-up democracy but also because it was combined with ethical socialism, an expression of his politics maintained over many years that aligned him with the shift in the party, with anti-austerity protestors and returning ex-members. When Corbyn voted against the Tory benefit cuts 'he was at one with the majority of Labour members on what they considered to be a moral issue,' notes Nunns.[491]

The significance of the renewal of ethical socialism among the party membership is that it connects to a long tradition within the labour movement. Eric Shaw clarifies how New Labour, while retaining the social democratic principle of redistribution, had abandoned ethical socialism in its policies and practice. The ethical socialist critique of capitalism was about more than social inequality, it also repudiated the way the system 'extolled the values of acquisitiveness, ruthless competitiveness and individual aggrandisement', derived from the practices of the market. In contrast, the welfare state was intended to be insulated from market forces and to embody the values of public service, solidarity, altruism and cooperation. This notion of the importance of the public service ethos had survived the decline of the industrial working class because it was 'historically deeply embedded in both the ideology and the culture of the Labour party'.[492]

Corbyn's ethical socialist values were apparent when he described socialism as a type of society where 'we each care for all, everybody caring for everybody else', appealing to a strongly-held popular desire for social support that seeks to restore collectivist priorities.[493] At the party conference in 2015, Corbyn posited the unifying ideal of 'shared majority British values' such as 'fair play for all', defined against the selfish individualism of hedge fund-backed Tory leaders, and attributed his election to the idea of 'a kinder politics and a more caring society'.[494] At the 2017 conference, he criticized the Tories not only for driving down wages, but also for their promotion of ruthless competitiveness and individual acquisitiveness: 'their disregard for rampant inequality, the hollowing out of our public services, the disdain for the powerless and the poor have made our society more brutal and less caring.'[495]

Ethical socialists seek to integrate the community through a sense of belonging and shared fate. While the revisionist right concluded in the 1950s that the future of social democracy was tied to the efficient management of the capitalist economy, the vision of ethical socialism persisted insofar as its values are embodied in the universalist aspects of the welfare state, which both secured a fairer distribution of life-chances and 'a mode of human interaction in which people related and behaved towards each other as equals in a spirit of mutual respect'. An important corollary to this principle for Labour is that the public domain should be insulated from market forces and commercial competition. Sustaining a large and expanding public sphere has come therefore to be seen as the principal institutional expression of ethical socialist values.[496] Hence the National Health Service stands as an oasis of egalitarian social relations in a capitalist society and has taken on the responsibility for the overall well-being of the public, even though that is not what was intended at its foundation. The difficulties faced by Thatcherite governments intending to dismantle it and its current centrality in the public response to the coronavirus pandemic is a testament to the tenacity of the social change begun in 1945. People continue to expect healthcare as a right of citizenship, not as consumers.

I found evidence of the persistence of ethical socialism at Labour's grassroots in interviews with members and supporters from a wide spectrum of party opinion. There was a surprising consensus on the need to impose redistributive taxation as a solution to the problem of extreme inequality, irrespective of members' views on Corbyn. This confirmed the extent to which the membership had repudiated New Labour's position that inequality is necessary for economic growth. The state, said interviewees, should enforce payment of taxation by corporations and the rich, while making social necessities universally available by taking them into public ownership. Some Labour members more clearly expressed ethical socialist ideas of creating a more humane and cooperative society. Julia, an adult education teacher, said socialism was 'where people are properly cared for ... a kinder, far more caring society', while Labour voter Catherine stipulated that certain things like housing, care work, and education should be kept within the public domain 'and not subject to the market process'.[497]

Members had a wide range of opinions on nationalisation, although there was a unanimous rejection of privatisation. Ideas which in the 1970s were championed by a minority in the labour movement have now become commonplace. Most wanted a mixed economy, while some had merged together ideas about increased efficiency, public accountability, and workers' control of management. Interviewees under 30 specifically advocated a non-statist form of nationalisation, such as workers' cooperatives, viewing public ownership as a way to create public accountability and allow democratic control by the people employed in it – close to a Bennite position and the outlook of anti-inequality social movements. They were more likely to think in terms of socialism as a movement of social empowerment allowing for greater individual freedom, as well as levelling power relations within society.[498]

The unifying role of ethical socialism in creating the basis of Corbyn's support was missed by political commentators, who assessed its component parts separately. Left cultural theorist Jeremy Gilbert, for example, wrote that while the Corbyn movement is 'a true grassroots mobilisation', it is at the same time 'a top-down project placing loyalty to a single individual at its centre, with almost no real debate on policy or strategy'. Within Corbynism, he argues, there are two opposed tendencies: 'a decentralised political movement that would like to build a more democratic and cooperative economy' coexisting with 'a top-down project focused entirely on maintaining Corbyn's leadership, which is largely proposing a return to the statist social democracy of the post-war era.'[499] However, while it is true that the difficulties Corbyn faced with the parliamentary party encouraged the concentration of power in the leader's office, conflicting with the ideal of membership empowerment, that is not the same as reinstating statist social democracy as a policy. I argue, against Gilbert's view, that despite the paucity of debate on policy and strategy within the left, Corbyn's supporters have developed a new politics that seeks to combine legislative power with the potential of participatory democracy. Their mutual reinforcement offers the possibility of implementing more radical and longer-lasting social change than state-centric reform alone.

Corbyn's ability to communicate Labour's socialist principles to the public in a way that connected them with the political fight against austerity was his great strength. The inclusivity of his message enabled him to make a human connection with crowds at rallies and events. When he visited the site of the Grenfell Tower tragedy, whose victims included many immigrants of colour, local residents and survivors flocked round him. By contrast, prime minister Theresa May spoke only to police and emergency services.[500] Whatever limitations Corbyn may have as a politician, what is important is the fact that many thousands of new members were attracted to Labour because of his leadership, and they felt empowered to participate in and take responsibility for the party's policies. However, their instinctive support for his ethical socialism did not translate into badly-needed political education on Labour's transformative economic vision and the building of a firmer base for the party's new left.

Brexit and the second leadership challenge

Thatcherite governments over the course of eighteen years had shifted the political consensus to a neoliberal mean, and New Labour accepted the constraints of this framework for its efforts at limited redistribution. Thatcher could not have carried through the economic and political changes she did without first discrediting social democratic ideas, and New Labour followed the same approach by constructing an image of 'Old Labour' and the welfare state as a tax-and-spend boondoggle. But what was novel about New Labour itself was 'first, the cool and deliberate way in which it attuned its policies and objectives so they corresponded as closely as possible to the contours of power, and, second, its very marked disinclination to challenge the wielders of private power'.[501] When political office is connected to the contours of power, it forms an incentive to resist challenges to the status quo. Most of the parliamentary party was selected under Blair, which screened out anyone who might disagree with New Labour's identification with the hierarchies and conventions of the existing state.

For this reason, the PLP and party bureaucracy were determined to overturn Corbyn's mandate from the membership. Immediately following the Brexit referendum in 2016, shadow cabinet members used the tactic of a series of highly public resignations in an attempt to force Corbyn to step down, and following that, 172 Labour MPs voted no confidence in him, triggering a second leadership election. Corbyn had campaigned for the party's Remain policy more energetically than any other politician, yet he was criticised for a 'lacklustre' approach. His decision to support the immediate implementation of Article 50 so as to trigger the Brexit leave process was attacked by MPs and by commentators in the corporate media, even though he qualified it with a call for negotiations to protect jobs and working conditions. His campaigning had brought him into closer touch with the electorate than most of his critics, and he attributed the referendum result to the anger of communities in the face of instability and deprivation caused by austerity. It is probable his reported 'seven and a half' out of ten support for the bloc reflected the views he had encountered, not just his own assessment of the EU.[502]

While his Article 50 decision was controversial, it could also be understood as stemming from his respect for popular democracy rather than a consideration of parliamentary tactics. Despite the actions of the administration at the party's offices in Southside, which shut down CLP and branch meetings while the second leadership contest was under way, Corbyn was re-elected with a larger majority. It subsequently emerged that the party's headquarters staff were openly hostile to Corbyn's leadership, and used their positions to suspend or exclude thousands of his supporters from the party during the leadership election.[503] His political orientation at that time could be seen as an attempt to overcome the political divisions within the party and to avoid the trap of playing off 'leavers' against 'remainers', instead focusing on the problems facing all sections of British society by accepting the referendum result and working to negotiate a political settlement with the EU.

The referendum had unleashed social forces that turned a Tory political project into a constitutional crisis. Cameron originally called it to counter the electoral threat from the anti-EU party UKIP, which was attracting support from the ultra-right of the Tories and its voters by blaming immigration for welfare cuts. The narrow victory of the Leave vote, however, transformed his attempt to deflect the political cost of austerity into a crisis of governmental legitimacy, and Cameron immediately resigned. The vote cut across party lines, superseded the constitutional sovereignty of parliament, and threw its authority into disarray. Conflicting interpretations of the mandate set the legislature and the executive in opposition to each other, and precipitated a constitutional crisis requiring the intervention of the judiciary.

The framing of the question presented to voters was the result of right-wing pressure for a misleading choice: it was changed from whether or not the UK should remain in the EU, to 'should the UK remain a member of the EU or leave the EU?' as though Leave was a simple answer to a complex question. Labour's position of 'remain and reform' was not on the ballot and got no media exposure. While the British establishment would have preferred to stay in the European Union, it was politically split. The business sector was opposed to severing ties with Europe, while the Leave campaign was bankrolled by hedge fund managers like Nigel Farage and Arron Banks who were accustomed to taking extreme risks with other people's wealth. Their adoption of a campaigning strategy that relied on racist imagery and language led predictably to a rise in violent attacks on immigrants.

The consolidation of a financialised economy had encouraged the right wing of the Tory party to envisage Britain as a European Singapore, with negligible regulation and worker rights, which Cameron and Theresa May accommodated in an attempt to counter the nationalist appeal of UKIP. Cameron had been playing up warnings of a migrant threat from the

Mediterranean only a year before the referendum, while as home secretary Theresa May had created a 'hostile environment' for immigrants. This was not new: the Tories had spent years trying to undermine Blair's ability to win elections 'by experimenting with different types of dog-whistle anti-immigrant rhetoric, often combined with demonisation of the EU', points out journalist Patrick Cockburn.[504] The Leave campaign built on this rhetoric, projecting the identity of a 'British public', British-born and majority white citizens defined in opposition to immigrant 'outsiders'.

The referendum's divisions brought to the surface the unmet needs of communities that had been sidelined for generations, areas with the lowest wages in the country and with a high proportion of unskilled jobs. The yes-no question polarised the outcome, framed by powerful elites with the idea of 'taking our country back'. An academic study found that the contraction of the welfare state after 2010 was a 'key driver' of the rise of UKIP and correlated closely with the Leave vote.[505] The highest Brexit vote was located in small towns in England and in areas in the North-east that had been deindustrialised, that had suffered disproportionately from austerity-driven benefit cuts, and where prospects for improvement were neutralised by corrupt and right-wing municipal authorities. Even before the coalition's imposition of austerity, financialisation under Thatcherite governments had encouraged a regional drain of resources to London and the south-east that was sustained under New Labour, with the consequence that the victims of globalisation found that their objections were ignored by the traditional processes of the political system. The Brexit campaign succeeded by blaming Brussels and the EU for the grievances of the 'left-behind' communities and their sense of political disempowerment.

Satnam Virdee and Brendan McGeever argue that a consequence of the Brexit campaign has been a 'politicisation of Englishness'. A latent longing for empire in the context of the structural decline of British capitalism activated racialised structures of feeling about national belonging and immigration, they maintain. Downward mobility, in the aftermath of a succession of class defeats under Thatcherite governments, combined to produce a politics of nationalist resentment that found its voice in the Brexit vote. New Labour's complicity in the neoliberal settlement also created the social and political conditions for the result. A narrative took hold which made the losers from globalisation the 'white working class', framing the consciousness of those in deindustrialised areas and 'othering' black and brown Britons as well as EU citizens.[506] However, the multiple motivations of the electorate coalesced into a 'Leave/Remain' identity, changing the nature of the 'other' to those who voted differently in the referendum.[507] This was reflected in

Nigel Farage's later decision to abandon UKIP because of its association with overt racism and launch instead the single-issue Brexit party.

A nation for the many

Labour was able to reassert its voice during the snap election called by Theresa May for June 2017 with the intention of improving her parliamentary majority and strengthening her hand against the far right of her party in the Brexit negotiations. In a presidential-style campaign May continuously repeated the slogan of a 'strong and stable' government. Opinion polls had indicated a 20-point lead for the Tories at the beginning of the campaign, but as election day approached their apparent lead began to decline as election rules enforced equal media time for the parties and more impartial reporting of Labour's policies. The result was that the Tories lost 13 of their 17-seat majority and Labour gained 30, leaving a hung parliament which was only resolved by an arrangement between May and Northern Ireland's Democratic Unionists.

The Labour Party's election manifesto, *For the Many, not the Few*, was popular with the electorate and signalled a clear break with neoliberalism. Its title referenced Percy Bysshe Shelley's poem *The Mask of Anarchy*, lines from which were quoted by Corbyn at the end of his election speeches: 'Rise like lions after slumber/In unfathomable number/Shake your chains to earth like dew/Which in sleep have fallen on you –/Ye are many, they are few.'[508] Although its economic proposals were moderate, and less radical than previous Labour manifestos, it challenged the austerity narrative by promising good local jobs in future-oriented industries; a new programme of council house building; free education; a working NHS; state-run infrastructure to create the foundation for successful businesses; minimising the social advantages of inherited wealth; and a reduction of the extreme inequality created by financialisation. The overriding message was a revival of collectivism, reversing the forty-year efforts of Thatcherite governments to dismantle the welfare state.

At a macroeconomic level, the manifesto's proposals were basically Keynesian, but it combined them with plans for new patterns of public ownership of industry and the decentralisation of economic power to local communities, together with the creation of a national investment bank linked to a network of new regional banks. Even though it was put together in the short time allowed by the calling of the snap election, the manifesto was successful in projecting a unifying narrative that countered the divisiveness of the Brexit vote and prevented the Tories from making it the central issue. It was leaked to the press a week before its launch, but this had the effect of publicising policies which polls found to be overwhelmingly popular. Clear majorities of voters supported renationalising the railways, the energy companies, Royal Mail, and the banning of zero-hours contracts, together with building 100,000 more council houses each year and abolishing university tuition fees.[509]

The expansion of the party membership created a new relationship with the electorate, enabling a mass get-out-the-vote campaign on election day in 2017. Mike Phipps discovered that 'many of the new intake were wholly new to formal political activity, like the canvasser in the marginal constituency of Hampstead and Kilburn whom I met on polling day, whose only experience of campaigning was donning a Corbyn t-shirt and starting random conversations with people on London's vast public transport network about the leader's ideas'.[510] The membership's efforts were complemented by a spontaneous surge of support: 3.5 million more people voted Labour in 2017 than had in 2015, vindicating the leadership's strategy of expanding the electorate to include those who had not previously voted. In most cases, the party had no idea who they were.

What the manifesto achieved through its concrete radicalism was to change the scope of political discourse in the election campaign, moving the political centre to the left and creating a space for the open discussion of social democratic values. Even some MPs not favourably disposed to Corbyn welcomed its message, which directly addressed how society could be made fairer. Its comparatively moderate agenda posed the restoration of a collectively caring society that matched principles deeply embedded in the labour movement, positing a reversal of the flow of wealth and power from the poor to the rich by taxing the rich to fund social welfare. It enabled Labour to build a new electoral coalition in 2017 that encompassed layers of the precariat, the young, the well-educated, and a large part of its traditional support in the manual working class.

Labour's strategy and 'new kind of politics'

Practical examples of some of the manifesto's proposals can be found in innovative Labour councils that have sought new ways to deal with the defunding of their communities by cuts in government support. One prominent case cited in the *Alternative Models of Ownership* report, commissioned by John McDonnell and released just before the election, is the 'Preston model'. It uses the spending power of the city's 'anchor' institutions, such as local government, hospitals and universities, to favour local supply chains, local businesses and cooperatives and so retain wealth in the community. Along with its new procurement policy, Preston is paying its council workers the real Living Wage, has advanced support for credit unions, a community bank, encouraged retiring business owners to sell their companies to their employees, and is creating a cooperative infrastructure similar to that of Mondragon in Spain (which has a federation of 257 worker cooperatives). All this was achieved in the absence of central government support, but the potential relocation of major government institutions outside of London could make them important contributors to local economies.[511]

The significance of this model to the left is that it signals a path to a more democratic and inclusive form of state. The potential of the Preston 'community wealth building' strategy is that it will reduce the influence of corporate outsourcing and reinstate local economic decision-making. Corbyn supporters Christine Berry and Joe Guinan elaborate this strategy much further through an approach to state power that would facilitate radical decentralisation and popular participation. They explain that this approach would encourage the building of local counterweights to the power of financial markets and create a social basis for a democratic transformation of the state so that central and municipal governments will work with and be accountable to local communities. Their perspective does not rely on central government to control the economy through nationalised industries, but instead advocates building new centres of power from the bottom up, diverting the circulation of capital from global corporations so as to retain it within local communities, and creating new forms of democratic community and public ownership that would be the foundation of a cooperative social metabolism.

De-privatisation, insourcing, regulating and taxing speculative financial activity would displace the stranglehold of the financial markets, and a larger worker-owned and cooperative sector would be a base for 'a new place-based economics and politics'. Public banking institutions would help grow this new economy. On a national scale, 'the NHS has the potential to become the backbone of an industrial strategy around the production of goods and services for health and community well-being,' which would keep public funds in circulation and anchor jobs. To break the Treasury stranglehold on spending and economic decision-making, its powers and budgets should be devolved to local councils, reversing the Thatcherite centralisation of economic power. Labour, they say, must 'purposely rebuild' local government strength as part of a strategy for building new sources of popular power. This doesn't exclude an important role for the central state, however, in taking control of banks, transport, or establishing the framework for a green economy. A left agenda should be aimed at 'transforming the state itself' so that its power can be used in a genuinely progressive and democratic way.[512]

Academic critics Matt Bolton and Frederick Pitts strongly opposed the Preston model, describing it as analogous to what they call Bennite economic 'protectionism', which they consider reactionary in the context of globalised trade and production; local wealth, they argue, can only be legitimated in the international market since they believe 'we live in a world structured and socially reproduced as and by capital, a social relation which exists as a world market' so that 'local wealth only appears as such through its validation as social, or global, wealth'.[513] Their key assumption is that the use-values needed to maintain a community are only accessible through the global market, as though all commodities have to pass through the portals of Amazon. However, if the surplus value produced in a community is redirected from the circuit of global accumulation into local supply chains, the Preston model will provide more jobs and local control over the economy, increase the tax base for local services and keep wealth in the form of both money and control over assets within the local area. It helps to consolidate productive capacity – especially the workforce – in a way that the building of an Amazon warehouse would not. The model is not socialism, but it has in practice improved people's lives in the immediate present, reduced unemployment in the city, and strengthened the hand of the labour movement in its struggle against local deprivation and government cuts.

The radical economist Robin Murray provided a solid theoretical foundation for the Preston model. He argued that the civil economy is divided between those parts driven by social goals, and those which are subject to the imperatives of capital accumulation. There is nothing intrinsic in components of the social economy (the household, the grant economy, the market, and the state) that drives them towards capital accumulation, he said. They are not separate economies but represent semi-autonomous and interrelated economic fields of force. 'As economies they are oriented to their own social goals; each can operate in the market in pursuit of their goals without being drawn into the vortex of accumulation.' He goes on to note that parallel to globalisation is a surge in civil economic activity – from non-profits to cooperatives – that can be seen as a counter movement to global neoliberalism. 'Globalisation of the mainstream economy and the tensions to which it has given rise has … provoked its opposite, an intensely local, self-governing, socially embedded alternative.' Murray's theories point to a strategy of transforming the state so that it supports the creative capacities of the social economy while resisting the demands of private capital, combining the theories of cooperative socialism with the idea of participatory democracy.[514] Moreover, cooperative self-government means sharing knowledge openly and rejecting the treatment of others as competitors, with the consequence of resisting the internalisation of entrepreneurialism as a self-image, which Dardot and Laval characterise as a 'double refusal' of neoliberal social relations and psychology.[515]

The Corbyn leadership evidently opened up a political space for a new theorisation of the socialist agenda that includes radical proposals for a transformative change in the structure of ownership and economic power, while addressing the challenge of integrating the state with the civil spheres of the economy. These issues enlivened the debates at the Momentum-organised 'The World Transformed' events that paralleled the party conferences and that have worked towards a coherent strategy for resisting global corporate power. An example of this fundamental re-thinking of policy was *Land for the Many*, a report on housing produced for the party. It goes beyond the proposals of the 2017 manifesto, pointing out that even 300,000 new house builds annually would not reduce house prices more than 7 per cent. It recommends that 'a Labour government should set an explicit goal to stabilise house prices, so that wages can catch up and the house-price-to-income ratio can gradually fall.' It set its sights on restricted land ownership which is at the root not only of social and political power in Britain, but also the whole economic model based on inflation of house prices and growing indebtedness of the poor. The immediate problem is that easily available mortgage credit, the high levels of speculative demand from buy-to-let landlords as well as financial elites, the reduction in social housing and the need by many to escape the insecurity of private rental accommodation have pushed up house prices to 'unprecedented heights'. Cheap bank credit and low property taxation has only benefited asset holders and allowed land rent extraction to drive up inequality.[516]

The report notes that acting to deflate the housing market in order to aid renters and the homeless risks households being stuck in negative equity and a consequent economic contraction. It therefore proposes the creation of community land ownership institutions that would buy the land beneath houses and lease it to home buyers. Along with proposals for tax reform that would replace council tax with a progressive property tax, as well as a surcharge on all properties owned by those who are not resident in the UK for tax purposes, the report suggests the Bank of England should use its macroprudential powers to encourage a shift in bank lending away from real estate towards more strategically useful sectors of the economy. The combination of community land ownership with bank intervention is significant because it gives a concrete example of how the new transformational politics envisages the role of the central state: to guarantee basic social needs like housing, healthcare, education, and heat, and to make structural reforms that facilitate participatory democratic control of the economy at the local level.

A Socialist Green New Deal

Labour's relative success in the 2017 election had alarmed the political establishment. Since the Tories no longer had an absolute majority, Theresa May was unable to negotiate a Brexit deal that would satisfy either Labour – who wanted to retain the worker rights and safeguards associated with the EU – or the far right of the Tories, who wanted to ditch those rights. Media attention was focused on the small group of anti-Corbyn Labour MPs who split away to form 'Change UK', joined by some dissident Tories, and an imaginary Liberal Democrat resurgence. The possibility of a future Corbyn-led government meant that the leadership focused on holding the parliamentary party together until the next election, avoiding disciplinary action on overt challenges from right-wing MPs. Brexit negotiations trapped the leadership in Westminster politics, which tended to dissipate the anti-austerity mass movement that had flocked to the party between 2015 and 2017.

The issue created major internal divisions, when the membership's generally anti-Brexit sentiment was leveraged by the party's centre-right with the intention of undermining Corbyn's support. Political confusion and division on the left enabled the right to sponsor a membership campaign for a second referendum at the party's 2018 conference. Shadow Brexit secretary Keir Starmer unilaterally introduced the idea that there would be a Remain option in a second referendum. His conference speech succeeded in shifting the emphasis of Labour's policy in such a way as to accentuate the divisions between remain supporters and MPs from leave-voting Labour constituencies in the north who warned at the time that the policy would lose the party votes in a new election.

Corbyn's opponents seized on his attempts to negotiate a compromise position to portray him as unprincipled, and they alienated Labour voters who saw it as trying to overturn a democratic vote. Another compromise involved easing the conditions for trigger ballots in constituency selections, rather than implementing mandatory reselection of MPs. This had the effect of stalling the effort to change the composition of the PLP, and at election time constituency parties were reluctant to use the trigger ballot process since it meant negative campaigning against the existing candidate. While wrangling over these issues, the left did little to turn outwards and build a socialist sensibility in the electorate on problems that directly affected it.

At the same time, new institutions like The World Transformed[517] and the Common Wealth think tank[518] were giving voice to the emergent political possibilities of an empowered membership, reaching far to the left of the leadership. Grassroots campaigns advocated bold ideas on climate change, free movement and abolishing private schools. Angus Satow co-founded one such campaign, 'Labour for a Green New Deal,' in the wake of the 2017 election, when it seemed as though a Corbyn-led Labour Party might soon be elected. 'Labour's membership gained confidence', he writes. 'With a party leadership that would actually listen to its members, a group of young climate activists could start a new campaign, organise in CLPs, and pass a radical vision for a fundamentally transformed economy, with ground-breaking decarbonisation targets at party conference.' But it had a downside: although the campaign pushed Labour further on climate than the 2017 manifesto, 'the rise of policy-based campaigns like ours masked our failure to arrest the continued decline of the trade union movement and community "red bases" of class power.'[519]

The 2019 party conference in Brighton was marked by the radicalism of the policies adopted on a wide range of issues – reducing the working week to four days; closing all immigration detention centres and allowing free movement after Brexit; establishing generic drugs manufacturing under the NHS to undercut drug company monopolies; and the flagship policy of a transformative Green New Deal that ties together decarbonisation of the economy with new skilled jobs and a reduction of inequality. An attempt to commit the party to an EU Remain position was rejected in favour of a compromise that pledged a second referendum between remaining in the EU and a Labour-negotiated Brexit after the election of a Labour government. All the resolutions were the result of organised grassroots campaigns, but what clearly accelerated the Green New Deal policy were the demands of the Extinction Rebellion protests that were taken on board by the party leadership, enlarging the political space for membership intervention at constituency level.

When thousands of protestors closed down important road junctions in London for several days, they brought climate change to the centre of political discourse.[520] The impact of the protests enabled Corbyn to get parliament to accept a declaration of climate change emergency, which in turn legitimised the protests, and at the same time he announced a more detailed 'Green Industrial Revolution' policy that linked reduced carbon emissions to a massive investment in renewable energy.[521] The effective campaigning of 'Labour for a Green New Deal' persuaded more than 128 constituency parties to send in supportive motions, putting the policy top of the agenda for the Brighton conference.

The 2019 election manifesto offered pragmatic and integrated solutions to many of the systemic problems created by years of neoliberal governments, in particular rebuilding public services and repairing the damage done to the NHS by ten years of austerity. Some of its proposals, such as free broadband, were thought to be far-fetched at the time but after the coronavirus lockdown are seen as far-sighted. However, the manifesto lacked a clear narrative that would have enabled the party to counter the ferocity of the political establishment's ideological assault after the election was called. The compromise with the 'People's Vote' campaign for a second referendum, backed by many of Corbyn's opponents, was seen as unconvincing: even traditional Labour voters who had backed Remain considered it an undemocratic attempt to overturn the original decision.

The Tories were working single-mindedly to leverage the erosion of class affiliation with its Brexit campaigning. Boris Johnson's expulsion of 'One-Nation' Tories from the Conservatives after becoming prime minister in June consolidated far-right control of the government. The prorogation of parliament and the Supreme Court's subsequent ruling of it as unlawful enabled him to construct a narrative of systemic obstruction of the 'people's will' and fed into a propaganda onslaught on Labour, accompanied by a weaponised disinformation campaign on social media funded by an infusion of cash from unaccountable oligarchs. According to academic studies, negative press coverage of Labour was more than double the levels identified in 2017.[522] The direct appeal of Tory strategists to English nationalism with their slogans of 'Get Brexit Done' and 'levelling-up' was directly aimed at leave-voting constituencies and succeeded in winning votes in areas like the northeast and Yorkshire. This contrasted with Labour's success in places like Preston and Portsmouth, where innovative Labour councils were connected with a local network of social enterprises and cooperative organisations. The loss of 59 Labour seats, giving the Tories an overall majority of 80, marked the decline of the traditional Labour vote in northern and midlands constituencies, magnified by the first-past-the-post electoral system.

Labour strategists were not able to address the sense of disempowerment in left-behind communities and their susceptibility to the right-wing tabloid framing of their problems. Corbyn's initial instinct to respect the referendum result had maintained the support of these communities in 2017, but the party itself was divided, and the turn to support a second referendum hindered its attempt to focus the election on economic issues. In the event, it could not overcome the appeal of the Tories' populist message. The referendum had been the catalyst for an anti-establishment politics that supported Labour when it was seen as the anti-establishment party, but voted for Johnson when he successfully portrayed Theresa May and Labour as part of the parliamentary establishment frustrating Brexit.

The new politics developed within Labour was premised on the expectation that a party with a socialist leadership could win a working parliamentary majority, or at least another hung parliament. The extent of the Tory victory in terms of parliamentary seats came as a bitter blow to activists and contradicted their assumption that the 2017 result could be replicated. Corbyn himself announced he would stand down as leader. Predictably, the centrist current in the party blamed Corbyn's leadership for the defeat – despite the fact that the Labour vote had fallen much further under New Labour. In terms of votes cast, Labour won 13.5 million in 1997, 10.7 million in 2001 and 8.6 million in 2010 under the leadership of Blair and Brown. The Labour vote recovered slightly to 9.35 million in 2015, and in 2019 it was 10.3 million. The exceptional year was 2017 when Labour won 12.9 million votes. The party's policies themselves were popular, but simply presenting them to the electorate was not enough to overcome the sense of many traditional Labour voters that the political system would not deliver change that benefited them. The very forces of capitalist opposition that left theorists had anticipated would attempt to derail a socialist government in power had succeeded in preventing Labour from getting that far.

In this chapter, I discussed how the mass protests against the way Tory austerity intensified the economic marginalisation of young people and working-class communities merged into Labour politics after the nomination of Corbyn for party leader. His leadership campaign restored social democratic ideals and ethical socialist principles, which formed a strong political bond between him and the membership. Corbyn's supporters formed a new political constellation inspired by the participatory ideals emerging from twenty-first century social movements as well as an older socialist tradition, seeking radical change 'through an exciting array of new and old democratic forms, from worker ownership and public banks to land trusts and municipal energy companies'.[523] But the enthusiasm of Labour members canvassing in December's dark evenings could not overcome the political establishment's sustained focus on Brexit or the media demonisation of Corbyn.[524]

Regardless of the loss of Corbyn as Labour leader, his tenure has already achieved a dramatic alteration of the terms of political discourse on state intervention in the economy. May's and Johnson's governments both had to take on board some of Labour's redistributionist policies in face of the growing crisis facing health services and the immediate issue of homelessness. The Johnson government was forced to announce unlimited panic spending on the NHS after the extent of its deterioration was exposed by the urgent demands of the Covid-19 pandemic. It was a belated recognition by the government of the danger to the public from its ideologically motivated rundown of state institutions and its wilful refusal to take early measures to arrest the virus's spread. It also tacitly confirmed the failure of austerity and the necessity for a restoration of a collectivist approach to social problems.

The significance of Corbyn's leadership role was primarily as a symbolic focus for the radicalised membership to challenge bureaucratic control of the party apparatus and to diminish the influence of the parliamentary party. However, he was unable to maintain discipline in the PLP and was forced to compromise, under immense pressure, with the Brexit remain lobby. The Labour left was consumed with defending the party against accusations of institutional anti-semitism, which diverted it from extra-parliamentary campaigning in working-class communities, and it never cohered around a clear political perspective that would have distinguished a transformative agenda from a rudimentary ethical socialism. Momentum activist Sabrina Huck comments that the void in its political outlook 'was filled with a focus on a vague set of values (such as "fairness" or "kindness"), which can easily be attributed to a wide range of Labour politicians. Members who have supported Corbyn for these reasons will not see the contradictions in now backing Starmer.'[525] The party missed an historic opportunity to elect its first woman leader in frontbench MP Rebecca Long-Bailey, who stood as the Corbyn continuity candidate. Her political agency was undermined by accusations of being directed by male advisers,[526] while Starmer was able to draw on a traditional privileging of male leadership within Labour to present himself as more 'electable'.

The membership was persuaded by a narrative that blamed party disunity for Labour's defeat and believed Starmer's promise that he would end factionalism, while continuing to support the policies of the 2017 manifesto. What Starmer's notion of electability meant in practice, however, was a refusal to challenge the government's disastrous handling of the pandemic, and the reorientation of the party to the political centre so as to attract back the votes of older and more socially conservative Labour supporters who had defected to the Tories in 2019. Since he professed their switch in allegiance to be the result of hostility to the former leader rather than the party's Brexit stance, Starmer distanced himself from the Corbyn left by removing its representatives from front bench positions, eventually removing the Labour whip from Corbyn himself. This won Starmer the approval of the media, but split the membership and made him more dependent on support from the right. The appointment of a right-wing general secretary, David Evans, facilitated a crackdown on constituency discussion of the leadership's actions, at a time when the pandemic prevented CLPs from meeting in person.

Initially the left sought to cooperate with Starmer's supporters to form a centre-left coalition that would continue to campaign for Labour's 2017 policies. Andrew Fisher, a former adviser to Corbyn, argued that 'the Left can play a constructive (and, when necessary, constructively critical) role that reflects both our influence and the position of the current leadership … the Labour Left must work constructively to build on the best of Corbynism's legacy, while organising to remove the structural factors that inhibited its success.'[527] However, anti-democratic factional activity by full-time party officials outraged members and polarised the rank and file. Members left in droves, while accusations of antisemitism were used to suspend left activists and whole constituency parties so as to ensure a right-wing majority of delegates at the 2021 conference in Brighton. Rule changes pushed through the conference with the support of Unison delegates diminished the influence of the membership and consolidated right-wing control of the party apparatus. While left resolutions were passed with little opposition for a £15 per hour minimum wage, a Green New Deal, an ambitious council housing programme, and a historic condemnation of Israel's repression of Palestine, the leadership made clear that they would be ignored at election time.

Because the party's disciplinary structure is now being used to enforce political conformity, the left is faced with the necessity of waging a strategic battle to build social power and legitimacy both inside and outside of this structure. However, the curtailing of party democracy has not killed the vitality of the socialist ideal, evidenced not only in the overwhelming votes for left policy resolutions, but also in the enthusiasm and political determination of participants in The World Transformed and at conference fringe events. Although activists have resigned in protest at the bureaucratic suppression of the left, young members especially are committed to continue fighting within the party.

Conclusion

The new form of the socialist ideal has evolved historically in three phases: from a utopian dream of a cooperative commonwealth, through a belief in a statist model of nationalised industries and welfare provision, to one of combining central state with local democratic power. These stages in the development of the ideal correspond to changes in the orientation of the labour movement to the state. Before 1940, organised labour was shut out of political power and the actual state was experienced as a repressive force. To bring about socialism, activists envisaged an imaginary state, existing above classes. But government intervention came to be perceived as a positive good after the establishment of full employment and the welfare state by the 1945 Labour government. The militant opposition of the organised working class to the problematic role of the Wilson government, and the failure of Keynesian methods of economic intervention, prompted Tony Benn when a minister to demonstrate that support from within the state could legitimise workers' initiatives for reorganising production so as to save jobs. The Corbyn leadership took this further by opening up a new discourse of combining elective power with local community organising in such a way as to curb the flow of wealth to extractive international capital.

The coronavirus pandemic has ushered in a new historical moment. It has fractured capitalist society along fault lines that were already apparent – its economic dependency on global supply chains and consumer spending, the hollowing-out of the state, the number of people on precarious agency and zero-hours contracts. It has also accelerated the spontaneous growth of grassroots collective organisation. Lockdowns made access to the basic necessities of life more difficult and made prominent people's interdependence. As a result, the initiative in restoring social connections amidst the chaotic disruption of the economy is coming from within civil society itself. Local aid groups sprang up across the country, independent of the central state, and a popular response to the calls of footballer Marcus Rashford for free school meals forced a government U-turn. This resurgence of collective activity is an important political phenomenon that normalises social solidarity and changes how people relate to the market.

What now for the Labour left? In their comprehensive study of the new left, *Searching for Socialism*, Leo Panitch and Colin Leys consider it unlikely that activists will soon find any other way forward than continuing the struggle inside the Labour Party, since efforts to establish alternative left parties have had little success. The central dilemma for democratic socialists, they say, is how to discover and develop 'new political forms' adequate to addressing 'the contradictions being generated by twenty-first century capitalism' and 'the popular capacities needed to overcome them'.[528] In fact, this has already begun to happen, since the failure of conventional Labour politics has fostered new approaches and creative ideas for resistance within the broader labour movement. The consolidation of right-wing control of the party apparatus has, ironically, forced the left to broaden its focus from winning positions in CLPs to a longer-term perspective of participating in shopfloor union struggles and social movements outside the Labour Party. Bringing together the strands of popular opposition to a rentier-dominated economy has changed the political battleground for implementing a transformative economic agenda from a national to a local level. Community Wealth Building projects are concrete examples of economic development that can short-circuit the extraction of wealth by rentier capitalism. They also posit the building of new democratic institutions that bypass political restrictions on local government.

This shift in grassroots discourse means that the new form of the socialist ideal developed by theorists encouraged by Corbyn's leadership has emerged at exactly the right moment. It orients activists towards the self-empowerment of communities, reimagining socialism as the transformation of social relations through popular agency, buttressed by structural changes in ownership through central state legislation. Christine Berry has outlined how the left can develop a hegemonic socialist discourse about how to solve the problems facing society. The conditions have to be created, she argues, by putting down roots in communities and participating in existing grassroots struggles – combining practical help with political education that situates individual problems in relation to larger systemic forces that require collective action.[529] Rather than abstract calls for building a mass extra-parliamentary movement, she insists that a more concrete approach to movement-building is needed. Campaigning groups should be organised around shared political identities (such as renters, debtors, or NHS patients), that empower them to tackle common problems, rather than putting pressure on government actors to do it for them. Transformative change will depend on the collaborative efforts of specific groups within communities to make a real difference in people's lives, not something premised on social-democratic control of the state.[530]

Workplace organising is important to building collective economic power. But this faces significant difficulties arising from past working-class defeats and economic downsizing. Before the pandemic, trade union density in the working population nationally had declined from 30.7 per cent in 1997, to 27.4 per cent in 2009, and 23.4 per cent in 2018.[531] That is not the whole picture, however: some of the drop in union membership was reversed by new forms of organising in the growing gig economy. Although the numbers of organised workers in these sectors do not match the loss of members in manufacturing, their extreme exploitation has fostered a fierce militancy: strikes at fast-food corporations like McDonalds, supported by the bakers' union, have been joined by spontaneous walkouts in networks of delivery riders and Uber drivers. A 'new generation of small, radical, insurgent trade unions' has sprung up, such as the 'United Voices of the World' (UVW), which led successful direct actions among cleaners in London offices despite tension with the established bureaucracies of large unions like Unison.[532] While this form of struggle can be highly effective, sustained organisation over the long term needs support from established union structures, and it also poses political struggles for workplace regulatory change at local and national level.

The economic aftermath of the pandemic, combined with the disruption caused by Brexit, threatens the return of widespread poverty and reduction of state benefits. But this takes place in the context of the activities of community groups that have already emerged to sustain civil society during the pandemic. Union strength is growing as more people turn to them to defend their health and safety at work. There will be direct action on job-related issues and resistance to the evictions of renters. The expansion of these support groups will pose the need for national coordination, the development of relations with other social movements, and the assertion of the groups' legitimacy against government efforts to contain them.

Things cannot return to the old 'normal': an unsustainable social and economic system has disrupted the environment to such an extent that climate-related disasters and viral pandemics will inevitably reoccur, and more frequently. The labour movement has an unprecedented opportunity to give direction to efforts to rebuild society, and the left has an important role to play by unlocking the creative thinking of Labour's rank and file on how to build a movement of counter-power and fulfil earlier promises of a movement-based party. The new formulation of the socialist ideal is essential to harnessing the values of equality, public service, and cooperative effort in the struggle to reconstruct the foundations of society so as to put public wealth over private profit. In the words of Jeremy Corbyn, 'I think it's called socialism'.[533]

Appendix
Labour Members and Supporters Speak

Interviews conducted by the author with Labour members and supporters in Liverpool, Luton, London and Birmingham during October 2016.

Question: What is your idea of socialism?

Alastair, *20s, student and musician, not LP member:* Welfare is a big part of what I think socialism is about, free health care available to everyone at all levels, free and accessible education, things like the minimum wage, limited number of working hours, I suppose it's a minimum quality of life that should be available to everyone at all levels and a distribution of wealth that supports that.

Anjona, *20s, works in voluntary sector, trade union activist, LP and Momentum member:* Socialism means people are free to achieve their maximum potential – a universal income plan and levelling the economic playing field. The state should provide necessities like the NHS and social care etc.

Corinna, *22, unemployed, not LP member:* One where migrants aren't scapegoated and we're not having people yelling in the street black or gay or something, where people have freedom of speech to say what they want about society but without that becoming inflammatory.

Danielle, *20s, student nurse, union activist, LP member:* Socialism is about everybody having a fair and equal chance in life, I'm from Cornwall and that is a place that's left behind, we have no money, we have no opportunities, socialism is about no matter where you're from, no matter who you are, what background or religion you are, that you are met with equality and you're able to succeed just the way anybody else does and also that life isn't about money and capitalism and we value our being over money. It's really important we have a free and comprehensive health care service, education should be free and there are things in life that we need to succeed, they are not things that are a privilege.

Kyle, *25, freelance musician, not LP member:* Socialism is about creating a fairer society. Opportunities for all, people from whatever background whether rich or poor should have the same sort of opportunities. Just receiving music lessons: it ends up quite unfair that those who can afford private music lessons have a big advantage over those who can't afford to have private music lessons. Just having some funding into that from the government in schools to have an initiative to learn an instrument, to gain a valuable skill, and have the opportunity to choose to do that or not, rather than saying if you can't afford that, you can't learn that skill.

Taj, *18, student, LP and Momentum member:* A future socialist society would have people empowered, it would have grassroots democracy, it would be less bureaucracy. A lot of the international corporations exploit poorer workers in poor countries, so there has to be a global resolution maybe from the UN, where there are limits on how companies treat employees, they have to be universal rights. I would be in favour of cooperatives rather than state ownership of industry: a lot of socialist theory has been discredited by the idea that big government has power, I'm more of the view that there can be a liberal socialist world where people can have their human rights respected, their views, their freedom of speech, and it's the people as a whole that have ownership of industries.

Kieran, *20s, GMB union official, Green party member:* Socialist society comes down to the level of freedom and control that people have got over their own lives, so there wouldn't be discrimination against people. Also there would be economic democracy as well as political democracy, so people would be running the companies they work for, and there would be democratic control over public services, and that doesn't necessarily need to mean nationalisation, it can also mean cooperatives and local level economic democracy. It basically comes down to there being economic and political equality and people having some sort of control either individually or collectively over their own lives.

Anna, *20s, student, Green party member:* Practically I see it as a very devolved way of living, so that small communities and stuff, that work for themselves but are also globally interconnected, because we've got technology, … it's going back to a smaller way of organising but still using technology, so it's fully-automated luxury communism!

Claire, *20s, advice worker for charity, Green party member:* A huge systematic change which basically means overthrowing capitalism, taking an intersectional approach to it as well, you get lots of different types of inequality and the structures that surround them; sharing out wealth, sharing out power from the base up. I would actually call myself an anarcho-communist in the sense that everything should be shared for the good of everybody, but also within that respecting individual freedoms, allowing people just to live to fulfil their lives and fulfil themselves rather than just working for the sake of working and making profit for other people.

Poppy, *20s, not LP member*: One where people are putting human needs before profits. That means we're striving for maybe self-development, knowledge development, character development, relationship development rather than just getting enough resources so we can survive.

Catherine, *30s, Labour voter*: We need to make choices about what should be held within the public sphere and the private sphere, I can see the benefit of the market in the sense that it generates income, but there's certain things like large infrastructure, care work, education should be kept within collectively-owned, state-owned, people-owned, people-controlled, and not subject to the market process. Housing should be taken out of the private sphere and took into the public sphere, and not be a place purely for the generation of profit.

Ian R., *early 50s, musician and songwriter, rejoined LP to vote for Corbyn*: Socialism is sharing, caring, looking out for each other. It's doing your bit to help those who can't help themselves. It's not just about taxing rich people, as a lot of people on the right seem to think. People should pay their fair amount of taxes, from the top all the way down to the bottom. Everyone should be contributing to society to make it fairer and more equal.

John, *51, retired car worker, ex-AEU member and shop steward, not LP member*: Socialism should be a freer society from banks and multinational companies where everybody should be able to enjoy life and paying for people to be kept in their places [homes]. One of the problems in this day and age is that people don't fight for anything, part and parcel of socialism is to go out to fight to change things.

Sandra, *early 50s, recent LP member*: Socialism is supporting working people to get to a place where they can have enough money so they can live comfortably and not have to worry about money all the time, every hour that God gives you to be able to exist. There's always going to be rich people and poor people but the rich should not get richer by taking advantage of poor uneducated people.

Desiree, *40s, works in social services on zero-hours contract, LP member*: Everyone manages to get along with people, they form communities. I'd like to see more international socialism as well, so right across the board, we're working on the same thing, we've got housing that's really affordable, everybody gets some form of a job, a chance of a career, of a profession. Schooling that applies to everyone, mixed communities, everyone gets a chance, and the health service, and elder care service. Everyone's a human being, it's not a policy of what's right or what's left, it's what's right for human beings.

David, *59, business manager tech company, not LP member*: I believe in a society where people are able to live a good quality life, have good social interactions with other people in society, be productive and collaborate and achieve good outcomes. I'd rather think of that as a productive way of seeing the future of society. Socialism has some negative connotations around state power, nationalisation and things like that have become a bit of a dogma and a taboo among left groups, that they are the road to a better society, and I don't think in all cases they are.

Ian B., *late 60s, teacher, rejoined LP to vote for Corbyn*: It's about people having control over their lives, especially economic control, more security, less inequality, availability of social housing and education, rent control, the state intervening in the markets at all levels, the nationalisation of things that would otherwise be natural monopolies. We have to have more services that are available for everybody, equal of wealth or status, such as the NHS.

Jim, *late 60s, retired civil servant, joined LP to vote for Corbyn:* The idea of socialism is that we're all in it together: we're all human beings, nobody is entitled to privilege above other human beings, everybody is entitled to things like clean water, sewage, food, shelter and all the rest of it.

Len, *late 60s, retired government worker, UNITE Community member, LP member:* For me the idea of socialism is people taking responsibility for power themselves. It has to be based on everybody being able to argue for their ideas, their vision of the way forward, on an equal basis with everyone else, so there is no sense of vested power interests determining that. What I would advocate is an equality of income and benefits accorded to everybody, without fear or favour.

Hugh, *70s, ex-Labour councillor, retired production engineer, LP member*: I don't like the regimes where they force it on people, it's got to grow on people, you have to encourage them to do the good things; I don't know what it's like to be in a regime like the Eastern bloc. Equal opportunities for everybody, to encourage people that don't have the same ideas that you have; the Russians turned corrupt because they were doing it for the wrong reasons, they should do it because it's a way of making a fair society, not a society that you were forced into, not because it was the right thing to do.

Andrew, *60s, retired urban planner, LP member*: Socialism as I understand it is a set of principles where wealth is better distributed throughout society. Does it require all the assets of society to be publicly owned? I don't think it does. I don't know of any economy in the world that functions on the basis of all factors of production being owned by everybody, where there's no private ownership as such. I think it's to do with the more equitable distribution of wealth throughout the country. There's a lot of work that needs to be done to try and curb some of the excesses of extreme wealth to make sure that if there are people who secure a disproportionate amount of assets they are challenged to put it back into society.

Jerry, *70s, retired dockworker, T&G staff rep, CND member, LP member*: Socialism, to me, is what's better for everyone rather than what's better for the few. It has a knock-on effect because we can create work. Socialism is basically a fair society. The class was 1945: we were bankrupt, yet we created the NHS, we also built up all sorts of things for society, we nationalised the railways. That's what socialism is all about, the betterment of the majority, not a small minority who control the resources.

Pat, *late 60s, retired schoolteacher, lifelong LP member*: There's an underclass of people now which is different from the underclass of the 1950s and 60s, when people were seen to be living in council houses, now the underclass is often the people who aren't even in work. Housing is such an issue for that element of people who don't have any job security. With the state having more control over people's lives, but only to ensure the equality. It would free up the lower levels of society, and basically the people who do too well out of society at the moment may well have to moderate their lifestyles a bit. There's enormous wealth being made, and those people buy the most expensive luxury items, but we don't have to produce those in great quantity, I see society in coming down to a middle, not a middle class, but a middle in terms of income level.

Graham, *70s, retired conservation officer, LP supporter*: I'm not too affected by the nature of how things are produced as long as they're produced in a system that's set by government, and that assures a certain amount of fairness and equality, and certainly the great inequalities we have at the moment to reduce those. One of the things that might be done is through taxation: VAT rates for a wide range of goods should be tailed down and more should go onto direct taxation, so you balance out the differences, the sheer inequalities that seem to have been generated over the last 30 years in terms of the wages of the rich compared to the wages of the average worker in an organisation.

Geraldine, *70s, retired adult education teacher, LP member*: When I was teaching, I'm obviously white middle class, all the people I was teaching, they had so many problems. Extreme poverty, you name it, they suffered from it, racism, the lot. One of them said to me we don't want to be treated differently from anyone else, we just want to be treated the same. People should be treated with the same respect, the same dignity. Life has moved on from all that [the era of the Beveridge report]; people are living longer, they're healthier, everything is more expensive, but the gap is getting wider all the time between the haves and have-nots. How you bridge that gap between people, the only way I found I could do it was this attitude of existing with people and walking their walk with them and trying to be sympathetic about what was going on, but not in any way say we're all the same, because we're not, and we've just got to face it. You've got to try in your own small way to try and improve and help other people in their lives.

Sandy, *70s, ex-teacher, ex-human rights worker, ex-Labour councillor, LP and Momentum member*: I think it would be a society that was just, where there was a division of good things in society divided fairly throughout society, where everybody had decent wages, decent quality of life, access to housing, NHS, legal services – at the moment it isn't just because some people are spending all their energies on just existing and don't have access to the good quality of life and that should be accessible to everybody in a socialist society, from each according to his means and to each according to his needs essentially. At the moment power isn't in the hands of the politicians, it's in the hands of global capitalism, so democracy is being taken away from people.

Julia, *61, background in adult education, LP member*: It's ultimately a far more equal distribution of goods and services where people are properly cared for at every stage in their life. We need a much fairer wage for everybody, industry should be owned by the workers so the people have the means of production. Work should be about producing goods and services we need, not excess wealth for the few which then gives them extra power. We would also have a kinder, far more caring society, we would have fewer social problems, social ills; an awful lot of criminality and cruelty is connected with poor distribution which means that a lot of people grow up in very poor circumstances and that causes all sorts of problems.

Further Reading

General

Foote, Geoffrey, *The Labour Party's Political Thought: A History*, New York: St Martin's Press, 1997

Harker, Dave, *Tressell: The Real Story of The Ragged Trousered Philanthropists*, London: Zed Books, 2003

Harvey, David, *A Brief History of Neoliberalism*, Oxford UP, 2005

Kynaston, David, *Austerity Britain: 1945-51*, London: Bloomsbury, 2007

Price, Richard, *Labour in British Society: An Interpretative History*, London: Routledge, 1990

Thompson, E.P., *The Making of the English Working Class*, New York, London: Vintage Books/Penguin Random House, 1966

Tressell, Robert, *The Ragged Trousered Philanthropists*, ed. Peter Miles, Oxford UP, 2005; also published by Penguin Classics, intro. Tristram Hunt, 2004

Labour after 1940

Addison, Paul, *The Road to 1945: British Politics and the Second World War*, Cape: London, 1975

Croucher, Richard, *Engineers at War: 1939-1945*, London: Merlin Press, 1982

Harris, Jose, *William Beveridge: A Biography*, Oxford UP, revised ed. 1997

Howell, David, *British Social Democracy: A Study in Development and Decay*, New York: St. Martin's Press, 1976

Jenkins, Mark, *Bevanism, Labour's High Tide: The Cold War and the Democratic Mass Movement*, Nottingham: Spokesman, 1979

McKibbin, Ross, *Parties and People: England 1914-1951*, Oxford UP, 2010

Miliband, Ralph, *Parliamentary Socialism: A Study in the Politics of Labour*, London: Allen & Unwin, 1961

Minkin, Lewis, *The Contentious Alliance: Trade Unions and the Labour Party*, Edinburgh UP, 1991

Morgan, Kenneth O., *Labour in Power 1945-1951*, Oxford UP, 1984

Morgan, Kenneth O., *The People's Peace: British History 1945-1990*, Oxford UP, rev. ed. 1992

Panitch, Leo, *Social Democracy and Industrial Militancy: The Labour Party, the Trade Unions and Incomes Policy, 1945-74*, London: Cambridge UP, 1976

Saville, John, *The Politics of Continuity: British Foreign Policy and the Labour Government, 1945-46*, London: Verso, 1993

Saville, John, *Memoirs from the Left*, London: Merlin Press, 2003

Shaw, Eric, *The Labour Party since 1945: Old Labour: New Labour*, Oxford: Blackwell, 1996

Thomas-Symonds, Nicklaus, *Nye: The Political Life of Aneurin Bevan*, London: I.B. Tauris, 2015

Labour after 1979

Benn, Tony, *Arguments for Socialism*, London: Cape, 1979

Benn, Tony, *Arguments for Democracy*, London: Cape, 1981

Heffernan, Richard, *New Labour and Thatcherism: Political Change in Britain*, London & New York: Macmillan, 2000

Heffernan, Richard and Mike Marqusee, *Defeat from the Jaws of Victory: Inside Kinnock's Labour Party*, London: Verso, 1992

Minkin, Lewis, *The Blair Supremacy: A study in the politics of Labour's party management*, Manchester UP, 2014

Panitch, Leo and Colin Leys, *The End of Parliamentary Socialism: From New Left to New Labour*, London: Verso, 1997

Shaw, Eric, *The Labour Party since 1979: Crisis and transformation*, London: Routledge, 1994

Shaw, Eric, *Losing Labour's Soul? New Labour and the Blair Government 1997-2007*, Abingdon, Oxon: Routledge, 2007

Wainwright, Hilary, *Labour: A Tale of Two Parties*, London: Hogarth Press, 1987

Wainwright, Hilary and Dave Elliot, *The Lucas Plan: A new trade unionism in the making?* London: Allison & Busby, 1982

Labour after 2015

Berry, Christine and Joe Guinan, *People Get Ready! Preparing for a Corbyn Government*, London: OR Books, 2019

Labour Party manifesto, *For the Many, not the Few*, 2017

Monbiot, George (ed.), Robin Grey, Tom Kenny, Laurie Macfarlane, Anna Powell-Smith, Guy Shrubsole, Beth Stratford, *Land for the Many: Changing the way our fundamental asset is used, owned and governed*, Labour Party, 2019

Nunns, Alex, *The Candidate: Jeremy Corbyn's improbable path to power*, London: OR Books, 2016

Panitch, Leo and Colin Leys, *Searching for Socialism: The Project of the Labour New Left from Benn to Corbyn*, London: Verso, 2020

Perryman, Mark (ed.), *Corbynism from Below*, London: Lawrence & Wishart, 2019

Seymour, Richard, *Corbyn: The Strange Rebirth of Radical Politics*, London: Verso, 2nd edition 2017

Useful websites

https://www.opendemocracy.net/en/

https://newsocialist.org.uk

https://labourlist.org

https://labourhub.org.uk

https://novaramedia.com

https://www.redpepper.org.uk

https://skwawkbox.org

https://labouroutlook.org

https://tribunemag.co.uk

NOTES

Introduction

1. David Hall, 'The UK 2019 election: defeat for Labour, but strong support for public ownership', University of Greenwich Public Services International Research Unit, January 2020, http://gala.gre.ac.uk/id/eprint/26848/
2. Interview with the author, October 2016.
3. Quoted in John Saville, *The Politics of Continuity: British Foreign Policy and the Labour Government, 1945-46*, London: Verso, 1993, p. 113.
4. Amy Black and Stephen Brooke, 'The Labour Party, Women, and the Problem of Gender, 1951-1966', *Journal of British Studies*, Vol. 36, No. 4 (Oct., 1997), pp. 419-52.

Chapter One

5. Quoted in John Saville, *The Politics of Continuity: British Foreign Policy and the Labour Government, 1945-46*, London: Verso, 1993, p. 113.
6. John Saville, (1993), p. 116.
7. *Hansard*, HC Deb, 7 February, 1946.
8. Samuel H. Beer, *British Politics in the Collectivist Age*, New York: Alfred A. Knopf, 1965, p. 130.
9. Geoffrey Foote, *The Labour Party's Political Thought: A History*, 3rd edition, New York: St Martin's Press, 1997, p. 38.
10. Quoted in Jonathan Rose, *The Intellectual Life of the British Working Classes*, New Haven, Yale, 2001, p. 312.
11. Samuel Beer, (1965), p. 130; Francis Williams, *A Prime Minister Remembers*, London: Heinemann, 1961, p. 88.
12. David Howell, *British Social Democracy: A Study in Development and Decay*, New York: St. Martin's Press, 1976, p. 132.
13. Simon Winder, a publishing director at Penguin, told the *Guardian*: 'We sold many more than usual of our Penguin Classics edition last year [2008], with sales going up from about 3,000 a year to more than 5,000, and this year it is carrying on the same way. It is incredible for such a serious classic. And there are several editions out there from other publishers, too.' https://www.theguardian.com/books/2009/may/02/ragged-trousered-philanthropists-left-wing-bestsellers
14. The TUC's official website states: 'In 1940, Penguin published the 1918 edition as a paperback for sixpence – around half an hour's pay for a male industrial worker, but twice that for a woman – and The Richards Press carried on reprinting the 1914 edition.

From 1941, after Hitler broke his pact with Stalin, and Russia joined the capitalist Allies, British Communists and Labour left-wingers pushed the Penguin [edition] in the armed forces and trade unions, and it was in its fifth printing by 1944. Reportedly, sales were massive, and the book contributed to the Labour Party's landslide election victory in 1945 …' http://www.unionhistory.info/ragged/ragged.php

15 Robert Tressell, *The Ragged Trousered Philanthropists*, London: Grant Richards, 1914, p. 1; ed. Peter Miles, Oxford UP, 2005, p. 7. In Bakhtin's terminology, Tressell made collective labour a 'chronotope' as the organising centre of the novel, that structures the narrative and gives meaning to its events. See M.M. Bakhtin, 'Forms of Time and of the Chronotope in the Novel,' in *The Dialogic Imagination*, ed. Michael Holquist, Austin: Univ. Texas, 1981, p. 250.

16 Robert Tressell, 1914 edition, p. 110; 2005 edition, p. 121.

17 Robert Tressell, 1914 edition, p. 293; 2005 edition, p. 402.

18 Dave Harker, *Tressell: The Real Story of The Ragged Trousered Philanthropists*, London: Zed Books, 2003, p. 121.

19 Dave Harker (2003) pp. 137, 140.

20 Julie Cairnie and Marion Walls (eds), *Revisiting Robert Tressell's Mugsborough: New Perspectives on The Ragged Trousered Philanthropists*, New York: Cambria Press, 2008, p. 175.

21 Dave Harker, (2003), pp. 138, 142.

22 Robert Tressell, *The Ragged Trousered Philanthropists*, ed. Peter Miles. Oxford, 2005.

23 Letter to Reg Johnson, *The Robert Tressell Family Papers*, in Julie Cairnie and Marion Walls, (2008), p. 180

24 Noel Thompson, *Political economy and the Labour Party: The economics of democratic socialism, 1884-1995*, London: UCL Press, 1996, p. 14.

25 Robert Tressell, 1914 edition, pp. 172-175; 2005 edition, pp. 213-217.

26 Robert Tressell, 1914 edition, p. 331; 2005 edition, p. 493. In Tressell's original manuscript, the oration is presented by a different character, Barrington, edited out of the novel by Jessie Pope. Brian Mayn comments: 'Barrington is a subtly developed character who plays a very important part at the end of the novel … By making Barrington a gentleman in disguise (a not infrequent phenomenon either in the fiction or the society of the time) Tressall [sic] is able to use him to provide a more sophisticated context for the discussion of socialism than could credibly be allowed to the self-educated Owen.' Brian Mayn, 'The Ragged Trousered Philanthropists: an appraisal of an Edwardian novel of social protest', *Twentieth Century Literature*, Vol 13, No. 2, July 1967.

27 Robert Tressell, 1914 edition, p. 332; 2005 edition, p. 494.

28 Robert Tressell, 1914 edition, p. 335; 2005 edition, p. 498.

29 Robert Tressell, 1914 edition, pp.336, 340; 2005 edition, pp.498, 502–3.

30 In his original manuscript, Tressell suggests that the way to achieve democratic control of the national organization of industry would be for the community to elect a parliament 'in much the same way as is done at present.' [2005 ed, p. 509] Through Barrington he argues that workers should stop voting for Liberals and Tories and instead 'fill the House of Commons with Revolutionary Socialists.' [2005 ed, p. 520] Both passages were cut from the 1914 and 1918 editions.

31 Anna Vaninskaya, 'Literature and Propaganda: The Socialist Utopia of Robert Blatchford', in Vieira, Fátima, and Freitas, Marinela, eds. *Utopia Matters: Theory*

Politics, Literature and the Arts, Porto, PT: U. Porto editorial, 2005, p. 75.
32   *Merrie England,* 1894; quoted in Samuel Beer, (1965), p. 133.
33   Quoted in Julie Cairnie and Marion Walls, (2008), p. 179.
34   John Bew, *Citizen Clem: A Biography of Attlee,* London: Riverrun, 2016, p. 66.
35   *Hansard,* HC Deb 23 November 1922 vol 159 cc44-166.
36   Arthur E. Morgan, *Edward Bellamy,* New York, 1944, p. 232. Morgan quotes Bellamy's own summary of his argument: 'As it is at present held to be the duty of all citizens to fight for their country, so then it is held their equally obvious duty to work for it, and it is considered self-evident that to be efficient, working requires system and unity of action quite as much as fighting. The nation has, in fine, been organized for peace as at present for war.' In 1948, meeting with Bellamy's son in London, Attlee described his government as 'a child of the Bellamy ideal.' John Bew, (2016), p. 100.
37   John Bew, (2016), p. 103.
38   From *Socialism Made Easy,* Chicago, 1908, republished in P. Berresford Ellis, *James Connolly: Selected Writings,* Harmondsworth: Penguin, 1973, pp. 150-151.
39   Richard Price, *Labour in British Society: An Interpretative History,* London: Routledge, 1990, pp 153-4.
40   Quoted in Richard Price, (1990), p. 155.
41   Ralph Darlington, 'Re-evaluating syndicalist opposition to the First World War, *Labour History,* 53:4, p.534
42   'Labourism' became a central concept in the New Left's analysis of the failure of the Labour government in the 1960s. 'The political values of Labourism,' explains Hilary Wainwright, 'stem from the combination of the values of trade unionism with those of parliamentary respectability. ... The working class, through the trade unions, provides the money and the votes but the actual process of change is a matter for Parliament and the state.' Its primary characteristic is the separation of industrial and political power. Hilary Wainwright, *Labour: A Tale of Two Parties,* London: Hogarth Press, 1987, p. 14.
43   Richard Price, (1990), pp. 163-4
44   Richard Price, (1990), p. 169; Aneurin Bevan, *In Place of Fear,* London: Heinemann, 1952, p.41
45   Henry Pelling, *A Short History of the Labour Party,* London, 1996, p. 71.
46   Matthew Worley, *Labour Inside the Gate: A History of the British Labour Party between the Wars,* London & New York: I.B. Tauris, 2005, p. 134.
47   C.R. Attlee, *The Labour Party in Perspective,* London, Gollancz, 1937, p. 59.
48   Ben Pimlott, *Labour and the Left in the 1930s,* Cambridge UP, 1977, p. 199.
49   Geoffrey Foote, (1997), pp. 164-5.
50   Paul Addison, *The Road to 1945: British Politics and the Second World War,* Cape: London, 1975, p. 4.
51   Despite the hostility of unions to the employment of married women in a time of recession, women still looked to the labour movement to further their interests, although this meant in practice an accommodation to the anti-feminist outlook of the labour leaders. Between the wars, organisations in the Labour party such as the Women's Labour League, the Women's Cooperative Guild and the Women's sections of the party represented over a million women members. Christine Collette, *The Newer Eve: Women, Feminists and the Labour Party,* Basingstoke, Palgrave Macmillan, 2009, p. 69.
52   Matthew Worley, (2005), pp. 184-5, 174; Pamela M. Graves, *Labour Women: Women*

in British Working-Class Politics 1918-1939, Cambridge UP, 1994, pp. 182, 187
53 Quoted in in Samuel Beer, (1965), p. 134; John Swift, *Labour in Crisis: Clement Attlee and the Labour Party in Opposition, 1931-40*, London: Palgrave, 2001, p. 23.
54 Ben Pimlott, (1977), p. 201.
55 Paul Addison, (1975), p. 46.
56 Ben Pimlott, (1977), pp. 86-7.
57 Matthew Worley, (2005), p. 204. But on p. 206: 'local parties could sometimes complain that their Spain committees received a 'lack of support' from the wider labour movement, suggesting a cause for the activist was not necessarily a cause for the broader membership.'
58 Ben Pimlott, (1977), p. 102.
59 Ben Pimlott, (1977), p. 197.
60 Ben Pimlott, (1977), pp. 112, 140.
61 John Bew, (2016), p. 215.
62 Clement Attlee, (1937), pp. 133, 280.
63 Eric Shaw, *Discipline and discord in the Labour party: the politics of managerial control in the Labour party, 1951-87* (Manchester UP, 1988), 29.
64 Clement Attlee, (1937), pp. 136, 268, 271.
65 Matthew Worley, (2005), p. 213.
66 Clement Attlee, (1937), pp. 57, 163.
67 Clement Attlee, (1937), pp. 177, 285.
68 Clement Attlee, (1937), p. 166.
69 Matthew Worley, (2005), p. 194.
70 Quoted in in Ben Pimlott, (1977), p. 149.
71 Quoted in in Matthew Worley, (2005), pp. 215-6. A.J.P. Taylor pointed out, 'Until 22 August 1939 the Labour movement from Right to Left retained its old principles or, if you prefer, its old illusions. It still held the outlook of Keir Hardie and E.D. Morel, of Brailsford and J.A. Hobson ... Imperialist capitalism was the cause of war. Socialists should oppose both war and capitalism.' Quoted in Ben Pimlott, (1977), 150.
72 John Swift, (2001), p. 125.
73 Matthew Worley, (2005), pp. 195, 148.
74 The Labour Party Constitution, Clause Four, 1918.
75 Ben Pimlott, (1977), pp. 174, 176.
76 Geoffrey Foote, (1997), p. 180.
77 Clement Attlee, (1937), p. 16.
78 David Howell, (1976), p. 97.
79 Ross McKibbin, *Parties and People: England 1914-1951*, Oxford UP, 2010, p. 134.
80 Steven Fielding, Peter Thompson and Nick Tiratsoo, *'England arise!': The Labour Party and popular politics in 1940s Britain*, Manchester UP, 1995, p. 85.

Chapter Two

81 Quoted in Francis Williams, (1961), p. 37.
82 *Daily Herald*, 4 September, 1939.
83 Ross McKibbin, *The Ideologies of Class: Social Relations in Britain 1880-1950*, Oxford UP, 1991, p. 290.

84 Ritchie Calder, 'Why? Why? Why?', *Daily Herald*, September 27, 1940.
85 Lewis Minkin, *The Contentious Alliance: Trade Unions and the Labour Party*, Edinburgh UP, 1991, p. 57.
86 Jim Tomlinson, 'The Labour government and the trade unions, 1945-51' in Nick Tiratsoo, ed, *The Attlee Years*, London: Pinter, 1991, p. 90.
87 Ross McKibbin, (1991), p. 291.
88 Steven Fielding, Peter Thompson and Nick Tiratsoo, *'England arise!': The Labour Party and popular politics in 1940s Britain*, Manchester UP, 1995, p. 80.
89 Paul Addison, (1975), pp. 129-130. He adds: 'The high levels of taxation on personal incomes also had a levelling effect ... Although wage-rates did not overtake the rise in the cost of living until July 1943, unemployment was virtually abolished, and wage packets increased rapidly because of overtime. Largely as a result of the war, the average wage income rose by 18 per cent between 1938 and 1947, while the average income from property fell by 15 per cent, and from salaries by 21 per cent.'
90 Quoted in Stephen Brooke, *Labour's War: The Labour Party during the Second World War*, Oxford: Clarendon, 1992, p. 43.
91 David Howell, (1976), p. 118.
92 '3 Years of Social Advance, says Attlee,' *Daily Herald*, London, 12 July 1943.
93 Steven Fielding et al, (1995), p. 85.
94 In his opening address to the 1944 party conference, Harold Laski called for 'electoral authority to enter in the fullest way we can upon the great task of building the Socialist and Co-operative Commonwealth. ... Only a Socialist Commonwealth can give us full employment. A Socialist Commonwealth is the necessary precondition of adequate health and nutrition, of a rational housing policy and security against the burden of old age. It is the only direction which permits the State-power to utilise to their full extent the immense and growing potentialities of science and technology. ... For no other system save that which is Socialist in its foundations can regard humble men and women as ends as well as means.' Labour Party, Report of 1944 Annual Conference, p. 110.
95 Quoted in Steven Fielding et al, (1995), pp. 81-2.
96 David Howell, (1976), p. 121.
97 Ralph Miliband, *Parliamentary Socialism: A Study in the Politics of Labour*, London: Allen & Unwin, 1961, p. 273; Ross McKibbin, *Parties and People: England 1914-1951*, Oxford UP, 2010, pp. 130, 132.
98 Tony Mason and Peter Thompson, 'Reflections on a revolution? The political mood in wartime Britain', in Tiratsoo, (1991), p. 65.
99 David Kynaston, *Austerity Britain: 1945-51*, London: Bloomsbury, 2007, p. 57.
100 Steven Fielding et al, (1995), p. 33.
101 Lewis Minkin, (1991), p. 58.
102 Labour Party, 1946 conference report, p. 14; Mason and Thompson, (1991), p. 56.
103 Stephen Brooke, (1992), pp. 67-8.
104 Selina Todd, *The People: The Rise and Fall of the Working Class*, London: Murray, 2015, pp. 128-30.
105 Bill Hunter, *Lifelong Apprenticeship: The Life and Times of a Revolutionary*, vol 1, 1920-1959, London: Index Books: Porcupine Press, 1997, p. 84.
106 Richard Croucher, *Engineers at War: 1939-1945*, London: Merlin Press, 1982, pp. 153,

145.
107 Richard Croucher, (1982), p. 353.
108 Kenneth O. Morgan, *Labour in Power 1945-1951*, Oxford UP, 1984, pp. 28-9.
109 Noel Whiteside, 'The Beveridge Report and Its Implementation: a Revolutionary Project?', *Histoire@Politique* 2014/3 (n° 24), pp. 24-37.
110 Bill Hunter, (1997), p. 86. Hunter adds that on the day the report was published, 'a queue a mile long formed outside the government bookshop in central London. Within three hours 70,000 copies were sold. Two weeks later the British Institute of Public Opinion published a survey which showed that 95 per cent of the public had heard of the report, with 88 per cent in favour, 6 per cent against, and 6 per cent undecided.'
111 Jose Harris, *William Beveridge: A Biography*, Oxford UP, revised ed. 1997, p. 413.
112 Jose Harris, (1997), p. 378.
113 The Beveridge Report, *Social Insurance and Allied Services*, London: HMSO, 1942, §445.
114 Jose Harris, (1997), pp. 416, 406-7.
115 Warwick University Digital Collection, 'Notes of statement by Sir William Beveridge to General Council at their meeting on 16 December, 1942', https://warwick.ac.uk/services/library/mrc/explorefurther/digital/health/beveridge
116 Jose Harris, (1997), p. 411.
117 The Beveridge Report, (1942), §7, §21, §294, §274, §130.
118 The Beveridge Report, (1942), §455, §459, §461.
119 Jose Harris, (1997), p. 415.
120 Warwick University Digital Collection, 'Trade Union Regional Conference on the Beveridge Report', Midland Federation of Trades Councils, 16 January 1943.
121 The *New Leader*, 19 December 1942.
122 Warwick University Digital Collection, 'From a member of the Fire Brigade Union', 10 December 1942.
123 Ross McKibbin, (2010), pp. 192, 132-3.
124 Nick Ellison, 'Consensus Here, Consensus There ... but not Consensus Everywhere: The Labour Party, Equality and Social Policy in the 1950s', in Harriet Jones, Michael Kandiah (eds), *The Myth of Consensus: New Views on British History, 1945-64* London: Macmillan, 1996, 23.
125 Jose Harris, 'The debate on State welfare', in Harold Smith (ed), *War and Social Change: British Society in the Second World War*, Manchester UP, 1986, pp. 251-2
126 Quoted in Paul Addison, (1975), p. 185.
127 Report of the Labour Party Conference 1942, pp. 133-4.
128 Jose Harris, (1986), p. 253.
129 Quoted in Paul Addison, (1975), p. 223.
130 Paul Addison, (1975), pp. 215-6.
131 John Campbell, *Nye Bevan and the Mirage of British Socialism*, London: Weidenfeld and Nicolson, 1987, pp. 96, 130-131.
132 Ralph Miliband, (1961), pp. 276-7.
133 Paul Addison, (1975), p. 256.
134 Clement Attlee to Harold Laski, 1 May 1944; quoted in Paul Addison, (1975), p. 272, and John Saville, (1993), p. 116.
135 Angus Calder, *The People's War: Britain 1939-45*, London: Jonathan Cape, 1969, p. 533.

136 Undated memo, Attlee papers (Churchill College) 1/24, cited in Addison, (1975), p. 26.
137 Paul Addison, (1975), p. 262.
138 Stephen Brooke, (1991), p. 313.
139 Steven Fielding et al, (1995), pp. 67-8.
140 Steven Fielding et al, (1995), pp. 76-77.
141 Labour Party, *Let Us Face the Future: A Declaration of Labour Policy for the Consideration of the Nation*, 1945.
142 Richard Croucher, (1982), pp. 344-5.
143 David Kynaston, (2007), p. 67.
144 Quoted in Peter Hennessy, *Never Again: Britain 1945-51*, London: Cape, 1993, p. 88.
145 David Kynaston, (2007), p. 68.
146 Quoted in Paul Addison, *Now the War is Over: A Social History of Britain 1945-51*, London: BBC/Jonathan Cape, 1985, p. 12.
147 Quoted in C.J. Bartlett, *A history of postwar Britain 1945-74*, London: Longman, 1977, p. 2.
148 Quoted in John Bew, (2016), 388.
149 David Kynaston, (2007), p. 80.
150 Ross McKibbin, (2010), p. 134.
151 Ross McKibbin, (2010), pp. 137-8.
152 The Beveridge Report, (1942), §458.

Chapter Three

153 Samuel Beer, (1965), p. 190.
154 Harry Leslie Smith, 'Hard rain and cold Yorkshire stone,' *New Statesman*, 31 October 2014. Later in life he became an outspoken defender of the welfare state and championed the rights of international refugees.
155 In 1946 alone, the government passed the National Insurance Act, the Industrial Injuries Act, the National Assistance Act, the National Health Service Act, and the first Housing Act.
156 Ralph Miliband, (1961), p. 307.
157 Steven Fielding et al, (1995), p. 77.
158 Lewis Minkin, (1991), p. 80. Known as order 1305, the Conditions of Employment and National Arbitration Order was passed in 1940 and effectively banned strikes, enforcing arbitration in any industrial dispute.
159 Lewis Minkin, (1991), pp. xiv, 9.
160 John Saville, (1993), pp. 82, 85.
161 Eric Shaw, *The Labour Party since 1945: Old Labour: New Labour*, Oxford: Blackwell, 1996, p. ix.
162 David Kynaston, (2007), p. 137.
163 Eric Shaw, (1996), p. 35.
164 Howard Webber, 'A Domestic Rebellion: The Squatters' Movement of 1946', *Ex Historia*, Exeter University, 2012, p. 130.
165 The flats, used as offices during the war, had in fact been offered by the Government to the Tory-led Kensington Council to use for public housing, but were refused. Minayo Nasiali, 'Citizens, Squatters, and Asocials: The Right to Housing and the Politics of

Difference in Post-Liberation France', *The American Historical Review*, Vol. 119, isue 2, pp. 434-59.
166 Kenneth Morgan, (1984), pp. 96-7, 99.
167 Harriet Jones and Michael Kandiah, (1996), p. 62.
168 Lewis Minkin, (1991), p. 73.
169 Kenneth Morgan, (1984), pp.140-141.
170 David Howell, (1976), p. 153.
171 Noel Thompson, (1996), p. 145.
172 Eric Shaw, (1996), p. 31.
173 Kenneth Morgan, (1984), pp. 139, 106.
174 Bill Hunter, (1997), p. 261.
175 Len Morgan, 'Too many bosses', *Tribune*, 7 March 1953.
176 Kenneth Morgan, (1984), pp. 204.
177 Quoted John Campbell, (1987), p. 191.
178 David Kynaston, (2007), p. 226.
179 Jonathan Schneer, *Labour's Conscience: The Labour Left 1945-51*, Boston: Unwin Hyman, 1988, pp. 147-8.
180 Jonathan Schneer, (1988), pp. 149-150.
181 Leo Panitch, *Social Democracy and Industrial Militancy: The Labour Party, the Trade Unions and Incomes Policy, 1945-74*, London: Cambridge UP, 1976, pp. 15, 21, 27.
182 Quoted in Ralph Miliband, (1961), p. 299.
183 Michael Foot, *Aneurin Bevan: A Biography; volume two: 1945-1960*, London: Davis-Poynter, 1973, p. 258.
184 John Campbell, (1987), pp. 199, 207.
185 Peter Hennessy, (1993), pp. 291, 434.
186 Kenneth Morgan, (1984), pp. 492-3.
187 Bill Hunter, (1997), p. 259.
188 Kenneth Morgan, (1984), pp. 495, 499.
189 Quoted in John Campbell, (1987), p. 316.
190 Quoted in Paul Addison, (1975), p. 277.
191 Samuel Beer, (1965), pp. 304-6.
192 Eric Shaw, (1996), p. 38.
193 Marvin Rintala, *Creating the National Health Service: Aneurin Bevan and the Medical Lords*, London & Oregon: Cass, 2003, p. 51.
194 John Campbell, (1987), pp. 167, 169.
195 Marvin Rintala, (2003), p. 113.
196 Michael Foot, (1973), p. 214.
197 David Kynaston, (2007), p. 148.
198 Marvin Rintala, (2003), pp. 59, 63.
199 John Campbell, (1987), p. 173.
200 *Hansard*, HC Deb 30 July 1958 vol. 592 cc1382-506.
201 David Kynaston, (2007), p. 327.
202 Charles Webster, '50 years of the NHS,' *History Today*, 00182753, July 98, Vol. 48, Issue 7.
203 https://www.theguardian.com/society/2018/may/28/overlooked-facts-of-nhs-history
204 Kenneth Morgan, (1984), pp. 296-7.
205 Jonathan Schneer, (1988), p. 153.

206 Steven Fielding et al, (1995), pp. 137-8.
207 Steven Fielding et al, (1995), pp. 96, 84, 90.
208 David Howell, (1976), p. 159.
209 Quoted John Bew, (2016), p. 460.
210 John Bew, (2016), p. 477.
211 John Bew, (2016), pp. 509, 555-6.
212 Paul Addison, (1975), p. 282.
213 Harriet Jones and Michael Kandiah, (1996), p. 10.
214 Lewis Minkin, (1991), p. 70.
215 Kenneth O. Morgan, *The People's Peace: British History 1945-1990*, Oxford UP, rev. ed. 1992, p. 107.
216 Ross McKibbin, (2010), p. 160.
217 Ross McKibbin, (2010), p. 164.
218 David Kynaston, (2007), p. 467.
219 Mary Davis, 'Women at Work,' London Metropolitan University, 2012. http://www.unionhistory.info/britainatwork/narrativedisplay.php?type=womenatwork.
220 In 1945 the vast majority of women remained ignorant of methods of birth control, despite the efforts of feminists during the wars to disseminate this information. The Labour Party itself suppressed discussion of the topic by Labour women so as not to offend Catholic voters, and because most male trade unionists were embarrassed by it. Harold Smith, 'British Feminists and the Labour Movement, 1919-1929', *The Historian*, November 1984, Vol. 47, No. 1, p. 26.
221 David Kynaston, (2007), p. 409.
222 Kenneth Morgan, (1984), pp. 302-3, 514.
223 John Saville, (1993), p. 171.
224 John Saville, *Memoirs from the Left*, London: Merlin Press, 2003, p. 87.

Chapter Four

225 Ralph Miliband, (1961), p. 25.
226 Clement Attlee, (1937), p. 211.
227 John Saville, (2003), p. 179.
228 Andrew Thorpe, *A History of the British Labour Party*, New York: St. Martin's Press, 1997, p. 130.
229 C.J. Bartlett, *A History of Postwar Britain 1945-74* London: Longman, 1977, pp. 116-17.
230 Ralph Miliband, (1961), p. 295.
231 Michael Foot, (1973), p. 90.
232 David Howell, (1976), pp. 144-5.
233 Kenneth Morgan, (1984), p. 70.
234 Jonathan Schneer, (1988), pp. 163, 179.
235 David Howell, (1976), pp. 146-7.
236 C.J. Bartlett, (1977), p. 87.
237 John Saville, (1993), p. 174.
238 Eric Shaw, (1996), p. 44.
239 Mark Jenkins, *Bevanism, Labour's High Tide: The Cold War and the Democratic Mass Movement*, Nottingham: Spokesman, 1979, p. 74.

240 Kenneth Morgan, (1984), p. 79.
241 Mark Jenkins, (1979), p. 83.
242 TUC, *Trade Unions and Wages Policy*, 12 January 1950, qtd in Leo Panitch, (1976), p. 35.
243 Leo Panitch, (1976), pp. 36, 273.
244 Mark Jenkins, (1979), p. 84.
245 John Campbell, (1987), p. 240.
246 Michael Foot, (1973), pp. 343-4.
247 John Campbell, (1987), p. 253.
248 Mark Jenkins, (1979), p. 34.
249 Nicklaus Thomas-Symonds, *Nye: The Political Life of Aneurin Bevan*, London: I.B. Tauris, 2015, p. 206.
250 Mark Jenkins, (1979), p. 296.
251 Quoted in Leo Panitch, (1976), pp. 39, 42.
252 Mark Jenkins, (1979), p. 291; Labour Party, *Let Us Win Through Together*, 1950.
253 Mark Jenkins, (1979), p. 297; Nicklaus Thomas-Symonds, (2015), p. 206.
254 Quoted in Nicklaus Thomas-Symonds, (2015), p. 208.
255 Nicklaus Thomas-Symonds, (2015), p. 199.
256 Eric Shaw, (1988), pp. 49, 292.
257 Kenneth Morgan, *The People's Peace*, p. 138.
258 Mark Jenkins, (1979), pp. 162, 167, 172.
259 Bill Webber at the NEC, qtd Eric Shaw, (1988), p. 37.
260 Mark Jenkins, (1979), pp. 173, 184.
261 A better term might be the sovereignty of the West German Federal Republic. The issue of German rearmament was a highly charged one, but British opposition melted away when it became clear that material US support for NATO was contingent on the creation of twelve West German divisions. C.J. Bartlett (1977), p. 85.
262 Campbell, (1987), p. 284.
263 Mark Jenkins, (1979), pp. 133-4.
264 Eric Shaw, (1988), p. 42.
265 Mark Jenkins, (1979), p. 190.
266 Nicklaus Thomas-Symonds, (2015), p. 224.
267 David Howell, *The Rise and Fall of Bevanism*, Leeds: ILP Square One Publications, 1973, p. 35.
268 Eric Shaw, (1988), p. 293.
269 David Howell, (1973), p. 16.
270 Mark Jenkins, (1979), pp. 261, 273.
271 Geoffrey Foote, (1997), p. 74.
272 David Howell, (1973), pp. 187, 169.
273 Nicklaus Thomas-Symonds, (2015), p. 234.
274 David Howell, (1973), p. 8.
275 Hilary Wainwright, (1987), p. 3.
276 David Howell, (1973), pp. 13-14.
277 Eric Shaw, (1988), p. 295.
278 Fielding et al, (1995), p. 210.
279 Mark Jenkins, (1979), p. 285.

280 Michael Foot, (1973), pp. 368-9.
281 Aneurin Bevan, *In Place of Fear*, London: Heinemann, 1952, pp. 119, 169.
282 Aneurin Bevan, (1952), pp. 75, 79.
283 Aneurin Bevan, (1952), pp. 85, 96.
284 Aneurin Bevan, (1952), p. 33.
285 Aneurin Bevan, (1952), pp. 3, 5.
286 Aneurin Bevan, (1952), p. 100.
287 Aneurin Bevan, (1952), pp. 31, 118.
288 Aneurin Bevan, (1952), p. 103.
289 Aneurin Bevan, (1952), p. 129.
290 David Howell, (1973), p. 37.
291 C.A.R. Crosland, *The Future of Socialism*, London: Jonathan Cape, 1956, p. 63.
292 C.A.R. Crosland, (1956), pp. 100, 196, 492.
293 C.A.R. Crosland, (1956), pp. 277, 518.
294 David Howell, (1976), p. 193.
295 David Howell, (1976), p. 215.
296 Amy Black and Stephen Brooke, 'The Labour Party, Women, and the Problem of Gender, 1951-1966', *Journal of British Studies*, Vol. 36, No. 4 (Oct., 1997), p. 425
297 Ralph Miliband, (1961), pp. 13-14, 327.
298 *New Reasoner*, Autumn 1959, number 10.
299 Dennis Dworkin, *Cultural Marxism in Postwar Britain: History, the New Left, and the origin of Cultural Studies*, Durham and London: Duke UP, 1997, p. 60.
300 E.P. Thompson, *The Making of the English Working Class*, London: Gollancz, 1963, p. 197.
301 E.P. Thompson, (1963), pp. 53, 70.
302 E.P. Thompson (ed), *Out of Apathy*, London: New Left Books, 1960, pp. 289, 297.
303 E.P. Thompson, (1960), pp. 301-2.
304 E.P. Thompson, (1960), p. 305.
305 *New Left Review*, 1, #6, Nov-Dec 1960, 'Missing Signposts', cited in Dennis Dworkin, (1997), p. 75.
306 Samuel H. Beer, *Britain Against Itself: The political contradictions of collectivism*, London and New York: Norton, 1982, pp. 120, 131.

Chapter Five

307 *Hansard*, HC Deb 15 June 1971 vol. 819 cc233-366.
308 Leo Panitch, (1976), p. 47.
309 Noel Thompson, (1996), p. 185.
310 David Howell, (1976), pp. 266, 276.
311 Noel Thompson, (1996), p. 192.
312 David Howell, (1976), p. 269.
313 Samuel Beer, (1982), pp. 152, 154.
314 Leo Panitch, (1976), p. 171.
315 David Howell, (1976), p. 265.
316 Leo Panitch and Colin Leys, *The End of Parliamentary Socialism: From New Left to New Labour*, London: Verso, 1997, p. 49.

317 'From Parliamentary to Popular Democracy,' Annual Conference, Welsh Council of Labour, 25 May 1968, quoted in Robert Jenkins, *Tony Benn: A Political Biography*, London: Writers & Readers Collective, 1980, p. 142.
318 Eric Shaw, (1996), p. 214.
319 Paul Dixon, *Northern Ireland: The Politics of War and Peace*, London: Palgrave Macmillan, 2nd ed. 2008, pp. 94, 108-9.
320 David Howell, (1976), p. 282.
321 Leo Panitch and Colin Leys, (1997), p. 27.
322 Benn called out the dualism of the rhetoric and practice of the Trotskyist Militant group in a debate with its leader, Ted Grant. Referring to the 'bloody settlement' that Grant predicted capitalists were preparing for workers, Benn replied: 'If I believed it, we wouldn't be here passing resolutions, we would be planning guerilla warfare.' Tony Benn, *Against the Tide: Diaries 1973-76*, London: Hutchinson, 1989, p. 20, entry for April 24, 1973.
323 Philip Armstrong, Andrew Glyn, and John Harrison, *Capitalism since 1945*, Oxford: Blackwell, 1991, pp. 230, 246.
324 Chris Wrigley, *British Trade Unions since 1933*, Cambridge UP, 2002, p. 43.
325 Mervyn Jones, *Michael Foot*, London: Gollancz, 1994, p. 335; Leo Panitch and Colin Leys, (1997), p. 53.
326 Leo Panitch and Colin Leys, (1997), p. 23.
327 *Hansard*, HC Deb 10 January 1974 vol. 867 cc178-321.
328 Leo Panitch and Colin Leys, (1997), p. 65.
329 Hilary Wainwright, (1987), pp. 164-5.
330 Raymond Williams (ed,), *May Day Manifesto 1968*, republished London: Verso, 2018, p.64. The manifesto drew attention to the growth of multinational companies and how their internal price adjustments could transfer profits to low-tax jurisdictions, enabling US-based corporations to dominate the European economy.
331 Michael Barratt Brown, 'The Institute for Workers Control', at http://www.workerscontrol.net/theorists/institute-workers'-control
332 Hilary Wainwright, (1987), pp. 305, 306.
333 Leo Panitch and Colin Leys, (1997), p. 39.
334 Tony Benn, *The New Politics: A Socialist Reconnaissance*, London: Fabian Tract 402, 1970, p. 28.
335 *Hansard*, HC Deb 02 August 1971 vol. 822 cc1084-150.
336 Quoted in Leo Panitch and Colin Leys, (1997), p. 58.
337 Jay Adams, *Tony Benn: A Biography*, London: Macmillan, 1992, p. 310; Tony Benn, *Office Without Power: Diaries 1968-72* London: Hutchinson, 1988, p. 366.
338 Noel Thompson, (1996), pp. 201-2.
339 Leo Panitch and Colin Leys, (1997), p. 121.
340 Noel Thompson, (1996), pp. 207, 243.
341 Noel Thompson, (1996), p. 247.
342 Leo Panitch and Colin Leys, (1997), pp. 81-3.
343 Leo Panitch and Colin Leys, (1997), pp. 73, 74, 85.
344 Hilary Wainwright and Dave Elliot, *The Lucas Plan: A new trade unionism in the making?* London: Allison & Busby, 1982, p. 250.
345 Leo Panitch and Colin Leys, (1997), pp. 98, 99.

NOTES 199

346 Coventry, Liverpool, Newcastle, N. Tyneside Trades Councils, *State Intervention in Industry: a workers' inquiry*, Nottingham: Russell Press, 1980, pp. 47, 49.
347 Leo Panitch and Colin Leys, (1997), pp. 98, 99.
348 Hilary Wainwright and Dave Elliot, (1982), pp. 101-7, 138.
349 Hilary Wainwright and Dave Elliot, (1982), pp. 8, 232.
350 Hilary Wainwright and Dave Elliot, (1982), p. 264.
351 Alan Thornett, *Militant Years*, London: Resistance Books, 2011, p. 360.
352 Leo Panitch and Colin Leys, (1997), pp. 86-7.
353 Quoted in Robert Jenkins, (1980), p. 214.
354 Noel Thompson, (1996), pp. 233-4.
355 Coventry, Liverpool, Newcastle, N. Tyneside Trades Councils, (1980), pp. 44, 145.
356 Mervyn Jones, (1994), p. 363.
357 Mervyn Jones, (1994), p. 366.
358 Andrew Thorpe, (1997), pp. 191, 194.
359 Tony Benn, *Fighting Back: Speaking Out for Socialism in the Eighties*, London: Hutchinson, 1988, p. 13.
360 Leo Panitch and Colin Leys, (1997), p. 105.
361 Labour party, 1979 conference report, pp. 292-3.
362 Hilary Wainwright, (1987), pp. 13-14.
363 Tony Benn, *Arguments for Socialism*, London: Cape, 1979, p. 42.
364 Hilary Wainwright, (1987), p. 56.
365 Leo Panitch and Colin Leys, (1997), p. 266.
366 Tony Benn, (1989), p. 50, entry for 26 June, 1973.
367 Tony Benn, (1979), p. 29.
368 Tony Benn, *Arguments for Democracy*, London: Cape, 1981, pp. 141, 128.
369 Quoted in David Powell, *Tony Benn: A Political Life*, London: Continuum, rev. ed. 2003, p. 129.
370 Tony Benn, (1979), p. 158.
371 Tony Benn, (1979), pp. 158-9.
372 Tony Benn, (1979), pp. 16, 161.
373 Tony Benn, (1981), p. 223.
374 Eric Shaw, (1996), p. 217.
375 Leo Panitch and Colin Leys, (1997), pp. 106-7, 128, 110.
376 Leo Panitch and Colin Leys, (1997), p. 170; Tony Benn, (1981), p. 11. Orthodox Marxists criticized the AES for failing to break from Keynesianism, considering that domestic reflation and import controls in effect advocated for an alliance between the working class and national capital. This would seem to be supported by Benn's foreword to Powell's biography (written for the first edition in 2001), where he touches on this contradiction in his position: 'if the trade union movement had not been demonized ... could we not have saved our manufacturing industry and built up an effective counterweight to the overwhelming power of the multinationals?' However, Benn is here clearly counterposing nationally-based manufacturing industry to international financial capital.
377 Leo Panitch and Colin Leys, (1997), p. 130.
378 Stuart Hall, 'Thatcherism: a new stage?', *Marxism Today*, February 1980.
379 Hilary Wainwright, (1987), p. 85.

380 Gregor Murray, *Trade Unions and Incomes Policies, British Unions and the Social Contract in the 1970s* (University of Warwick, 1985), 631; online at http://wrap.warwick.ac.uk/39312/1/WRAP_THESIS_Murray_1985.pdf
381 Leo Panitch and Colin Leys, (1997), p. 153.
382 Labour Party, 1979, *The Labour Way is the Better Way*
383 Hilary Wainwright and Dave Elliot, (1982), p. 260.

Chapter Six

384 Interview with the author, October 2016.
385 Kenneth Morgan, (1992), p. 450.
386 Philip Armstrong et al, (1991), pp. 308, 317.
387 Eric Shaw, *The Labour Party since 1979: Crisis and transformation*, London: Routledge, 1994, p. 153.
388 Pierre Dardot and Christian Laval (trans. Gregory Elliott), *The New Way of the World: On Neoliberal Society*, London: Verso, 2013, pp. 229, 252.
389 Richard Heffernan and Mike Marqusee, *Defeat from the Jaws of Victory: Inside Kinnock's Labour Party*, London: Verso, 1992, p. 10.
390 Mervyn Jones, (1994), p. 449.
391 Michael Foot, 'The Labour Party and Parliamentary Democracy', *Guardian*, September 10, 1981; quoted in Leo Panitch and Colin Leys, (1997), p. 192.
392 Eric Shaw, (1988), p. 246.
393 Jad Adams, *Tony Benn: A Biography*, London: Macmillan, 2nd ed. 2011, p. 412.
394 Hilary Wainwright, *Labour: A Tale of Two Parties*, 52, 69.
395 Labour Party, *Emergency programme of action*, 1983. This was not a fantasy: Norway placed its oil revenues in a sovereign wealth fund which now tops $1 trillion, as opposed to Thatcherite governments in Britain which squandered them on tax cuts. The interest from the Norwegian fund is invested in social welfare.
396 Richard Heffernan and Mike Marqusee, (1992), p. 30.
397 Andrew J. Richards, *Miners on Strike: Class Solidarity and Division in Britain*, Oxford: Berg, 1996, p. 100.
398 Richard Heffernan and Mike Marqusee, (1992), p. 61.
399 Quoted in Jim Phillips, *Collieries, Communities and the miners' strike in Scotland, 1984-85*, Manchester: Manchester UP, 2012, p. 110.
400 Eric Shaw, (1996), p. 170.
401 Richard Heffernan and Mike Marqusee, (1992), p. 67.
402 Eric Shaw, (1994), p. 50.
403 Andrew Thorpe, (1997), p. 220; Eric Shaw, (1988), p. xi.
404 Labour Party, *Britain Will Win with Labour*, 1987.
405 Stuart Hall, 'Blue election, election blues,' (1987), in *Selected Political Writings*, London: Lawrence and Wishart, 2017, pp. 242-3.
406 Marc Wadsworth, 'Celebrating Black Sections,' *Guardian*, 6 October 2008. The four MPs were Diane Abbott, Bernie Grant, Paul Boateng, and Keith Vaz.
407 Richard Heffernan and Mike Marqusee, (1992), p. 99.
408 Stephanie L. Mudge, *Leftism Reinvented: Western Parties from Socialism to Neoliberalism*, Cambridge MA: Harvard, 2018, p. 344.

409 Richard Heffernan and Mike Marqusee, (1992), p. 302, 304.
410 Eric Shaw, (1994), pp. 187, 190.
411 Lewis Minkin, *The Blair Supremacy: A study in the politics of Labour's party management*, Manchester UP, 2014, p. 83.
412 Lewis Minkin, (2014), p. 663.
413 Colin Leys, 'The British Labour Party's Transition from Socialism to Capitalism,' *Socialist Register* vol. 32, 1996, p. 8.
414 Stephanie Mudge, (2018), p. 293. Clinton had won the presidential primary with the sponsorship of the Democratic Leadership Council (DLC), which had been formed with the aim of marginalising the progressive wing of the Democratic party. It presented a manifesto emphasising 'opportunity, free markets, progressive taxation, crime and punishment, and work-friendly welfare'. The rhetoric of 'fairness' was deliberately replaced by the phrase 'equal opportunity, not equal outcomes' – which was understood by Jesse Jackson as an attack on civil rights concerns.
415 Richard Heffernan, *New Labour and Thatcherism: Political Change in Britain*, London & New York: Macmillan, 2000, p. 22.
416 Hilary Wainwright, (1987), pp. 168, 202
417 Sylvia Bashevkin, 'From Tough Times to Better Times: Feminism, Public Policy, and New Labour Politics in Britain', *International Political Science Review*, London: 2000, vol. 21 No. 4, p. 413.
418 Sylvia Bashevkin, (2000), pp. 417, 419.
419 Andrew Connell, *Why did Frank Field Fail? New Labour and welfare reform, 1997-8*, Cardiff University, unpublished PhD thesis, 2008, pp. 135-7.
420 Paul Routledge, profile of Ed Balls, *Independent*, March 8, 1998, quoted in Mudge, (2018), p. 347.
421 Stephanie Mudge, (2018), p. 348.
422 Richard Heffernan, (2000), p. 71.
423 Labour Party, *Britain will be better with New Labour*, 1997.
424 Richard Heffernan, (2000), p. 164.
425 Pierre Dardot and Christian Laval, (2013), pp. 216, 260, 263.
426 Leo Panitch and Sam Gindin, *The Making of Global Capitalism: The Political Economy of American Empire*, London: Verso, 2012, pp. 241-2.
427 Simon Lee, 'Gordon Brown and the British Way of Risk-Based Modernisation', *Observatoire de la société britannique* #10 | 2011, §10, 11.
428 Eric Shaw, *Losing Labour's Soul? New Labour and the Blair Government 1997-2007*, Abingdon, Oxon: Routledge, 2007, p. 139.
429 Eric Shaw, (2007), pp. 58, 55, 168.
430 Eric Shaw, (2007), p. 165.
431 Eric Shaw, (2007), p. 129.
432 Andrew Connell, (2008), p. 189.
433 Pierre Dardot and Christian Laval, (2013), pp. 245, 248.
434 Eric Shaw, (2007), p. 93.
435 Eric Shaw, (2007), p. 207.
436 Tony Wood, 'Good Riddance to New Labour,' *New Left Review*, March-April 2010, 18
437 Nicholas Shaxton, 'The finance curse: how the outsized power of the City of London makes Britain poorer,' *The Guardian*, October 5, 2018.
438 Eric Shaw, 'Assessing New Labour,' *British Politics*, 2011, vol:6 iss:1, 120.

439 Alan Finlayson, *Making Sense of New Labour,* London: Lawrence & Wishart, 2003, p. 94
440 Eric Shaw, (2007), pp. 63-4, 69.
441 John Tomaney, 'End of the Empire State? New Labour and Devolution in the United Kingdom,' *International Journal of Urban and Regional Research,* September 2000.
442 Tony Wood, (2010), p. 22.
443 Lewis Minkin, (2014), p. 510.
444 Nigel Morris, 'Blair's frenzied law making: a new offence for every day spent in office,' *Independent,* August 16, 2006.
445 Lewis Minkin, (2014), p. 685.
446 Chris Harman, 'The crisis in Respect,' *International Socialism* 2:117, Winter 2008
447 Patrick Wintour: 'Labour membership halved,' *Guardian* August 3, 2004.
448 Eric Shaw, (2007), p. 111.
449 Lewis Minkin, (2014), p. 702.
450 Simon Lee, (2011), §17.
451 Colin Hay, *The Failure of Anglo-liberal Capitalism,* Basingstoke, Palgrave Macmillan, 2013, pp. 39-40, 18.
452 Tony Blair, *The Third Way: New Politics for the New Century,* London: Fabian Society, 1998, p. 5.
453 Eric Shaw, (2007), p. 200.
454 Stephanie Mudge, *Leftism Reinvented,* 57-8.
455 Richard Heffernan, (2000), p. 178; Colin Hay, *The Political Economy of New Labour: Labouring under false pretences?* Manchester UP, 1999, p. 42.
456 Anthony Giddens, 'The rise and fall of New Labour,' *New Statesman,* 12 February, 1999.
457 Mark Bevir, *New Labour: A critique,* London: Routledge, 2005, p. 153; Connell, (2008), p. 26. More recently, history professor Glen O'Hara wrote an ideological defence of New Labour in the *Guardian*: 'No government that rebuilt the public sphere, radically improved the state healthcare system, improved maintained schools and took on homelessness can possibly be painted only in those terms [of neoliberalism].' 'New Labour was far more leftwing than it is given credit for', *Guardian,* 20 November 2018.
458 David Harvey, *A Brief History of Neoliberalism,* Oxford UP, 2005, p. 65.
459 Pierre Dardot and Christian Laval, (2013), p. 277.
460 Francesca Polletta, 'Breaking Point: Protests and Revolutions in the 21st Century,' *Journal of International Affairs,* Vol. 68, No. 1, pp. 83-4.
461 Eric Shaw, (2007), pp. 31, 188, 206.

Chapter Seven

462 BBC, 'No Such Thing as Corbynism', 13 December 2019, www.bbc.com/news/av/election-2019-50789271/no-such-thing-as-corbynism.
463 Larry Elliot, 'Alistair Darling: we will cut deeper than Margaret Thatcher', 25 March, 2010, https://www.theguardian.com/politics/2010/mar/25/alistair-darling-cut-deeper-margaret-thatcher
464 Craig Johnson and Sunil Rodger, 'Did Perception of the Economy Affect Attitudes to Immigration at the 2010 British General Election,' *Social Science Quarterly,* Volume 96, Number 5, November 2015.

465 Jeremy Green and Scott Lavery, 'The Regressive Recovery: Distribution, Inequality and State Power in Britain's Post-Crisis Political Economy,' *New Political Economy,* 2015, 20:6, 894-923, https://doi.org/10.1080/13563467.2015.1041478.

466 For example, the entry of the predatory Blackstone group into the London property market, arguably the leading global corporate residential landlord. See Hodkinson, SN, Beswick, J, Fields, D et al. (3 more authors), 'Speculating on London's housing future: The rise of global corporate landlords in 'post-crisis' urban landscapes,' University of Leeds, 2016, https://doi.org/10.1080/13604813.2016.1145946.

467 https://weownit.org.uk/public-ownership/nhs.

468 Patrick Wintour, 'Ed Balls: George Osborne's plan is failing but Labour cannot duck reality,' *Guardian,* 13 January, 2012.

469 Hannah Aldridge, Peter Kenway and Theo Barry Born, 'What happened to poverty under the Coalition?', New Policy Institute, April 2015. Aggregate real government spending on welfare and social protection decreased by around 16% per head. At the district-level, spending per person fell by 23.4% in real terms between 2010 and 2015, with the sharpest cuts in the poorest areas. See also Thiemo Fetzer, 'Did Austerity Cause Brexit?' University of Warwick Working Paper, 2018.

470 George Parker, Political Editor *Financial Times,* 6 June, 2013.

471 John Cassidy, 'Jeremy Corbyn's Victory and the demise of New Labour,' *New Yorker,* 13 September 2015.

472 Conrad Landin, 'Labour Left Wins Out at Party Election,' *Morning Star,* 21 August 2014.

473 'SNP wins 56 of 59 seats in Scots landslide', BBC News, 8 May 2015, https://www.bbc.com/news/election-2015-scotland-32635871.

474 The Lib Dem support of university tuition fees lost them a lot of support, and the anti-austerity, anti-racist and gender equality politics of the Greens in this election also attracted some alienated Labour voters. The Lib Dems lost 5.4 million votes compared to 2010, while the Greens picked up 892,3383. Brendan Prendiville, 'The Green Party: "Green Surge" or Work in Progress?', *French Journal of British studies,* XX-3 2015.

475 Amelia Gentleman, 'Labour vows to reduce reliance on food banks if it comes to power', *The Guardian,* 17 March 2015.

476 Alex Nunns, *The Candidate: Jeremy Corbyn's improbable path to power,* London: OR Books, 2016, p. 75.

477 Adam Bienkov, 'Labour oppose almost nothing in George Osborne's budget', Politics.co.uk, 9 July 2015.

478 Alexander Sehmer, 'MP says he would 'swim through vomit' to oppose 'sickening' welfare bill', *Independent,* 21 July 2015.

479 Alex Nunns, (2016), quoted pp. 141-2.

480 Nadia Khomami, 'What does Jeremy Corbyn think?', *Guardian* 12 September 2015.

481 Alex Nunns, (2016), p. 259.

482 Selma James and Nina Lopez, Global Women's Strike, August 2016, https://selmajames.net/2016/08/04/security-forces-and-corbyn-guardian-letter/

483 'Selma James & Women of Colour GWS sign letter: We stand with Jeremy Corbyn – just as he always stood with us', 10 December 2019, https://globalwomenstrike.net/selma-james-women-of-colour-gws-sign-letter-we-stand-with-jeremy-corbyn-just-as-he-always-stood-with-us/.

484 Phil Burton-Cartledge, 'A Tale of Two Crises,' in Mark Perryman (ed.) *Corbynism from Below* London: Lawrence & Wishart, 2019, p. 67.
485 Alex Nunns, (2016), p. 15.
486 Liam Young, *Rise: How Jeremy Corbyn inspired the Young to Create a New Socialism*, London: Simon & Schuster, 2018, pp. 98, 190.
487 Professor James Curran, *Guardian*, 13 September 2015; https://www.theguardian.com/politics/2015/sep/13/how-rank-outsider-jeremy-corbyn-re-energised-a-tired-party.
488 Richard Seymour, *Corbyn: The Strange Rebirth of Radical Politics* London: Verso, 2nd edition 2017, p. xvii.
489 Richard Seymour, (2017), pp. 227-9.
490 'Jeremy Corbyn's Labour conference speech: readers' verdict,' *Guardian,* 29 September, 2015.
491 Alex Nunns, (2016), p. 15.
492 Eric Shaw, 'Assessing New Labour,' *British Politics*, 2011, vol:6 iss:1 p. 119.
493 'Jeremy Corbyn – End Austerity Now,' 15 June 2015, https://www.youtube.com/watch?v=DK36ps3L-aU
494 Nicholas Watt, 'Corbyn declares his values,' *The Guardian* 30 September 2015
495 https://labour.org.uk/press/jeremy-corbyn-speech-to-labour-party-conference/
496 Eric Shaw, (2007), pp. 35, 39.
497 Interviews with the author, October 2016.
498 Interviews with the author October 2016.
499 Jeremy Gilbert, 'Labour can win. But first it must explain what Corbynism means,' *Guardian* 24 July, 2017, https://www.theguardian.com/commentisfree/2017/jul/24/labour-can-win-corbynism-movement-philosophy.
500 https://www.buzzfeed.com/marieleconte/this-is-what-happened-when-theresa-may-and-jeremy-corbyn
501 Eric Shaw, (2011), p. 123.
502 Sarah Pine, 'Corbyn: 'Article 50 has to be invoked now',' *LabourList* 24 June 2016, https://labourlist.org/2016/06/corbyn-article-50-has-to-be-invoked-now/
503 The Labour Party, *The Work of the Labour Party's Governance and Legal Unit in relation to antisemitism, 2014-2019*, March 2020. It is noteworthy that the narrative of antisemitism that has so bedevilled the party originated from within this faction, which has strong connections with the media and political establishment.
504 Patrick Cockburn, 'Brexit Britain is facing a deep crisis of self-confidence. It will only end in tears – and rising nationalism', *Independent,* 7 December 2018.
505 Thiemo Fetzer, 'Did Austerity Cause Brexit?' University of Warwick Working Paper, 2018.
506 Satnam Virdee and Brendan McGeever, 'Racism, Crisis, Brexit', *Ethnic and Racial Studies*, 2018, vol. 41, No. 10, pp. 1802-1819
507 Sara B. Hobolt, Thomas J. Leeper, James Tilley, 'Divided by the Vote: Affective Polarization in the Wake of Brexit', London School of Economics and University of Oxford, 2019
508 Labour Party, *For the Many, not the Few*, 2017. The phrase was actually introduced by Tony Blair to replace Clause IV in the party constitution, which currently calls for the creation of '*a community in which power, wealth and opportunity are in the hands of the many, not the few…*' But its adoption by the Corbyn platform gave it a new meaning that reflects mass support for social change, returning it to its Shelleyan roots.

509 Jason Beattie, 'Poll shows people LOVE Labour's manifesto policies - but don't rate Jeremy Corbyn as a Prime Minister,' *Daily Mirror*, 12 May 2017, http://www.mirror.co.uk/news/politics/poll-shows-people-love-labours-10404216
510 Mike Phipps, *For the Many: Preparing Labour for Power*, London: OR Books, 2017, p. 9.
511 Labour Party, *Alternative Models of Ownership*, June 2017, https://labour.org.uk/wp-content/uploads/2017/10/Alternative-Models-of-Ownership.pdf
512 Christine Berry and Joe Guinan, *People Get Ready! Preparing for a Corbyn Government*, London: OR Books, 2019, pp. 155, 31, 69, 137, 140.
513 Matt Bolton and Frederick Harry Pitts, *Corbynism: A Critical Approach*, Bingley: Emerald Publishing, 2018, p. 141. This is fake Marxism: the authors confuse the term wealth with the concept of value and make no distinction between large-scale and small-scale capital circulation. It makes no difference to capital if value is realised locally or internationally.
514 Robin Murray, 'Global Civil Society and the Rise of the Civil Economy', in Mary Kaldor, Henrietta L. Moore, Sabine Selchow (eds), *Global Civil Society 2012: Ten Years of Critical Reflection*, London: Palgrave Macmillan, 2012, pp. 145, 161.
515 Pierre Dardot and Christian Laval, (2013), p. 320.
516 George Monbiot (editor), Robin Grey, Tom Kenny, Laurie Macfarlane, Anna Powell-Smith, Guy Shrubsole, Beth Stratford, *Land for the Many: Changing the way our fundamental asset is used, owned and governed*, Labour Party, 2019.
517 https://theworldtransformed.org/.
518 https://www.common-wealth.co.uk/.
519 Angus Satow, 'Jeremy's leadership was transformative – particularly on climate', *LabourList*, 3 April 2020, labourlist.org/2020/04/jeremys-leadership-was-transformative-particularly-on-climate/.
520 David Graeber, 'What does climate emergency mean?', Labour Briefing 2 May 2019, http://labourbriefing.squarespace.com/home/2019/5/2/z0vv4cel28gckbq982vv490ne465hc.
521 Sienna Rodgers, 'Labour movement builds focus on 'green industrial revolution' plans,' *LabourList*, 16 May 2019, https://labourlist.org/2019/05/labour-movement-builds-focus-on-green-industrial-revolution-plans/.
522 Loughborough University, General Election 2019 Report, 7 November–11 December 2019, https://www.lboro.ac.uk/news-events/general-election/report-5/.
523 Christine Berry and Joe Guinan, (2019), p. 192.
524 Luke Pagarani, 'Labour failed to engage older voters – and after 100 hours canvassing, I know why', *Guardian*, 21 December 2019, https://www.theguardian.com/commentisfree/2019/dec/21/labour-older-voters-corbyn-local-socialism
525 Sabrina Huck, 'Where next for the Labour left? The reorientation of Momentum', *LabourList*, 29 April, 2020; https://labourlist.org/2020/04/where-next-for-the-labour-left-the-reorientation-of-momentum/
526 Kate Proctor, 'Corbyn's heir fights on all fronts in Labour race,' *Guardian*, 6 March 2020, https://www.theguardian.com/politics/2020/mar/06/rebecca-long-bailey-the-pyjama-loving-heir-to-corbynism.
527 Andrew Fisher, 'I was at the heart of Corbynism. Here's why we lost', OpenDemocracy, 10 September 2020, https://www.opendemocracy.net/en/opendemocracyuk/i-was-heart-corbynism-heres-why-we-lost/.
528 Leo Panitch and Colin Leys, *Searching for Socialism: The Project of the Labour New Left from Benn to Corbyn*, London: Verso, 2020, p. 255.

529 Christine Berry, 'Lessons from the 2019 election result', 20 December 2019, https://www.christineberry.net/2019/12/long-read-lessons-from-the-2019-election-result/.
530 Christine Berry, 'The radical potential of the Corbyn project,' *Red Pepper*, 20 September, 2019; www.redpepper.org.uk/the-radical-potential-of-corbynism/.
531 Source: www.gov.uk/government/collections/trade-union-statistics.
532 Jack Shenker, *Now We Have Your Attention: The New Politics of the People*, London: Bodley Head, 2019, pp. 89, 84.
533 'Jeremy Corbyn – End Austerity Now,' 15 June 2015, https://www.youtube.com/watch?v=DK36ps3L-aU

Index of Names

Addison, Paul 24, 45, 69
Armbruster, G.H. 10, 11
Attlee, Clement 2, 9, 10, 11, 18, 22, 24, 26, 27, 28, 29, 30, 32, 33, 35, 44, 45, 47, 48, 52, 61, 69, 79, 80, 82, 83, 84, 85, 95, 115

Baldwin, Stanley 23
Balls, Ed 136, 139, 152
Barratt Brown, Michael 106
Banks, Arron 162
Beer, Samuel 10, 53
Bellamy, Edward 3, 16, 17, 18, 26
Benn, Tony 3, 5, 98, 99, 100, 101, 102, 104, 105, 106, 107, 108, 109, 110, 111, 112, 113, 114, 115, 116, 117, 118, 119, 120, 122, 127, 128, 130, 148, 155, 175
Berry, Christine 166, 176
Bevan, Aneurin 21, 25, 27, 35, 45, 46, 57, 60, 61, 62, 64, 65, 66, 67, 74, 79, 80, 81, 82, 83, 84, 85, 86, 87, 88, 89, 90, 91, 99, 112
Beveridge, Sir William 40, 41, 42, 43;
Beveridge Report 5, 32, 33, 39, 44, 45, 48, 51, 52, 54, 63
Bevin, Ernest 22, 23, 24, 26, 27, 29, 30, 33, 40, 55, 62, 71, 76, 77
Bevir, Mark 146
Bewley, Bill 14
Blair, Tony 4, 5, 126, 132, 134, 135, 136, 140, 141, 142, 143, 144, 145, 146, 148, 149, 161
Blatchford, Robert 3, 15, 16, 31
Blatchford, Winifred 18
Bolton, Matt 167

Brown, Gordon 4, 5, 126, 132, 135, 138, 140, 144, 145, 150, 152
Burton-Cartledge, Phil 156
Bush, George W. 143
Bussey, E.W. 42

Calder, Ritchie 33
Calderbank, Michael 154, 158
Callaghan, James 98, 114, 115, 120, 121, 126
Cameron, David 151, 162
Campbell, John 62, 80
Cassidy, John 152
Castle, Barbara 50, 80, 101
Chamberlain, Neville 32, 33, 36
Churchill, Winston 33, 44, 45, 48, 65, 73
Citrine, Walter 22, 27
Clarke, Charles 131
Clarke, Otto 62
Clegg, Nick 151
Clinton, Bill 134, 135, 136, 140, 146, 149
Coates, Ken 106
Cockburn, Patrick 163
Cole, G.D.H. 20, 81
Connell, Andrew 147
Connolly, James 19, 20
Cook, Robin 143
Corbyn, Jeremy 1, 4, 6, 143, 149, 150, 151, 153, 154, 155, 156, 158, 160, 161, 162, 164, 170, 171, 172, 173, 174, 175, 177
Cousins, Frank 85, 101
Cripps, Francis 108

Cripps, Stafford 22, 25, 26, 27, 30, 56, 57, 69, 79
Crosland, Anthony 91, 92, 94
Crossman, Richard 30, 80, 84, 91
Croucher, Richard 39

Dalton, Hugh 23, 24, 26, 29, 30, 56, 61
Dardot, Pierre 136, 148, 168
Darling, Alastair 150
Deakin, Arthur 44, 78, 79, 81, 82, 83
De Leon, Daniel 19
Denington, Mrs. E. 47
Driberg, Tom 37
Durbin, Evan 23

Eckstein, Harry 64
Eden, Anthony 86
Edwards, Bob 60, 61
Estcourt, Dr Peter 67
Evans, David 174

Farage, Nigel 162, 164
Feather, Victor 107
Fielding, Steven 31, 36, 37,
Fisher, Andrew 174
Foot, Michael 15, 80, 104, 114, 126, 127, 129
Foote, Geoffrey 86
Franco, Francisco 76

Gaitskell, Hugh 23, 74, 75, 78, 79, 82, 83, 84, 85, 86, 87
Galloway, George 143
Giddens, Anthony 146
Gilbert, Jeremy 160
Glasier, Bruce 35
Gould, Bryan 132
Greenwood, Arthur 32, 84
Griffiths, Jim 64
Guinan, Joe 166,

Hall, Stuart 94, 106, 120, 131
Hardie, Keir 35
Harman, Harriet 135, 154
Harvey, David 147
Hattersley, Roy 102, 132

Hay, Colin 146
Healey, Denis 114, 119, 126, 127
Heath, Edward 103, 104, 105, 110, 117
Heffer, Eric 14, 110
Heffernan, Richard 136, 146
Hewitt, Patricia 138
Hitler, Adolf 27, 76, 84, 90
Hodgson, Geoff 109
Hogg, Quintin 47
Holland, Stuart 108, 109
Howell, David 11, 35, 58, 77, 103
Huck, Sabrina 173
Hunter, Bill 38, 39, 59, 63

James, Selma 155
Jay, Douglas 23
Jenkins, Mark 79, 81, 86, 88
Johnson, Boris 171, 172, 173
Jones, Harriet 70
Jones, Jack 14, 106, 109, 113
Jones, Lord Elwyn 50

Kandiah, Michael 70
Keynes, John Maynard 22, 24, 47, 79
Khrushchev, Nikita 92
Kinnock, Neil 5, 126, 127, 129, 130, 131, 132, 133, 134, 135, 149
Kynaston, David 36, 51, 71

Lansbury, George 27
Laski, Harold 22, 44, 47
Laval, Christian 136, 148, 168
Lawson, Hugh 62
Lawther, Will 82
Leslie, Chris 154
Leys, Colin 110, 134, 175
Livingstone, Ken 127
Lloyd George, David 21
Long-Bailey, Rebecca 173

MacDonald, Ramsay 21, 22, 26
Maclean, John 20
Macmillan, Harold 47
Major, John 139
Mandelson, Peter 131, 132, 142
Mann, Tom 20, 21, 93

Marwick, Arthur 50
Masheder, Philip 50
Mason, Roy 59
Mason, Tony 37
May, Theresa 160, 162, 163, 164, 169, 172, 173
McDonnell, John 165
McGahey, Mick 130
McGeever, Brendan 163
McKenzie, Grant 35
McKibbin, Ross 33, 34, 36, 43, 51, 71
Meacher, Michael 128, 132
Mikardo, Ian 46, 49, 80, 109
Miles, Peter 15
Miliband, David 152
Miliband, Ed 152
Miliband, Ralph 36, 54, 75, 93, 94, 106
Minkin, Lewis 34, 37, 55, 70, 134
Moran, Lord 65
Morgan, Kenneth O. 56, 57, 59, 60, 63, 69, 70, 77
Morris, William 13, 18, 93, 95
Morrison, Herbert 23, 24, 26, 30, 33, 36, 47, 48, 60, 62, 66, 68, 71, 76, 80, 82
Mosley, Oswald 24
Mudge, Stephanie 146
Murdoch, Rupert 142
Murphy, J.T. 20
Murray, Robin 167

Nasser, Gamal Abdel 86
Neira, Patricia 158
Nkrumah, Kwame 76
Nunns, Alex 154, 155, 156, 158

O'Neill, Terence 102
Orwell, George 64

Panitch, Leo 110, 175
Pelling, Henry 22
Phillips, Morgan 77
Phipps, Mike 165
Pitts, Frederick 167
Platts-Mills, John 77
Pollock, Allyson 141
Pope, Jessie 12, 15,

Price, Richard 21
Rae, John 51
Rashford, Marcus 175
Reeves, Rachel 153, 154
Richards, Grant 12,
Rintala, Marvin 66
Roberts, Ernie 106
Rogers, Jack 42
Ruskin, John 18
Russell, Bertrand 30

Samuel, Raphael 94
Satow, Angus 170
Saville, John 9, 55, 72, 76, 93, 94
Scanlon, Hugh 101, 106,
Scargill, Arthur 130
Seymour, Richard 157
Shaw, Eric 27, 55, 56, 85, 133, 148, 158
Shawcross, Christine 153
Shelley, Percy Bysshe 164
Sheppard, Roland 15
Shinwell, Emanuel 44, 82
Skinner, Dennis 128
Sommerfield, John 14
Smillie, Robert 21
Smith, Harry Leslie 53
Smith, John 134
Starmer, Keir 151, 169, 173, 174
Stephen, Campbell 42
Strachey, John 91

Tatchell, Peter 127
Tawney, R.H 118
Thatcher, Margaret 113, 120, 121, 122, 123, 124, 125, 129, 130, 133, 137, 138, 161
Thomas-Symonds, Nicklaus 81
Thompson, Edward 50, 93, 94, 95, 106
Thompson, Noel 15
Thompson, Peter 31, 37
Thornett, Alan 112
Tiratsoo, Nick 31
Tomlinson, Jim 34
Topham, Tony 106
Tressell, Robert (Robert Noonan) 3, 11, 12, 14, 15, 16, 17

Virdee, Satnam 163

Wainwright, Hilary 87, 110, 112, 116
Warbey, William 50
Webb, Beatrice 40
Whelan, Charlie 136
Whiteside, Noel 39
Wigzell, Claire 158
Williams, Raymond 106
Williamson, Tom 82
Willink, Henry 64

Wilson, Harold 98, 99, 100, 102, 103, 104, 107, 109, 113, 114, 115, 119, 120
Worsthorne, Peregrine 50

Young, Liam 156
Young, Michael 60

Zilliacus, Konni 77

About the Author

Martin R. Beveridge got his start in political activism at the age of 14. Since then, he worked as a printer for a socialist newspaper, became a socialist writer, and is active in the Labour Party, Momentum, Unite the Union, and various US citizens' groups.

His experiences inspired him to write and interpretation of Labour Party history that foregrounds the role of its members, and to examine how social and political change has shaped discourse on the left. His work has appeared in *Jacobin* magazine, and he regularly blogs on current events at coloneldespard.wordpress.com. He divides his time between the UK and the US.